Progress in Parapsychology

Edited by J. B. RHINE

Progress in Parapsychology

THE PARAPSYCHOLOGY PRESS

COLLEGE STATION, DURHAM, NORTH CAROLINA 27708

Andrew S. Thomas Memorial Library
MORRIS HARVEY COLLEGE, CHARLESTON, W. VA.

97121

Second Printing 1973
THE FOUNDATION FOR RESEARCH ON THE NATURE OF MAN
Library of Congress Catalog Card Number 76—140922
ISBN 0-911106-03-0

PRINTED IN THE UNITED STATES OF AMERICA
BY THE SEEMAN PRINTERY DIVISION
OF FISHER-HARRISON CORPORATION, DURHAM, N. C.

To honor the memory of

PROFESSOR WILLIAM McDOUGALL, F.R.S.
1871-1938

on the centenary of his birth

this book is respectfully dedicated.

Professor William McDougall

McDougall's Contribution to Parapsychology

William McDougall led the way in making parapsychology a successful scientific study. He would therefore, if he were alive today, be among the first to appreciate the developments this book reports. So it seems most appropriate to dedicate the volume to his memory.

Professor McDougall, however, would not have considered himself a parapsychologist (or psychical researcher). This field did not occupy his full time and attention even for a semester. He neither offered a course in it nor wrote a book about it. Yet his interest in it was so profound and enduring that he could write in his autobiographical sketch, "If I had not found it necessary to earn some income, I should perhaps have chosen to give all my time and energy to this field."

He was of course first of all a psychologist—the leading one in the English-speaking world, according to the historian A. A. Roback—and his academic career extending from the University of London (via Oxford and Harvard) to Duke University was a distinguished one. Yet even in his own experimental researches, which encompassed several areas of psychology and biology, parapsychology was never his main preoccupation.

Rather, what made McDougall the leading founder of parapsychology as a science was his forthright search for the key to man's nature with respect to the physical world, a search that, as his book Body and Mind, in *1911* indicated, became the major drive of his intellectual life. This persistent unswerving quest led him logically to consider those puzzling psychical occurrences belonging to parapsychology that so obviously challenged physical explanation. Such happenings seemed to suggest a solution to the problem of man's nonphysical nature that could be checked by scientific test—the only test McDougall would accept. His resolute action in holding the attention of a reluctant science on these promising but unorthodox claims until they were fairly explored was timely and essential to the emergence of parapsychology. There was no one else equal to the task, no one ready to take the responsibility, and none who so much needed the evidence of parapsychology for his intellectual purpose.

* * * *

McDougall joined the Society for Psychical Research when he was thirty. He reviewed books, served on the Council, and was otherwise active. In 1920 he was elected to the presidency of the Society, and on moving to Harvard that year he was elected to the presidency of the American Society for Psychical Research. Shortly thereafter, following a split in the A. S. P. R. organization, he helped to establish the Boston Society for Psychic Research and presided over it in the years that followed until in 1927 he left the Boston area for Duke University.

This was indeed a period of unequalled leadership. It was especially important for psychical research to be headed by a distinguished professor who was a Fellow of the Royal Society, but it was much more significant to have him be a psychologist of international reputation. No member of that profession at the time, either in Britain or America, had the purpose, interest and independence of mind to take so bold a stand on so unorthodox a branch of inquiry.

It was therefore the fact that McDougall was the kind of psychologist he was, with a major interest in the mind–body question, that led him to look into the claims of parapsychology as possible sources of the knowledge he was seeking. The great majority of the members of his profession were trying to fit psychology into the academic pattern with the older sciences, and parapsychology was too unconventional and uncertain to compete.

McDougall's move to Harvard was timely for American psychical research. The Margery mediumship came to prominence in 1923 and the Scientific American magazine asked

McDougall to serve on the committee appointed to investigate the claims of puzzling physical phenomena occurring in her darkroom seances. Most men would have been deterred by the consideration of what his American colleagues in psychology would think or how Harvard University would regard the matter, especially since the investigation had become a very public affair. McDougall did not hesitate to give both time and serious attention to the investigation. The turmoil over the claims and counterclaims of this fantastic mediumship was tremendous, but McDougall rode out the storm calmly and meanwhile quietly sponsored experimental research in telepathy in the Harvard Psychology Laboratory. Gardner Murphy was one of the young psychologists who worked with him, and later George Estabrooks produced what turned out to be the best laboratory experiment in parapsychology up to its time (republished in the Journal of Parapsychology in 1961).

* * * *

During these Harvard years a grand plan for the advancement of parapsychology was developing in McDougall's mind. In his address at Clark University in 1926, one of a series of lectures he himself had helped to set up, he argued persuasively that psychical research should be made a legitimate university study. To no one's surprise, neither Harvard nor Clark responded to the proposal, but when a year later McDougall transferred to Duke as chairman of the newly established psychology department in the new university, he found there a wholly favorable situation in which to implement his plan.

On my arrival at Duke in 1927 for a short period of study under McDougall's direction, he asked me to continue there to conduct research in parapsychology. The initiative was definitely his, even though he was strongly backed by the university's president, Dr. W. P. Few. Fortunately his support was steadfast through the trying years that accompanied the ESP research developments. He helped to establish a course in parapsychology and joined in founding the

Journal of Parapsychology. His influence, too, brought the first financial support from outside the University (the McDougall Fund was established).

And he was a willing participant in it all. He entered heartily even into the less conventional developments such as a "field trip" to investigate a medium, a horse or a dog reported to be "psychic." When the medium, Eileen Garrett, offered her services as a research subject, he promptly accepted, and while he turned her over to me, he remained a most interested observer and counselor. He shared also in the conclusion that while her performance showed what was then called "supernormal knowledge" (ESP) we could not safely draw a conclusion as to whether the information was received via ESP from deceased or from living sources.

Without hesitation, too, McDougall accepted the study of mediumship as a thesis topic for the Ph.D. degree, wisely requiring only that the study be designated as one aimed at the development of methods and not at a conclusive result. So it was that John F. Thomas got his Ph.D. in psychology under McDougall at Duke for a thesis on mediumship.

However, it was only when he was especially intrigued by a new finding that Prof. McDougall would take time from his own work to try the experiment himself. But when the PK research with dice-throwing methods began, he carried out an independent experiment on it with his family, although he did not publish a report of it himself. (Mind Over Matter, L. E. Rhine, p. 61)

In judging McDougall's involvement in the field, it would be well to turn to his preface to my book Extrasensory Perception. There he states that the program at Duke had gone far (it was eight years after the Clark address) to justify the policy he had recommended of admitting psychical research to the University. Three years later and only a year before the end of his life he wrote, in the editorial for the first issue of the Journal of Parapsychology, "This movement to acclimatize psychical research in the universities . . . has prospered undeniably." And so it did appear, even in 1937.

But how much does it really matter that parapsychology did not qualify for the current stage of psychology departments in American universities, in McDougall's day or ours, whether at Duke or any other American university? Eventual accommodation would after all seem to be only a matter of time. McDougall's idealization of psychology and of parapsychology's place in it still seems reasonable enough for 1926. No one could have known then how difficult a branch of inquiry the field has turned out to be.

However, one easily appreciates today what a fortunate mistake McDougall's overoptimism in timing was in opening the way for the Duke experiments, even though the setting was not a permanent one. McDougall himself saw, in his last years, the emergence of some of the problems that required "preventive separation" and he reluctantly approved the move. But there was no slightest dimming of his vision of the distant unity of the behavioral sciences, parapsychology and all. He and President Few even envisioned together a still larger integration of sciences in a projected Institute for the Study of Man, but it had to remain a dream.

* * * *

Naturally this sketch can reflect only one of many aspects of William McDougall's life and influence. Yet in realizing that this one branch of his interest owed very much to the total magnitude of the man, one comes at length to appreciate what it really was that constituted his major contribution to parapsychology: not a significant deed or great theory or high rank—no outstanding experiment or book or discovery. Rather it was primarily in being the man he was that McDougall became, to a degree not even recognized at the time, the principal creative figure in the emergence of the science of parapsychology. The splendid image of the exploring mind he brought to psi research from his exceptionally broad training, magnificent intellect, and varied experience provided an ideal set of values for that formative study to emulate. How fortunate an imprint it was for a nascent science!   —J. B. R.

Contents

McDougall's Contribution to Parapsychology	vii
Note on Statistics	2
Introduction: Dimensions of Progress *J. B. Rhine*	3

Part I   NEW APPROACHES

Preface	13
ESP Experiments with Mice *Pierre Duval and Evelyn Montredon*	17
A Quantum Process in Psi Testing *Helmut Schmidt*	28
Psi Application *Robert Brier and Walter V. Tyminski*	36
EEG Alpha Rhythm in Relation to ESP Scoring Patterns on Variance *Rex G. Stanford and Birgit E. Stanford*	53
IBM Cards in ESP Testing *Milan Ryzl and Marie Balounova*	62

Part II   MIND OVER MATTER

Preface	69
PK in the Laboratory: A Survey *Louisa E. Rhine*	72
A Help-Hinder Comparison *Sara R. Feather and Louisa E. Rhine*	86

PK on a Pendulum System — W. E. Cox — 97

PK Effect on a Plant Polygraph System — Robert Brier — 102

Retarding Fungus Growth by PK — Jean Barry — 118

Part III   FACTORS IN PSI TEST PERFORMANCE

Preface — 125

The Effect of the Checker on Precognition — Sara R. Feather and Robert Brier — 129

Response Bias and ESP Test Performance — Rex G. Stanford — 136

Psi Experiences and Test Performance — Joyce N. Jones and Sara R. Feather — 145

The Effect of Belief on ESP Success — Thelma S. Moss and J. A. Gengerelli — 152

Sex Differences in Mass School Tests — Robert Brier — 161

Testing Before and After Talks on ESP — Louisa E. Rhine — 171

Part IV   MAIN LINES OF CONTINUITY

Preface — 181

Some Psychological Variables in Psi Tests — Dallas E. Buzby — 184

Factors Affecting Precognition — John A. Freeman — 192

Mood and Precognition — James C. Carpenter — 203

Part V   PARAPSYCHOLOGY IN PERSPECTIVE

Preface   217

Parapsychology During the Last Quarter of a Century   221
   Robert H. Thouless

Psi and Psychology: Conflict and Solution   236
   J. B. Rhine

Parapsychology and Physics   258
   Remy Chauvin

Guiding Concepts for Psi Research   262
   J. B. Rhine

Appendixes

Appendix A   295
   Position Effects

Appendix B   296
   Selecting Precognition Targets

Appendix C   298
   Psi Missing

Appendix D   299
   Stacking Effect

Appendix E   301
   The Variance Test of Significance

Glossary   303

Indexes   307

ACKNOWLEDGMENT

The manuscript editor of this book was Patricia Tucker. She was assisted by Joyce N. Jones and Barbara Schmidt-Nielsen. Carol Schaber prepared the illustrations. Dorothy H. Pope, editor of the Parapsychology Press, has rendered supervisory aid.

Dr. Louisa E. Rhine and Dr. Robert Brier gave important editorial assistance.

Progress in Parapsychology

NOTE ON STATISTICS

The probability that a given result will occur by chance provides a measure of the significance of research findings that is useful in parapsychology as in other scientific fields.

A proper probability statement might read, "The odds are 100 to one against the chance occurrence of so large a deviation from mean chance expectation as this"; or "A difference this great or greater can be expected to occur by chance alone only once in 50 such experiments."

Rather than burden the text with numerous repetitions of such probability statements, the editors have adopted the formulation, "odds against chance." Wherever the phrase appears in this volume it should be taken to represent the full statement.

In most scientific fields, a finding is considered sufficiently unlikely to have occurred by chance to be considered "significant" if the chance odds against it are as much as 20 to one. Parapsychologists have adopted a more conservative standard, requiring that odds against chance occurrence be at least 50 to one before a result is said to be significant.

Introduction: Dimensions of Progress

"What is new in parapsychology?" This is a naturally recurrent question for anyone interested in the field of psi research. For the great many who cannot visit the widely separated research centers and who cannot read all the reports of that work in the scientific periodicals, some way is needed to bring reader and researcher closer together. This book undertakes to do that.

Progress in Parapsychology is a biennial harvest of "the most of the best" of what is going on in this new realm of discovery. It scans recent developments on the many advancing frontiers of this expanding and challenging field. The fruits of original researches, still in the words of the authors themselves, have been selected and presented both for the scholar and, with the help of glossary and appendices, for the general reader.

The way these reports were selected is important. More than fifty papers were presented at the six Review Meetings of the Institute for Parapsychology during the 1968-1969 period. These papers were carefully selected from among reports submitted by researchers in many parts of the world. The 20 papers included in this book were further selected from that group as giving the most representative survey of the field. Then, in addition, five of the principal addresses to these meetings were selected to provide a broad evaluative background.

The resulting book takes up where its predecessor, *Parapsychology Today*, left off, and covers in a similar way the march of parapsychology through the succeeding biennium of psi research. This collection, however, is more than an account or even an emphasis on what is merely new. Progress is more than novelty alone. It may help therefore in introducing these many diverse contributions to indicate other aspects of progress, some of which might be obscured by the more readily observable advances.

* * * *

Let us look first, however, at what is outstandingly new. The report on precognition tests with mice that opens the series is outstanding for its many-sided novelty. Not only is it the first successful work with this species in psi research but it is also the first published scientific report of precognition in animals. Then too the method of using a completely automated system of testing is new for animal tests in parapsychology. These are not all the "firsts" in this paper, and even the parapsychologist is a little startled by so much innovation in a single experiment. This naturally leaves one more strongly inclined than usual to suspend judgment until independent confirmation is reported. However, as this volume was going to press word came of at least one such confirmatory report.

Another major innovation of the period was the design of electronic equipment that automates the whole operation of psi testing with human subjects. The apparatus not only provides random targets and records the subject's responses automatically but automatically checks and analyzes results as well. The beauty of this new advance is that it leaves the experimenter practically free of all responsibility during the test except for the attention he needs to give to the subject's psychological requirements. This innovation is already leading to something of a new trend, one that is spreading in several directions. For example, the reports in this volume cover electronic testing only for precognition and clairvoyance, but the next volume will show the program carried further into still another type of psi ability.

One of the new steps reported here leads off into quite a different direction. It is an advance toward the practical application of psi ability. The aim is to use statistical methods to concentrate the thin yield of information given in most of the psi experiments and thereby to increase the predictive

Introduction: Dimensions of Progress 5

value of the data. Not only the methods themselves but the particular area of application is of interest in this case. Research workers in parapsychology since Professor Charles Richet have often found the equipment used in games useful in their tests, so it is not surprising that in this case the casino provided the proving ground for the new attempt at reliable prediction.

Still other lines of novelty depend on methods and devices borrowed from neighboring fields of science. In one the brain-wave equipment or electroencephalograph (EEG) was used; in another, the IBM card was used in an ESP test procedure that allowed excellent control throughout the experiment. Novelty has also come to the psychokinetic (PK) side of the field of parapsychology with the introduction of a new electrically-timed mechanical system as the target to be influenced.

* * * *

Novelty, of course, is relative; the case of the PK research just mentioned illustrates the point. In considering where the PK reports belonged there was a question of which is more important, to have the experiment conducted with a machine as new and different as this one, or to have these results as confirmation of findings in an earlier PK experiment with a mechanical target system. Fortunately we have both effects in these reports, and one may take his own choice of emphasis, but I think the more experienced parapsychologist will stress confirmation value as first. To him the major advancement of this two-year period is the steady support given to past discoveries. This represents the type of progress most appreciated.

The main reason for grouping the PK papers into one section is that the PK research is somewhat more in need of confirmatory support than the ESP side of the field, and there are fewer workers dealing with it. For instance, the PK tests with plants (attached to a polygraph) as targets have been awaiting confirmation of the novelty stage which was reported in *Parapsychology Today*. Likewise the PK research on fungus growth as reported in this book provides much needed support for earlier publications reporting the effect of PK on living tissues. The help-hinder tests in dice-throwing PK experiments also carry on from earlier work on this same tug-of-wills type of test.

Understandably then the line of progress that stands out most in these PK papers is the display of continuity—progress in confirming the case already made for the various lines of PK represented. It is here that the historical paper included in the PK section contributes the background needed for the experimental studies. It brings out the soundness of the case for PK as an elemental psi function, but shows too how limited the concept is, how much remains to explore of just such questions as those on which these experiments touch.

* * * *

Incidentally the PK section also represents a third line of progress, that of extending parapsychology to bring additional psi phenomena under study, where the ESP side of the field has long had the lead. The first reliable evidence of psi back in the 1930's had to do with the clairvoyant type, but precognition promptly followed and then telepathy was pursued as far as presently seems possible. On the PK side, however, only the PK effect on moving targets (e.g., rolling dice) has so far been firmly established. Research has not yet produced a good experiment to confirm the PK of static inanimate targets (although reports of spontaneous physical phenomena suggest that it may occur) and some of the claims of demonstration are close to acceptability.

This volume includes reports of some further progress, even if in only two papers, into the PK of *living* targets. Actually this may signal a turning point, although plainly parapsychology has a long way to go in the PK "hemisphere" to match its explorations in ESP. The signs are good for a PK era ahead.

* * * *

The fourth dimension of progress is mainly concerned with what everyone in the field wants most to know—what psi really is and how it works—its nature and control. Hap-

Introduction: Dimensions of Progress 7

pily, most of the experiments reported here turned up some point that adds knowledge on this question, some condition affecting success, or a clue to what hinders psi performance.

Differences in psi test results according to the sex of the subject are among the more persistent factors that differentiate levels of scoring rate. Another, and a close second, is the subject's belief or disbelief in psi ability. Some little progress has also been made in associating ESP success with certain physiological conditions. *Parapsychology Today* reported a correlation with GSR or skin resistance; in this book the report concerns one of the brain waves, the alpha rhythm. Much more is also being learned about the correlation of psi with measurable mental states such as the subject's moods, special abilities, interests, habits and preferences. These psychological variables make a big difference in whether subjects consistently score above or below the expected chance level, i.e., whether they hit or avoid the targets. Many familiar mental factors, operating unconsciously, are now known to induce a difference in score levels known as the psi differential effect (PDE), a discovery that is probably the most illuminating finding of the last quarter century of parapsychology.

Two main lines of findings emerge, one having to do with *how much* psi ability the subject shows, and the other with the direction the ability takes—whether it registers in the way the subject intends by giving scores above chance, or unconsciously reverses its direction and goes below chance, causing psi-missing. (For a discussion of psi-missing see Appendix C.) Methods now register the evidence of psi either way and correct for this reversal of direction. As a result the psi differential effect has become a useful tool in this double relation of measuring both amount and direction of psi.

Some of the reports on conditions that affect the scoring rate in psi tests bring out the usefulness of the PDE with fascinating clarity. In one of the researches reported in this book, for example, all the evidence of psi occurred in one limiting condition, which was the first of the four runs on each record sheet. Another variable in the same experiment divided the results from these first runs into two opposite trends. Half of the results gave a positive deviation (above chance) and the other half a deviation just as negative (below chance). Thus the experimenter could see in one and the same experiment how these two different factors combine to produce the results, one by giving a measurable amount of psi exchange and the other by putting the evidence into opposite directions of deviation. When one learns what distribution of results to expect, as he may by applying proper statistical methods to his pilot experiment, he can make use of the negative deviation quite as well as the positive one.

Evidently the authors of most of these papers have been getting deeper into the functioning of this delicate unconscious process. They have been discovering that results which once were mystifying, some that cancelled themselves so that only chance results could normally have been reported, can now be efficiently handled and profitably interpreted. This is the most rewarding progress there is in any research field.

* * * *

There has been a fair development in parapsychology of still another kind. This is evident from the non-experimental papers in the final section, and might be called "progress in perspective." The advances indicated in these papers take one or another of three main directions: into the historical perspective of past progress; into the growth of relations between parapsychology and neighboring fields; and into the internal perspective on factors that make for the organizational unity of parapsychology as a field.

Because the historical sketch of PK is needed for an adequate appreciation of the recent work, one background paper is in the PK section. Another paper holds up to the lamp of history one of the most lamentable difficulties of parapsychology, its long quarrel with general psychology. The illumination however seems to the author to have revealed enough of the etiology of the problem to warrant prescription. If the prescription is correct, historical perspective will have had a most fruitful and useful influence.

On the frontiers of parapsychology's relation to other studies, not only psychology but even physics comes into review. Obviously no section of nature can be adequately studied entirely apart from all the rest, even in the most isolated laboratory imaginable. In the very nature of things interrelationships are eternally present and must eventually be faced and considered. The essay on the relationship to physics presents a temperate approach, reasoned from appreciation of both fields, and in a way that offers progress in understanding.

Parapsychology must be expected as a matter of course to have in principle only the closest possible relations with psychology, and for that matter, too, psi must logically be assumed to have *something* in common with physical nature since its phenomena show interaction. Such interaction implies some kind and degree of underlying unity. In any case, the dividing lines between the sciences, however convenient, are always relatively artificial. Perhaps the present "progress reports" on interrelationships go as far as the present stage permits, and they wisely leave the questions open. Affirmations have only tentative value.

The inner perspective outlined in the final paper will be perhaps meaningful for those concerned today about psi research—how it can be managed, sustained, guided, improved and advanced in these times and in the years ahead. More than ever before, parapsychology now is a field of its own. It has an organized approach and a discipline, with standards, methods, and an integrated body of knowledge. But continued progress will depend on the growth of an educated and shared understanding of what a science requires of its personnel and its culture if it is to explore the unknown areas of man's nature that parapsychology has now learned to claim as its territory.

—J. B. R.

Part I
New Approaches

Preface

Novelty is the single unifying aspect of the five papers of this section—that and their psi involvement. The very diversity of these researches is remarkable in itself; such a combination of differences could hardly have been assembled in a scientific book on parapsychology before. Even the professional background of the authors is far-ranging—psychology, biology, physics, biochemistry, philosophy and engineering—although some of the authors are now primarily parapsychologists.

The first paper, which won the William McDougall Award for outstanding work in parapsychology published in 1968, fairly bristles with unique features. The authors introduce another species, the mouse, to psi research, and also a method of testing this animal for precognition. These are notable advances, although some unpublished attempts have been made by at least one other worker. The authors borrowed completely automated test apparatus from the laboratory of animal psychology, another first in parapsychology, making it possible to credit the results solely to the animal by eliminating the need for the experimenter to be present during tests.

Probably the most important new feature in this experiment was the first general use of what the authors call "random behavior." This innovative concept was essential to the success of the experiment. It provided a safe method of eliminating—before the results were checked—all those trials in which the mouse could not be expected to have exercised ESP. The safe and proper elimination of this "chaff" made the yield of "grain" significant. Earlier work at Duke with cats, reported by Dr. Karlis Osis and Esther Foster, had introduced the idea; the French workers put it to systematic use for the first time.

One of the authors is an internationally known biologist

and the other his student. They prefer, for professional reasons, that their real names not be used. The senior author has published a number of contributions to parapsychology; in some of them in which younger colleagues were involved, as in this instance, he has used the name of Pierre Duval.

* * * *

The principal feature of the next report is in the way it takes over the psi-testing operation and handles it with modern electronic equipment, even to providing a basis for the various analyses of results and checks on the adequacy of the controls. The experimenter, Dr. Helmut Schmidt, designed and assembled his apparatus at the Boeing Scientific Laboratories in Seattle, where he was a senior research physicist. Dr. Schmidt left Boeing in 1969 to join the staff of the Institute for Parapsychology, where he is now the Director.

The advantages of the Schmidt equipment are many. It relieves the experimenter of constant precautions against error or fraud during the test, enabling him to give full attention to the subject, and automatically provides for multiple analyses of the data by computer. Still another advantage lies in what the machine will test. This paper reports on tests of precognition and clairvoyance; work on adaptations for testing other types of psi will follow as the full range of the machine's potential is explored.

The embodiment of so much in the apparatus itself represents a major advance, not of course in our understanding of psi but in shortening the long road that leads to such understanding. Parapsychology research is not likely ever again to be the same.

* * * *

The third paper, instead of describing new apparatus, introduces a redesigning of older methods that promises to bring psi ability nearer to reliable use. The authors have in fact resorted to some of the oldest methods of psi testing—the use of dice and cards—as the means of testing their methods in the practical proving ground of the casino.

Dr. Robert Brier, who was for four years the Ralph Drake Perry Research Fellow at the Institute for Parapsychology, is now teaching at the New School for Social Research in New York City. Walter V. Tyminski, a former engineer, is the publisher of *Rouge et Noir*.

Brier and Tyminski used a new combination of statistical devices to concentrate the precognition effects thinly dispersed throughout a mass of test data. Even the limited success in improving the efficiency of psi ability which they have demonstrated is an important step, although it leaves psychological problems of maintaining adequate performance on the part of the subjects for other lines of research to develop further. These and later experiments by the same authors bring the day of application closer.

* * * *

The next report returns to complicated apparatus, in this instance the electroencephalograph (EEG). The EEG is now standard equipment in brain physiology; its records are familiar to the general public as patterns of brain waves. A number of laboratories have explored for connections between EEG and ESP, but this is the first report of significant success. Dr. Rex Stanford, a psychologist who was for a time on the staff of the Institute for Parapsychology, is now in the Division for Parapsychology of the Department of Psychiatry at the University of Virginia. With his wife as co-author, Dr. Stanford reports that while he failed to find a direct measurable relation between ESP and brain waves, he discovered a significant relation between extreme shifts of alpha rhythm recorded by the EEG and variance in the run scores of the ESP tests. As later publications will indicate, this has served to bring the EEG into a current wave of greater use in parapsychology.

* * * *

One of the authors of the fifth paper, Dr. Milan Ryzl, is the winner of an earlier McDougall Award. Dr. Ryzl, a former biochemist, and his assistant, Marie Balounova, a school teacher, both formerly of Prague, are now lecturing and writing in this country. Dr. Ryzl is the author of *Parapsychology: A Scientific Approach*, 1970.

The authors adopted the IBM punch card as a test device, which meant that the results could be checked and analyzed directly by computer. They combined with these conveniences the two-experimenter (double blind) arrangement for controlling their comparative tests of precognition and clairvoyance and the comparative use of hypnosis.

* * * *

One characteristic of these five papers not yet mentioned is that they all have to do with the ESP type of psi. However, the absence of a PK paper in this section does not mean that nothing really new has come up in that branch of the field, but mainly that the PK reports have been more advantageously grouped together in a single section. That common linkage well overshadows their novelty. But while the five papers in Part I do represent new developments they have, like the rest of the book other research values as well, just as most of the other researches break some new ground.

—J.B.R.

PIERRE DUVAL AND EVELYN MONTREDON

ESP Experiments with Mice

The great achievements in medicine and biology made possible by experiments with animals lead us to hope that parapsychology can profit in a similar way from the study of psi in animals. Parapsychology, like medicine, needs a "guinea pig." This report describes experiments with a method of detecting and measuring psi ability in mice.

Stories of animal feats that suggest psi ability have persisted through the centuries. Many reports of cats, dogs, birds, and even toads that found their way home from great distances over strange territory have accumulated in the literature, but no well controlled conclusive test for a psi factor in homing behavior has yet been devised.

Some parapsychologists have, however, turned their attention to animal psi, and a few laboratory investigations have produced encouraging results. The Russian physiologist Bechterev successfully tested a number of dogs for telepathy (1), with the help of the noted animal trainer Durov. Later in England, Richmond tried to influence the movements of paramecia by psi (2). Richmond divided the field of a microscope into four sections and by shuffling cards determined the quadrant into which he would attempt to "will" the animal to move. He reported success, but neither his nor Bechterev's experiments have been confirmed by others. The questions remain of what form of psi ability was operating, and in Richmond's tests, whether the animacule shared in whatever psi ability had been demonstrated.

Presented in absentia at the Winter Review Meetings of the Institute for Parapsychology, December 30, 1967, and January 4, 1969. Complete report (except for work covered in addendum) in *Journal of Parapsychology*, September 1968.

One of the first experimental studies of animal ESP was the work with cats done by Osis and Foster at the Parapsychology Laboratory at Duke University in 1952 and 1953 (3, 4). In the first experiment, Osis placed the animal in an enclosure which completely hid the observer. A long, covered passage was constructed with obstacles staggered along the way to disorient the cat, and two plates of food were put at the end of the passage. The experimenter tried to influence the animal to go to whichever plate had been selected in advance as the target. Significant results were obtained, presumably by telepathy, but of course the animal might have been using clairvoyance.

Osis and Foster then designed a test specifically for clairvoyance. Only one of the two dishes contained food, but the experimenters did not know which dish had been randomly selected. A strong blast of air eliminated olfactory cues. Results were positive here too, and with the human beings no longer aware of the target, the test presumably, but not conclusively, demonstrated clairvoyance in the animal.

In both cat experiments, most of the successes came early in the test. Many of the animals soon began to go consistently to either the left or the right regardless of target, so that results fell off. However, Osis and Foster noted that an animal, after developing a habit pattern, occasionally deviated from it, and when the animal did this, it scored a much higher percentage of hits than in the nondeviant responses.

For example, a cat with a strong tendency to choose the plate on the left (probably having found food there the first time) tended to be correct when it occasionally selected the plate on the right. It was as if the subtle ESP impression had a better chance to break through into expression when a strong habit pattern was interrupted. It seemed that what might be called "random behavior"—behavior contrary to habit—was likely to be an expression of ESP.

These observations pointed to the animal as the source of the psi effect, but the possibility was not entirely eliminated that what appeared to be psi in the animal might in-

ESP Experiments with Mice

stead be psi on the part of the experimenter. No test of ESP in animals yet reported had entirely eliminated either the human element or all possibility of sensory cues. We therefore built a completely automatic apparatus to exclude the human element.

PROCEDURE

Mice were chosen as test animals partly because they are small enough to be easily handled. The necessary stimulus was a mild electric shock, and the apparatus was designed to test whether the animal could avoid the shock by "guessing" which half of a cage would not be electrified.

A center partition which the mouse could easily jump divided the experimental cage constructed for the tests. The cage floor was composed of copper wires through which a weak electric current could be sent. Two live wires permanently under high voltage were connected to the center partition. A system of photoelectric cells, projectors, and mirrors was arranged to give the position of the animal at

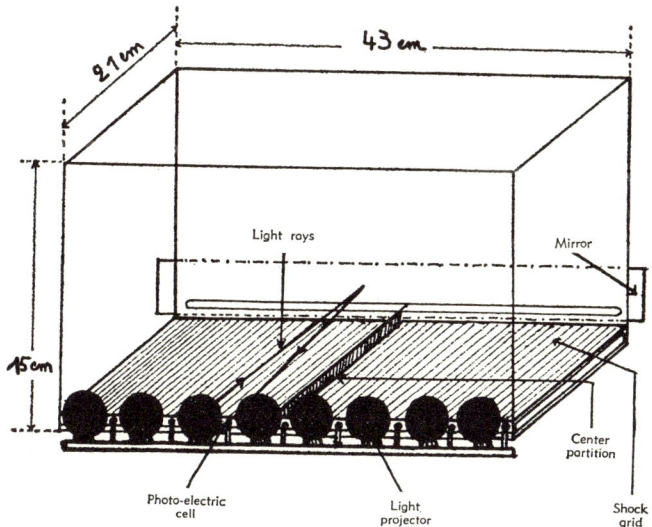

FIG. 1. Experimental cage used in mouse experiments.

all times by means of interference with the light rays (see Figure 1).

The cage was put in a quiet room kept at a suitable temperature. To decrease any possible preference for one side or the other, the cage was placed in a lightproof, soundproof box with orifices in the walls of both cage and box for ventilation.

The rest of the equipment was in another room, with a hall about six feet wide, two doors, and walls about 50 cm thick separating the two rooms. This equipment consisted primarily of a random target selector, a generator of electric pulses of adjustable voltage and duration, some recording apparatus, and safety devices (see Figure 2).

Adjustable characteristics of the apparatus were: duration and voltage of shock, voltage of the current in the center partition, frequency of trials, frequency of runs, interval between the selection of the section of cage floor to receive the cur-

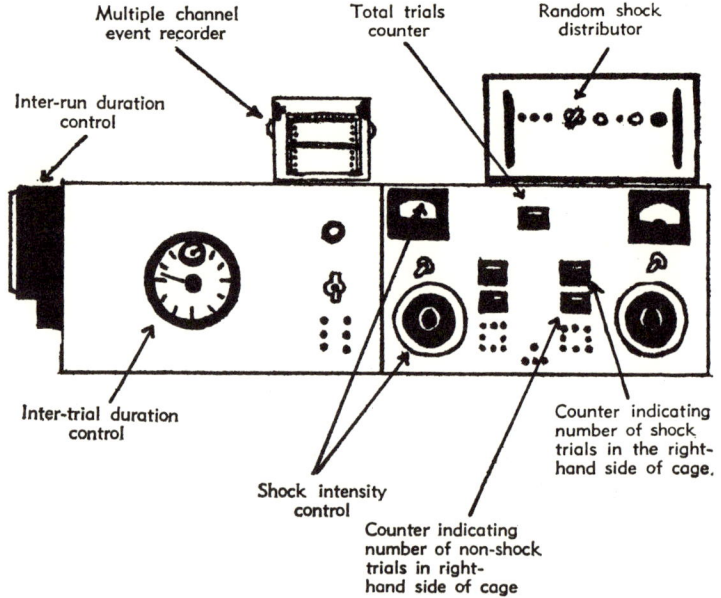

FIG. 2. Mechanical apparatus used in mouse experiments.

rent and the moment of delivery of the current to the cage floor.

The electronic selector was a multivibrator which determined randomly which of the two floor sections would deliver the next electrical stimulus. The animal would receive an electric shock if it was in the part of the cage selected, but not if it was in the other section.

There were four counters: the first recorded how many times an animal was shocked in one cage section; the second, how many times the animal was not shocked in that section; the third and fourth counters did the same for the other cage section.

The accuracy of the results recorded by these counters depended upon the system of light projectors and photoelectric cells. To make sure that there was no "dead spot" in any part of the cage, no place where an animal would fail to cut off at least one light beam, a mirror was positioned to double each light beam.

There was another problem. If, after an animal had been shocked in one side of the cage and the shock duly recorded, the animal jumped to the other side of the cage before the electrical charge stopped, first the shock and then the nonshock counters would be activated during one trial. The two counters for the other side of the cage would also be activated, so that the record would show the mouse had been both shocked and not shocked on each side of the cage during a single trial.

To prevent this, delay relays were connected to the pulse counters so that once a counter had recorded that the animal was or was not in the part selected for the shock, the other counter could not operate, whatever the animal might do, for five seconds (the duration specified for each shock) from the time of shock $+ 1/100$ of a second. Since this time of $1/100$ of a second is very short compared with the reflex time of the animals, it can be taken as a mathematical point in time, and the record will show only which side of the cage the animal was in at that point, leaving the probability of shock at the start of each trial at one chance in two.

Those same delay relays enabled us to record only one pulse even if the animal, after leaping away from the electrical stimulus, jumped back within less than five seconds into the activated part of the cage and felt the same shock a second time during the single trial.

Finally, an animal that jumped into the activated part of the cage after the current had begun to flow got a shock in order to reinforce its motivation to try to escape the stimulus, but since it had been in the nonshock half of the cage at the start of the trial, a pulse was recorded only on the nonshock counter.

In summary, which side of the cage would receive the current was decided by the target selector, and 1/100 of a second later, before the animal could possibly react to the current, a counter recorded whether the animal was or was not in the activated half of the cage. If the animal was there, the shock it got was recorded on the corresponding counter. If it was not in that half at the beginning of the trial, the fact was recorded on the nonshock counter even if during the five-second interval it jumped into the activated section of the cage and was shocked there.

At the end of each run, the counters provided a record of what had happened, with all the trials properly scored. The record showed, for example, that during a run of 100 trials the mouse had been shocked 28 times in the left half of the cage, 20 times in the right half; and not shocked 25 times in the left half, and 27 times in the right half.

The counter, however, did not show variations in the mouse's and in the selector's behavior during a run. A system was therefore connected to the counters to record the immediate details at all times. Thus, the experimenter could see which half of the cage had been selected and whether the animal was shocked or not at each trial. This device also permitted the randomness of the selector to be checked.

A fifth counter was connected to the selector to record how many times the selector operated, i.e., the number of trials in the run. The number of the results recorded by the four other counters combined should obviously equal the figure given by the fifth. Thus, there was a check on the accuracy of the recording systems after each run.

Another device was a test lamp placed in a window of the apparatus which came on when the random selector was activated but before the electric current was turned on, indicating whether the right or left half of the cage was going to receive the electric charge. This lamp could be seen by the experimenter but not, of course, by the mouse in its cage in another room. The lamp, which had been installed for use in a future experiment, was ignored by the experimenters when they were present, and furthermore, approximately half of the trials took place at night when no one was in the laboratory. This lamp introduces the possibility, however remote, of clairvoyance on the part of the animal or of telepathy between the animal and the experimenter. While it seems difficult to even consider that the animal could get information clairvoyantly or telepathically about the oncoming shock from the action of the lamp, there is this faint possibility.

Four pens connected to the selector and counters traced lines on a strip of paraffin paper whenever pulses were received. The paraffin paper unwound at a constant speed. The first pen showed if the left side of the cage had been selected; the second showed if the mouse was in the left side of the cage during the trial moment after the left side was selected; the third showed if the animal was in the right side at the trial moment when the right side had been selected; and the fourth showed if the right side of the cage had been selected. Since it was impossible for lines to be inscribed at the same time by both Pens 1 and 3 or both 2 and 4, this system provided a check on the operation of the apparatus as a whole.

RESULTS

As the test was designed, the psi ability of the mice could be measured by comparing the number of shocks and the number of nonshocks at the end of each run. These two numbers should not differ statistically if chance alone were operating, since theoretically the mouse had one chance in two of being shocked during each trial.

Analysis did not show any overall significant psi effect. In most cases, the animal behaved in an almost purely mechanical manner: it remained in one side of the cage until it was shocked; then it jumped to the other side until another shock caused it to jump once again.

To detect any possible evidence of psi, it was necessary to isolate the responses which were not purely mechanical or easily explainable by the conventional laws of physiology. Analysis on this basis showed three different kinds of responses: (a) mechanical, (b) static, and (c) random.

Static behavior trials were those in which the mouse did not change sides but remained on the same side of the cage, either because it did not feel the electrical stimulus, or because it was too frightened or too tired to jump over the center partition.

Some random behavior, different from the other two kinds of behavior and reminiscent of that noted by Osis and Foster, was observed in the data, and it was there that we looked for evidence of psi.

Random behavior occurred when the mouse, after successfully avoiding the shock during one trial, moved for no apparent reason into the other side of the cage before the next trial. If the animal then received a shock on this second trial, we called it "negative random behavior," because if it had remained in the "good" side of the cage, it would not have been shocked. If the move caused the animal to avoid shock in the second trial also, we called it "positive random behavior."

The number of positive random responses should equal the number of negative random responses in chance series. If the results were to turn out otherwise, psi could explain the difference, a very important question which is discussed below.

Further tests were made with the same apparatus, therefore, and the data analyzed by comparing the negative and positive responses in the trials where the animal exhibited random behavior. Three wild mice and one domestic mouse were each given 25 runs, each run consisting of 100 to 140 trials.

The mice exhibited random behavior in 612 of these trials. By chance alone, the mouse would have been shocked in about half of them (306), but this was not the case. Analysis showed that the mice had avoided the shock 53 times more than one would expect by chance (odds against chance: more than 1,000 to one). This significant result can be attributed to psi, for the animals apparently used precognition or clairvoyance in order to make these correct choices of response.

These results seem to justify the interpretation that electric shock disturbs the animal so much that it sometimes resorts to what we have called a "random" response in order to avoid another. Since the number of positive responses was much higher than the number of negative ones in the total number of random responses, and since nothing in the apparatus we used can explain this difference, we do not hesitate to attribute the results obtained to the psi abilities of the mice tested.

If one supposes that the animals had been getting some sort of sensory cue to which side of the cage was selected by the mechanism in spite of the thickness of the walls separating the selector from the cage, the results would have improved from trial to trial during each run, but no such improvement was observed. In this connection it should be added that a window in the cage room faced a street, and that near the selector in the other room was a machine for testing the effect of psychokinesis on radioactive disintegration. This machine was permanently in operation, and the fans used to cool the internal circuits were quite noisy. If there was a noise that could give the mouse a clue to the side selected by the mechanism, any such noise, if it penetrated the soundproof box around the cage at all, would have been covered by strong background noise.

Signals of electrical nature could not have warned the mouse of the side selected since the record was made within

1/100th of a second, and experimental precautions were taken to insure that no current of any kind should pass through the wires connecting the selector to the cage during that brief interval.

Since the cage room was locked during each run and the apparatus operated completely automatically, no sensory information could pass between the animal and the operator. In fact, the operator, who did not need to follow the experiments, was not aware during a trial of the behavior of either the selector or the mouse.

With the human role thus excluded, the experiment strongly suggests that mice have psi ability, either of the precognitive or clairvoyant type. There still remains, of course, the need to study the nature of this ability, and that is a most difficult task.

DISCUSSION

The equipment designed for this research made it possible to test animals for psi ability by an entirely automatic procedure. In our opinion, the experimenter could not contribute to the results because, as stated above, the experimenter was ignorant of the action of the random selector even when he was present. It seems plausible to conclude that the results, although they might possibly be due to clairvoyance, were more probably achieved by precognition on the part of the animal. In any case, it may be possible to distinguish more sharply between these two types of psi by an indirect method we plan to try.

Addendum

A confirmatory series has not been completed at the time of writing, but the data so far collected may be of interest here. Following the procedure described above, ten wild mice have been tested at the rate of five a day over a period of five months, each mouse being given 150 trials per session. In the 8,314 trials that show random behavior, there were 258.5 more hits than could be expected by chance alone (odds against chance: more than 1,000,000 to one).

LITERATURE CITED

1. Bechterev, Vladimir. "Telepathy and Animals." *Questions of Personality Study and Education*, 1920, No. 2, 230–78. (In Russian.)
2. Richmond, Nigel. "Two Series of PK Tests on Paramecia." *Journal of the Society for Psychical Research*, 1952, **36**, 577–88.
3. Osis, Karlis. "A Test of the Occurrence of a Psi Effect between Man and the Cat." *Journal of Parapsychology*, 1952, **16**, 233–56.
4. Osis, Karlis, and Foster, Esther. "A Test of ESP in Cats." *Journal of Parapsychology*, 1953, **17**, 168–86.

HELMUT SCHMIDT

A Quantum Process in PSI Testing

A notable feature of the three experiments reported here is the use of a quantum process to produce random targets for psi tests. Physicists consider quantum processes the most elementary source of randomness and assume axiomatically that they are quite unpredictable. Determining a target sequence by a simple quantum process therefore satisfies the physicist's demand for reliable randomness in target generation.

The fact that subjects scored significantly above chance expectation in long runs of predicting these targets challenges the physicist's assumption that quantum theory completely describes nature.

The equipment designed for these experiments offers other advantages. The target generator design permits easy verification of electronic operation and randomness. Automatic devices to record predictions, targets, and hits eliminate possibilities of error or fraud, and present the results in a form suitable for computer analysis. These features guarantee a high degree of precision and considerably reduce the experimenter's workload. The equipment is portable, enabling subjects to work wherever they prefer, and safety devices protect the machine from misuse or overload, so that the experimenter need not even be present during tests. Brightly colored lamps display the target instead of numbers, making it easy for a subject to follow his performance and maintain his interest.

Includes papers presented at the Winter Review Meetings of the Institute for Parapsychology, December 30, 1967, and January 4, 1969. Complete reports in *Journal of Parapsychology*, June 1969 and December 1969.

Precognition Experiments

The aim throughout these experiments was to test subjects only under favorable psychological conditions. Efforts were made to keep the subjects happy, slightly challenged, and confident of success. Although the total number of trials for each experiment was specified in advance, each subject was asked to work only when, where, and for as long as he felt in a good mood for it. The atmosphere was deliberately kept informal.

Although the tests could be run without direct supervision, the experimenter was present most of the time during the reported tests.

The first two experiments do not differentiate between precognition and psychokinesis. While a subject could use either to achieve positive results, the experiments are reported as tests of precognition as a matter of convenience.

The future event to be predicted was the lighting of one of four different colored lamps. Since the lamps are lighted in random sequence, a subject without psi ability will choose correctly in approximately a fourth of his trials, and a significantly higher score can be taken as evidence of psi.

APPARATUS

The die is the most familiar random target generator, but for these experiments an "electronic die," or quantum mechanical random number generator, was designed. Besides guaranteeing a high level of precision, it has the advantage of speed, and its reliability is easy to check.

The target generator consists of a radioactive source (strontium 90), a Geiger counter, and a four-step electronic switch controlling the four lamps (see Figure 1). The strontium 90 delivers electrons randomly at the average rate of ten per second to the Geiger counter. A high frequency pulse generator advances the switch rapidly through the four positions. When a gate between the Geiger counter and the four-step switch is opened, the next electron that reaches the Geiger counter stops the switch in one of its four positions (whichever one it happens to be in when the electron regis-

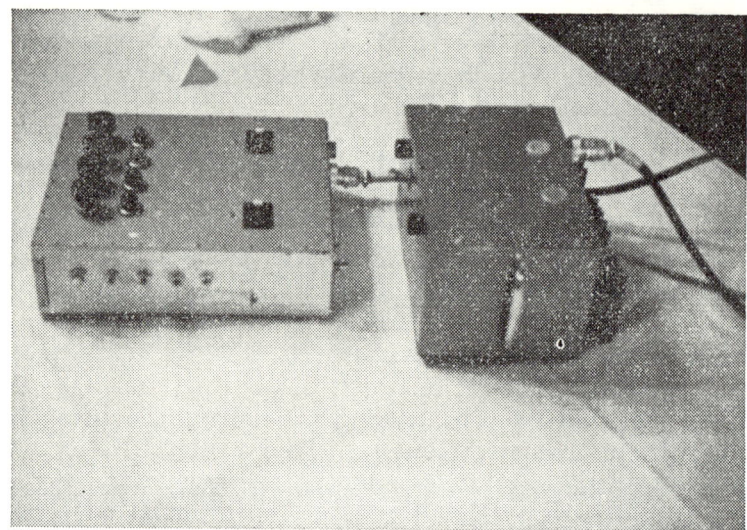

Fig. 1. Two-part device used in precognition testing: (left) console with four pushbuttons, four lamps, and recording mechanisms; (right) random number generator for determining which of the four lamps will light after a pushbutton is pressed.

ters) and illuminates the lamp corresponding to that position. Each lamp, therefore, has a one-fourth probability of being the next target, the choice depending on when an electron registers on the Geiger counter, which is the random result of a typical quantum jump.

The target generator is housed in a $9 \times 11 \times 4$-inch metal box with the four lamps, four corresponding pushbuttons, and two mechanical reset counters on top. The pushbuttons serve a dual purpose: a subject registers his prediction by pressing one of the buttons, and pressing a button triggers the lighting of a randomly selected lamp.

After the switch stops, there is a locking-time interval of approximately half a second to allow one of the mechanical counters to advance a step to record the number of trials made and the other to advance if there has been a hit, that is, if the lamp that lights next corresponds to the pressed button. Furthermore, voltage pulses on output channels activate a tape-punch to record which button was pressed and which number generated. As soon as the half-second locking time elapses, the machine is ready for the next trial.

If the subject presses buttons too rapidly for recording, the apparatus rejects the second choice. To forge a recording, a subject would have to open the sealed unit, advance the non-reset counters, and punch properly coded holes in the paper tape.

Reliability Check: To verify the random nature of target generation, a button was automatically activated by a time clock at the rate of between one and two counts per second, and the resulting numbers were recorded. Computer evaluation of five million numbers thus obtained on 100 different days over an 18-month period before, between, and after these tests showed no deviation from ideal randomness.

Preliminary Tests

Preliminary tests were run in order to find good subjects and favorable working conditions. Almost a hundred people volunteered. Among these, Dr. DW, a physicist, led with a score of 2,065 hits out of 7,600 trials, 165 more hits than would be expected from chance (odds against chance: 150,000 to one). Unfortunately, DW was not available for the experiments, and the three experimental subjects were chosen from among the other high scorers.

The results of the preliminary testing were not, of course, included in the results to be reported.

First Experiment

The three subjects of the first experiment were JB and KMR, both professional mediums, and OC, a student psychic. The mediums were chosen from among the high scorers because they were accustomed to doing psychic work over long periods and because of their strong motivation to demonstrate psi ability; the student psychic was selected partly because a broken foot limited his activities, leaving him with ample time to concentrate on the experiment.

A total of between 55,000 and 77,000 trials in all was specified.

PROCEDURE

The subjects performed the tests in their homes, working only when conditions seemed to be psychologically favorable.

The paper-tape recorder was connected and the electromechanical reset and non-reset counters switched on during the tests, but not between tests when the subjects were allowed to play with the apparatus to try their momentary precognitive skill. All of the events recorded on the tape, and only these, were included in the evaluation.

Convenience and the mood of both subject and experimenter determined the number of trials made on each of the many test days.

RESULTS

OC, the student psychic, made 22,569 trials on eleven days between February 20 and March 9, 1967, scoring 285.75 hits above chance expectation (odds against chance: 27,000 to one).

JB, a medium, made 16,250 trials on five days between March 22 and April 7, 1967, scoring 90.5 hits above chance expectation (odds against chance not considered significant).

KMR, the second medium, had practiced two different approaches to the tests. One approach was to do as the others did—wait for an intuition before pressing one of the buttons. KMR's other method was to use only the button for the red lamp, trying to "catch only red lights."

KMR made 24,247 trials in two sessions, one April 19-20, the other May 24, 1967, scoring 315 hits above chance expectation (odds against chance: 94,000 to one). His remarkable score clearly points to psi ability, but what kind of psi is not so clear. He himself believed he was using psychokinesis to make the red lamp light, and this belief is supported by the fact that among the random targets generated during his trials, the number 4, the target number that lights

A Quantum Process in Psi Testing 33

the red lamp, came up with significantly increased frequency. On the other hand, he may have pressed the button when his precognition told him subconsciously that the lamp would probably be the next to light.

The three subjects' total of 63,066 trials produced a total of 691.50 hits above mean chance expectation, a result that cannot reasonably be ascribed to chance (odds against chance: 500 million to one).

Second Experiment

One of the mediums who took part in the first experiment, KMR, was unavailable for further tests and was replaced by SC, the 16-year-old daughter of OC.

PROCEDURE

At the beginning of each session, the subjects were given the option of either trying to choose the lamp which would light next (trying for high score), or trying to choose one of the three lamps which would not light (trying for low score). A different code was used for each of the two modes of operation so the computer could distinguish between the two types of tests. A total of either 20,000 or 40,000 trials was specified.

OC, who tried for only high scores, made 5,000 trials, scoring 66 hits above chance. JB tried for high scores in 5,672 trials, scoring 123 hits above chance; and for low scores in 4,328 trials, scoring 126 below chance. SC, who tried only for low scores, made 5,000 trials, scoring 86 below chance.

The three subjects' total of 20,000 trials produced a total deviation of 401 hits in the desired direction (odds against chance: ten billion to one).

DISCUSSION

JB's score in the second experiment shows notable improvement over her performance in the first experiment. JB attributes the difference to some type of learning process. However, shortly before the second experiment JB took a few tests for psychometric ability (ability to get information by free-association to a token object), and demonstrated outstanding ability in this type of ESP. This success raised JB's self-confidence and at the same time reduced the experimenter's prejudice against professional mediums, creating more favorable psychological working conditions for the second experiment.

Clairvoyance Experiment

The highly significant results in the two experiments described above could have been achieved by means of either precognition or psychokinesis. A third experiment was designed to exclude psychokinesis by predetermining the sequence in which the lamps would light. Positive results might indicate either clairvoyance or precognition, but to simplify reporting, the experiment is treated as a test of clairvoyance.

The subject's task was, as in the two precognition experiments, to press the button corresponding to the lamp he thought would light next.

The apparatus devised for this experiment has the same external appearance as that used in the precognition experiments, in order to minimize possible bias in favor of either piece of equipment.

The difference is that a paper tape programmed with more than a hundred thousand numbers taken from random tables and further shuffled by computer replaces the random number generator. A tape reader, which can be positioned outside the test room, feeds the predetermined target numbers into the box, causing the appropriate lamps to light.

The target is thus a prepunched hole in the paper tape in front of one of the tape recorder's reading contacts.

Six subjects were chosen by preliminary testing, and a goal of either 15,000 or 30,000 trials in all was set.

Subjects were invited to try either for a high score by pressing the button for the lamp they thought would light next, or for a low score by pressing the button for a lamp they thought would not light. The two types of trial were

PROCEDURE

The procedure was the same as in the precognition experiments.

RESULTS

The six subjects made a total of 15,000 trials. Of these, 7,091 high-score trials produced 108 more hits than would be expected from chance alone; and 7,909 low-score trials produced 152 fewer hits than chance expectation (odds against chance of the total deviation in the desired direction: more than a million to one).

Conclusions

Both types of experiments produced significant scores, and all three experiments gave comparable results. While one might assume that it is easier for subjects to score high on the clairvoyance type of test than on the precognition tests, these experiments gave no support for such an assumption.

ROBERT BRIER AND WALTER V. TYMINSKI

Psi Application

Men have been trying to put their psi abilities to practical use since the dawn of human culture. Not only the histories of magic and occultism but also those of religion and the healing arts are, in large part, stories of attempts to exercise powers beyond the sensorimotor range. Precognition played a prominent role, even in politics, throughout ancient and medieval times. But inability to control the more or less unconscious functions of psi exchange has always seriously limited the application of psi to practical ends and even today is a major obstacle to parapsychological research.

One of the first attempts to approach the problem scientifically was Cadoret's use of a sampling technique to determine if a subject was psi-hitting or psi-missing (1). (See Appendix C for explanation of psi-missing.) Cadoret asked a subject to make a number of trials at locating a penny in a 5 x 5 matrix, then used a sampling of the calls as a prediction of whether the rest of that subject's trials would average above or below chance.

Hallett followed Cadoret's lead by analyzing samples of data from previous experiments to see if the sample would accurately predict the scoring direction in the remaining data (3). He concluded that a variety of techniques could be used to predict from a sample the direction of scoring in the remainder of the data, not only from run to run but also from one part of a single run to the rest of that run.

Neither technique, however, could be useful unless ESP were operating at a high level of efficiency. ESP scoring

---

Presented at the Spring Review Meeting of the Institute for Parapsychology, May 3, 1969. Complete report in the *Journal of Parapsychology*, March 1970.

Psi Application

levels can often be improved by various methods—putting the subject in a favorable state by bolstering his confidence, making the test situation more challenging and interesting, helping the subject to relax, etc.—but none of these methods is reliable.

The authors decided to try a statistical method, the "majority-vote" technique, to see if they could concentrate the ESP hits scattered throughout a large mass of data onto a smaller area to improve the percentage of hits.

Majority-vote Technique: The technique is similar to clarifying a weak signal by repetition. The subject makes a number of calls on the same target, and the call most frequently made is taken as the single call for scoring a hit or a miss. For example, if a subject makes 1,000 calls on evenly divided, concealed, red and black cards, he should score 500 (50%) hits by chance alone. A score of 540 hits, while convincing as evidence of ESP, would hardly be high enough for practical application which demands a far higher level of reliability. But if the subject can consistently score 5.4 hits in ten trials, and if he calls the same 100-card deck ten times so that he makes ten calls for each card, then if the hits are distributed evenly and the majority vote of the calls on each card is taken as a single call on that card, his percentage of hits on the single 100-card deck should be higher. By thus concentrating a relatively low percentage of hits in the large 1000-trial area onto the smaller 100-trial area, theoretically he should achieve a higher percentage of hits.

Foster, while not the originator of the majority-vote technique, used it to test American Indian children (2). Foster's ultimate target was the yes-or-no answer to a question. The subjects were given decks of black and red cards, each card in an opaque envelope. The task was to sort the envelopes, putting the ones they thought held black cards into an appropriate area if they thought the answer was yes, and to avoid doing so if they thought the answer was no. If the subject succeeded in the color matching to a significant degree, this could be taken as an answer to the question.

Unfortunately, when Foster used this method with children who had done well on other ESP tests, he obtained no evidence of ESP. The virtue of his method, however, was that the experiment was so designed that success on a normal ESP test would presumably yield information about an event other than the ESP test. A major obstacle to the use of this method was that it gave no information about the direction of scoring. A subject might indicate significantly that the answer to the question was no, when the correct answer was yes.

Ryzl reported winning a lottery by the majority-vote technique combined with the use of a code (5), but gave no statistical results in his report. More recently, Ryzl tried psi application using his high-scoring subject, PS, and the technique of repeated calls on concealed green or white cards so coded that calls could be translated into sets of three-digit numbers (4). The majority vote determined the final call. After a large number of calls, the report stated, five previously selected three-digit numbers were correctly identified.

Among the many problems the majority-vote technique entails is the problem of bias in calling, as when, for psychological reasons, a subject tends to call one color more than the other. A high percentage of guesses for one color seemingly due to ESP may actually represent only bias.

Another problem is the position effect. (For an explanation of position effects see Appendix A.) If the subject calls a number of runs and consistently shows a decline effect—scores positively in the beginning and at chance or below at the end—the majority vote will not show 54% on each card; it might, for example, show 80% hits on the first 20 cards but only 28% on the last 20. Here the 80% overall scoring on the first 20 cards would give no better result for those cards than the 54% in the other case, since both 54% and 80% accuracy on each call would theoretically produce 100% accuracy. With decline, the last 20 cards could not be correctly identified, but with a consistent 54% on each card, the majority vote should accurately identify the last 20 cards as well. Consistent decline and other position effects thus may detract from the efficiency of the majority vote system. However, position effects can also be used to increase efficiency. For example, if the data show overall scoring at chance and analysis of position effects shows that the hits are concentrated in one portion of the runs, a sample would show where the hitting is localized. That information can then be used as a prediction of where to look for hits in the rest of the data.

The present research on psi application began with a series of preliminary studies designed merely to find promising methods and tests. The results suggested that the majority-vote technique magnifies whatever ESP is in the data, and that the direction of the deviation from chance can be predicted on the basis of a sample portion of data. (See the *Journal of Parapsychology*, March 1970, for details of the preliminary studies.)

This preliminary work and the work of the previous researchers justified further research. To bring the experiment closer to a life situation, the authors decided to use a gambling casino. The excitement of gambling would help sustain the subject's interest through a long series of tests, and the results would lend themselves to clear statistical treatment. The events to be predicted—spins of roulette wheels and hands of cards—satisfy the mathematical requirements (randomness, clear determination of probabilities, etc.) for a scientific experiment, as witnessed by the close connection between the history of probability theory and the problems confronting gamblers in evaluation of odds. Also, the interests of the two authors (one in pure research and the other in psi application in the gaming world) made the casino an obvious choice as a testing ground.

An Attempt at Application: Four Pilot Series

PROCEDURE

The task was to predict which color the ball would land on in the first fifty spins of a particular roulette wheel in a specified casino on a specified future evening. The subject,

HB, made ten 25-trial runs, calling either red or black. The ten runs were divided in half. The five runs in each group were treated as five sets of trials for the same 25 targets, and the majority vote of the five trials on each target determined whether the prediction for that spin was red or black.

The first 25 spins of the roulette wheel at the casino on the specified evening were checked against one set of 25 predictions to see if the subject's precognition had been psi-hitting or psi-missing, but no bets were placed. Bets were then placed on red or black on the next 25 spins. The bets were made according to the predictions in the play set if the test set had indicated psi-hitting, but were placed on the opposite color if the test set had indicated psi-missing. When making the guesses, the subject had not been told which runs would be used to make up the test set of predictions and which would make up the play set, in case the knowledge might cause the subject to score differently on the two kinds of trials. The subject had merely been asked to visualize which of the two symbols, R or B, would eventually be entered in the final column on the record sheet.

Because the time is short between spins of the wheel (usually about 30 seconds) and the casino crowded, the psi-application method was simplified. The majority vote of the trial runs 1, 3, 5, 7, and 9 were used as predictions for the first 25 spins. When the results of these were obtained, they were used to indicate the predictive value of the majority votes of runs 2, 4, 6, 8, and 10 for the next 25 spins of the wheel. This method is illustrated in Figures 1–3, which are sample record sheets from the Pilot 1 test discussed below.

PILOT 1

The standard American casino roulette wheel has 18 black numbers, 18 red numbers, and 2 green numbers (0 and 00). If a bet on either red or black wins, the player wins an amount equal to the bet. The house advantage lies in the green numbers; if the bet is on red or black and a green number is the result, all other bets are lost. Thus, the

Psi Application

house advantage is 2/38, or 5.26%. Considering this house advantage, one would expect by chance slightly fewer than 12 hits per run of 25. This can be seen by the fact that 25 (number of guesses) × .0526 (house advantage) = 1.32, which is the average number of bets in every 25 spins the house takes. This leaves 25 − 1.32 = 23.68 as the average number of spins in 25 which by chance will not be green and on which the player has a one-half probability of winning. The number of hits expected by chance is 23.68 × .5 = 11.84.

The test set of 25 predictions yielded 13 hits. Since this was above chance, above-chance scoring on the next set of 25 predictions was expected. The play set of predictions produced 18 hits (odds against chance: 100 to one).

PILOT 2

The same procedure was followed the next evening. Once again the subject made the ten 25-trial runs, and majority votes gave predictions for 50 spins of the roulette wheel. The 25 test-set predictions from the five odd-numbered runs were matched against the first 25 spins of the wheel. The result was 15 hits, more than 3 above mean chance expectation; positive scoring was therefore expected on the second 25 spins of the wheel, and bets were placed according to the predictions provided by the even-numbered runs. Thirteen hits were obtained, again an above-chance value.

PILOT 3

The next day, the casino opened at 1:00 P.M., remained open until 6:00 P.M., then closed and reopened at 9:00 P.M. This gave two first-fifty spins of the wheel on that day, and the usual procedure was followed for both.

At 1:00 P.M. the set of predictions from the odd-numbered runs was matched against the first 25 spins, resulting in 12 hits, almost exactly chance. The next 25 spins were therefore expected to be within the range of chance and in fact yielded only 10 hits. While this application indicated that ESP had not influenced the predictions, it was considered moderately successful, since one of the functions of the system is to indicate when conditions are unfavorable for psi application.

PILOT 4

That same evening, the test set of 25 predictions gave 12 hits, again very close to chance, leading to the expectation that the play set would also give chance results. There were in fact only 12 hits in the play set of predictions, which was in accordance with expectation.

Discussion of Pilot Series

In two of the four attempts at application, the test set of predictions indicated that positive scoring should be expected, and in both cases the expectation was fulfilled on the play set. In the other two applications, the test set gave chance level results, suggesting that the play set would also be near chance, and this expectation was also met. These results were sufficiently successful to warrant further research.

The results also supported the hypothesis that the majority-vote technique can be used to concentrate the ESP in a given mass of data onto a smaller mass of data to improve the accuracy of the results. In Pilot 1, for example, the percentage of hits went from an average of 54% in five individual runs to 72% after the five runs had been consolidated into a single set of predictions by the majority-vote technique. The hypothesis finds support not only in these empirical results, but also in statistical theory. Given an above-chance scoring rate, probability theory would lead one to expect that the majority-vote technique would improve efficiency. Indeed, the relationships between the percentage of hits in a group of data of a given size and the percentage of hits one would expect when the majority-vote technique has been applied can be formulated, and it may have to be in order to define the optimal conditions for applying the technique to ESP research.

It may be worth noting that the testing conditions in the pilot series were far from ideal. Although the subject was interested in the project and highly motivated, she had done ten runs in each sitting. By the time she got to the 20 runs for Pilots 3 and 4 the novelty had probably worn off, which may account for the decline in evidence of ESP.

Confirmatory Series 1

In the confirmatory series, the same method of arriving at predictions was adapted for predicting the results in a craps game. Craps is a dice game in which the person throwing ("shooting") a pair of dice has a 50–50 chance of winning. (Winning bets, however, are paid at less generous odds, and this is where the casino makes its profit on the game.) Whether or not the shooter wins his hand ("makes a pass") depends upon the number of spots on the uppermost faces of both dice.

The predictions were whether the shooters would or would not make their passes on a series of hands when WT was present, whenever that might be. A test time was not specified; only WT's arrival at the table would determine the start of the test sequence.

Predictions were made for 40 hands, of which 20 were to serve as the test set and the remaining 20 as the play set. WT made ten 20-trial runs. The runs were concentrated by the majority-vote technique, five into predictions for the first 20 hands and five into predictions for the next 20. After the predictions had been determined, WT tossed a coin to decide which 20 predictions would be used as the test set and which 20 the play set. These decisions, of course, had not been taken when WT made the trials, in case the knowledge might make some difference in his calls on the two kinds of trials.

Since 20 is a small number for one-half probability trials and since any deviation from chance on the first 20 hands would represent a relatively large percentage, a score of less than ten was to dictate a psi-missing strategy for the 20 play trials and a score above ten, a psi-hitting strategy. A test set score of exactly ten (chance) would dictate no strategy in terms of psi-hitting or -missing.

RESULTS

The 20 test predictions yielded nine hits, so the psi-missing strategy was adopted and the play predictions were reversed. Fourteen, or 70%, of the 20 reversed play predictions were hits (odds against chance: 20 to one).

DISCUSSION

Here too, the statistically suggestive results indicated that the method of application was effective. There were also clear indications that increasing the number of trials would improve the significance. If, for example, the percentage of hits had dropped only five points from 70 to 65, which is still an impressive percentage, the test-prediction results would not have been statistically significant because the number of trials was so small.

Confirmatory Series 2

Another experiment was conducted using the same basic procedure, this time adapted for predicting the results of hands of baccarat. Baccarat is a card game in which either the player or the banker wins, and each has an approximately equal chance. The winner is determined by the total values of the cards dealt to the player and the total dealt to the banker. The cards completely determine the play; that is, the players make no decisions except the size of the bet and whether to bet with the player or the banker. The subject was ADK, who had previously demonstrated ESP ability. Predictions for five 200-hand sessions were derived by majority-vote technique from ADK's 200 runs of trials.

PROCEDURE

Instructions and 20 ESP record sheets were sent by mail to the subject, who lived at a distance from the experimenters. Each sheet specified a future date and a time of day that would determine which hands of baccarat would be the targets. The first sheet, for example, read: "First 50 hands, Evening at .... Hotel, 2/21/69." The subject filled in ten 25-call runs of trials on this and the other record sheets, predicting whether the player or the banker would win. She knew that the first 50 hands played on each specified evening would somehow determine which of her guesses were correct, but she did not know which five of her ten runs on each sheet would be consolidated into predictions for the first 25 hands and which for the second. She was told that the correct answer would be entered on the sheets next to each of her trials after the play. (The results of the first 25 hands were eventually entered on her record sheet five times, once next to each of the calls in the odd-numbered runs, and the results of the next 25 hands next to calls in the even-numbered runs.)

Before the subject filled out the record sheets, it had been determined that runs 1, 3, 5, 7, and 9 on each sheet would be consolidated by majority vote into 25 predictions for the first 25 hands of the evening, and that these predictions would serve as a test for the occurrence of psi and would determine whether the predictions yielded by consolidation of the even-numbered runs would be played as they stood or reversed.

The 20 completed record sheets were divided into five sets of four sheets, each set of four providing predictions for one session. The targets for a session were the first 200 hands played at the baccarat table on each of the specified evenings. Predictions from the first sheet in each set were matched against hands 1–50; from the second, against hands 51–100, etc., in each of the sessions. The first 25 predictions for a session were used as a test for predicting whether the remaining 25 would give positive or negative results. The experimenters decided that they would consider a test set score of 11, 12, 13, or 14 (close to mean chance expectation) to mean that psi was not operating. If the test score was 15 or above, predictions for the remaining 25 hands would be bet as they stood; if the test score was 10 or below (psi-missing), the predictions would be reversed.

Two of the five sessions, Sessions 3 and 4, were not scorable; one because the casino closed unexpectedly on the

Psi Application

Table 1
Results of Confirmatory Series 2

Session	Hands	No. of Hits in Test Run	No. of Hits in Play Run
1	1–50	13	9
	51–100	17[a]	16
	101–150	10[a]	16[b]
	151–200	15[a]	11
2	1–50	11	10
	51–100	11	13
	101–150	13	15
	151–200	12	14
3	1–50	12	16
	51–100	13	12
	101–150	13	11
	151–200	15[a]	16

[a]Sufficient to meet criterion for play strategy on the remaining guesses (play sections).
[b]After reversing predictions.

specified day, the other because the experimenter could not be present to record the results.

RESULTS

Table 1 shows the results for the three scorable sessions. Four of the twelve sample runs gave scores sufficiently high or low to meet the definition of psi occurrence. The four corresponding play runs had 59 hits, 9 above chance (the same odds against chance as before: 20 to one).

DISCUSSION

Both attempts at confirmation gave results that were positive and suggestive odds against chance.

In addition to producing evidence of ESP, the experiment pointed to something that may be even more important in psi application. When playing the baccarat hands in Series 2, WT noticed that the result of the first trials in a five-trial play segment seemed at times to give him a basis for predicting the number of hits in the remaining trials in that segment. It seemed that the predictions were producing a minimum of three hits out of each five; that is, the scores for the five-trial segments of the play runs were so consistently above chance that if the first two trials in a segment were both misses, the remaining three were relatively likely to be hits.

If the four play runs in Series 2 are divided into a total of 20 segments, each of these 20 segments have an approximately one-half probability of producing an above-chance score by chance. One would therefore expect the score for ten of the 20 segments to be above chance and ten to be below chance. Actually, 16 of the scores were above chance (odds against chance: 100 to one).

With this observation, it was logical to look at the remaining psi-application data to see if they too showed this effect. The pilot series had two ten-segment play runs and Confirmatory Series I provided one run of 20 trials on craps hands, for a total of 14 five-trial segments. By chance, the results of seven of these 14 would be positive; in fact eleven of them were positive, (odds against chance: 20 to one). Thus the five-trial segments of the various play runs in these psi application experiments were consistently above chance to a marginally significant degree.

General Discussion

The results of these experiments are clearly encouraging, but major improvements are needed. In the work done so far, the basic technique has been a combination of sampling and majority vote.

The sampling was in the use of the odd-numbered runs to get sets of test predictions and the even-numbered runs to get the play sets. If a subject should alternate between above- and below-chance from run to run, this sampling

Psi Application

technique would not be effective, but no such case has been reported in the literature.

In principle, it would be better to evolve a truly random sampling technique, but this would require relatively large numbers of runs to ensure against the possibility that a random-sampling technique might by chance select an unusual distribution of runs. With only ten trial runs to provide both test and play predictions, a random-sampling technique could conceivably select as the five runs for making the test set the first five runs the subject made. If the decline effect were present, the test predictions would then strongly indicate psi-hitting, but the play set would yield below-chance scores, which would be disastrous in many application situations. One could, however, avoid such possibilities by restricting the sampling technique so that the runs selected for making the test predictions would have to include approximately the same number of runs from first and second halves of the subject's run session, etc.

One might also apply a sampling technique within the runs. Position effects could thus be detected and perhaps utilized, as was done in a crude way with *post hoc* analysis of these data after attention had been drawn to the segment-score consistency.

These are only broad general indications of possible improvements in sampling techniques. They do not touch on the many fine points which must be considered.

The majority-vote technique was used to reduce five predictions of the same target to one prediction. This attempt to increase the percentage of hits by concentrating the hits in a number of trials into a smaller number of trials was successful. In each of the series, the technique did raise the hit percentage in the individual runs to a higher level in the derived predictions.

If each prediction had been based on ten, rather than five, trials, it is quite possible that the percentage of hits in the final predictions would have been still higher. What constitutes the optimum number—what number of "votes" will give the most dependable majority vote—is still an open question.

In the above experiments, success was measured by the statistical significance of the results. When the ultimate goal is successful application of ESP, a yardstick more closely akin to efficiency may be more appropriate. In casino roulette, for example, the house has a more than 5% advantage over the player. A subject who could use his ESP to maintain a 54% average of hits for a run of 100,000 bets on red and black would lose money because of the house advantage. His attempt at psi application, although a successful demonstration of psi, would fail as an application of psi.

If, by using his 100,000 predictions as trials and applying majority-vote technique to derive from them predictions for 20,000 plays, he could raise his hit level in the 20,000 predictions by as little as 2% to 56%, he would win; his attempt at psi application would succeed, although a 56% scoring rate on 20,000 trials is statistically less significant than a 54% scoring rate on 100,000 trials. Obviously there are measures of success more useful than statistical significance for psi applications in a casino.

Nor is a casino situation the only such case. In trying to send or receive a message by ESP, for example, statistical significance would not necessarily be useful in measuring success as a practical matter. Successfully transmitting 15 of the letters in a 37-letter message would be highly significant statistically, but might very well fail to convey any idea of what the message was about. On the other hand, success in transmitting four of the letters in a five-letter message would usually be quite adequate to convey the message. While successful as an application, getting four out of five letters correct has less statistical significance than getting 15 out of 37 letters correct. Other situations in which statistical significance is not the most useful yardstick for measuring the success of a psi application are not hard to find.

Another interesting aspect of the work reported here is the experimental design structure. The design of most psi experiments allows for the possibility that, for any number of reasons, the results will go contrary to those achieved in earlier work. Changes in attitude of an experimenter or subject, altered test conditions, variations in the composition of a test group, even the experience gained by any or all parties in previous experiments, are only a few of the variable factors that can reverse the direction of results. And of course any psi experiment must allow for the occurrence of psi-missing.

The sampling technique should enable the experimenter to correct for shifts of the subject's psi ability from psi-hitting to psi-missing, especially when the sample includes as large a proportion of the whole as 50%. As employed here, the technique was able to detect psi shifts from one session to another; it would have failed only if the subject had frequently alternated between hitting and missing from run to run.

Thus far, attention has been focused primarily on method. Even more important in any psi research project is the subject. If he cannot demonstrate his psi ability under experimental conditions, there is nothing for even the most sensitive of experimental methods to detect. Thus, anything which helps the subject evince psi ability will help speed psi research. On this score, the psi-application technique evolved in the reported work offers another advantage. Most subjects want very much to do what the experimenter asks them to do and are discouraged if they score negatively when positive scoring is desired. With the above psi-application technique, the experimenter can assure subjects that either psi-missing or psi-hitting is welcome, which may remove a psychological handicap.

The majority-vote technique can also help to lessen a psychological handicap inherent in the casino situation and some other practical situations where psi might usefully be applied. When a player is having a run of good luck (which could mean he is responding by ESP), the casinos have a strong interest in throwing him off his stride, and have developed some effective techniques for interfering with his psychological state. Casino employees may stop the play to examine the dice, change dealers, offer the player free drinks, or use other devices to distract a player who is winning heavily. But if the player can use precognition as a guide, he can determine his play before coming to the casino and make his predictions under conditions most favorable for him. In fact, he need not expose himself to the casino's influence at all. (A detailed description of the relationship between parapsychology and casino psychology can be found in the book, *Winning at Casino Gaming* [6]).

LITERATURE CITED

1. Cadoret, Remi. "The Reliable Application of ESP." *Journal of Parapsychology*, 1955, **19**, 203–27.
2. Foster, A. A. "ESP Tests with American Indian Children." *Journal of Parapsychology*, 1943, **7**, 94–103.
3. Hallett, S. J. Unpublished data cited by Cadoret.
4. Ryzl, Milan. "A Model of Parapsychological Communication." *Journal of Parapsychology*, 1966, **30**, 18–30.
5. Ryzl, Milan. "Training the Psi Faculty by Hypnosis." *Journal of the Society for Psychical Research*, 1962, **41** (No. 711), 234–52. (Edited and reviewed by G. W. Fisk.)
6. Staff of Rouge et Noir, Inc. *Winning at Casino Gaming*. New York: Rouge et Noir, Inc., 1966.

REX G. STANFORD and BIRGIT E. STANFORD

EEG Alpha Rhythm in Relation to ESP Scoring Patterns on Variance

The question of the optimal state of mind for ESP performance is frequently raised. Usually the test subject's mental state has to be inferred either from the way he acts or from what he says about his state of mind. With the apparatus on hand today, however, it is no longer necessary to depend entirely upon such observations or verbal reports for records of the mental changes occurring in the individual. The brain-wave record, or electroencephalogram, for instance, provides a simple method for recording certain rapid changes of electrical activity occurring in the brain that are related, at least in some respects, to the mental state of the individual (7).

A number of parapsychologists have suggested that a relaxed state of mind is likely to facilitate ESP performance. Rhea White made a point of this in her excellent discussion of old versus new methods of response in ESP experiments. In much of the early, non-quantitative work on ESP, White notes, ". . . specific techniques are made an integral part of the method for achieving a relaxed state" (8, p. 29). Deliberate attempts were made to still the body and the mind. This was not the entire method, but was an important part of it.

In certain spontaneous ESP cases in which, initially, only a somewhat vague impression occurs, the individual is sometimes able to bring into consciousness more complete details by maintaining a relatively undisturbed, steady state of "concentrated introspection." Sudden action or disturbance

---

Presented at the Autumn Review Meeting of the Institute for Parapsychology, September 2, 1967. Complete report in *Journal of Parapsychology*, March 1969.

sometimes seems to interfere with bringing further details into consciousness (6).

Thus it is quite possible that by maintaining a steady, undisturbed, or relaxed state of mind, one can facilitate the emergence into consciousness of psi material.

It has been recognized for about fifty years that the brain wave known as alpha rhythm, a relatively large, 8-13 cycles per second wave, is associated with relaxed wakefulness. This rhythm is likely to be present in the occipital (visual cortex) region of the brain, especially when the eyes are closed while the person is awake and is not attempting to visualize any image. When a person is alerted by a sensory stimulus and begins to focus his attention upon a sensory situation or upon purely internal imagery, the alpha rhythm is likely to disappear or to give way to the more rapid wave known as the beta rhythm. Under these circumstances alpha activity is blocked. Conversely, a recorded beta wave or simply an absence of alpha giving way to an alpha rhythm over a period of time suggests that the person is moving from a state of focused, alert attention to one of more relaxed wakefulness wherein the mind is free of effort to visualize or otherwise reorganize the thought processes.

In view of these findings it is not strange that parapsychologists should take an interest in a possible correlation between alpha activity or alpha activity changes and ESP performance. Cadoret's electroencephalogram (EEG) recordings made during clairvoyance tests with seven subjects showed more ESP hits during periods of relatively slow EEG activity, predominantly alpha rhythm, than when EEG activity was relatively fast. The difference was marginally significant (1).

The purpose of the present experiment was to see if Cadoret's finding could be confirmed and to explore other possible correlations of EEG and ESP.

PROCEDURE

EEG recordings were made on 11 male subjects ranging from junior high school age to middle age while the subjects were taking down-through clairvoyance tests. Pre-experimental plans had stipulated a total of 60 ESP runs with simultaneous EEG recording. Thus the average number of runs per subject was five to six, the actual number for each subject depending on the time available for working with him.

On all but five of the EEG-ESP runs, bipolar EEG recording was employed. In this experiment that meant the electrical potential changes occurring in the occipital (visual) area of the subject's cerebral cortex were referenced to (measured relative to) electrical changes in the frontal area of the brain. Recording of EEG was always done on the subject's left side. With five of the EEG-ESP runs monopolar EEG recording was employed. Electrical changes in the occipital region of the brain were referenced to a relatively stable area, the ear lobe.

The EEG records were made with scalp electrodes and a Grass Model 5c polygraph. Recording was simultaneous with the ESP run.

Each ESP run consisted of the subject's calling a deck of cards by the down-through clairvoyance method. Each deck consisted of 24 cards; six of each of four geometrical symbols—star, square, circle, and three wavy lines—as found in the conventional ESP deck. (The fifth ESP symbol, the cross, was not used.) Subjects were given a different deck of cards for each run. Each deck was thoroughly shuffled, cut, and sealed in a cardboard box before being presented to the subject.

Subjects were shown their scores after they called each deck.

Before beginning the initial session with each subject, the experimenter explained that the purpose was to determine whether any special state of mind was associated with ESP performance and that we were using the EEG recording to measure the state of mind of the subject. The subject was told that we did not expect to find any direct connection between ESP and brain waves; that is, he was told there was no reason to think that brain waves act like radar in detecting the cards. In short, the explanation given was truthful, but not specific enough to reveal the hypothesis.

Subjects were also assured that the test situation was harmless and that there was no danger of their being shocked by the apparatus. A strong effort was made to make each subject feel at ease in the somewhat "medical" situation. The subject relaxed in a reclining chair and called each card deck with his eyes closed in a darkened room.

EEG activity was measured for its "alpha index" by one experimenter, BES, who was not allowed, while measuring the EEG, to know the ESP score associated with that run. The other experimenter, RGS, was unaware of the results of the EEG measurements when scoring the ESP tests. ESP tests were scored twice to insure accuracy. Each subject's EEG record was scored twice, and the two measurements averaged. Details of the measurements which allowed us to obtain an index of alpha activity can be found in the full technical account of this experiment in the *Journal of Parapsychology*, March 1969.

RESULTS

According to the hypothesis based upon the Cadoret work, each run was analyzed to see whether the half-run showing the greatest preponderance of alpha activity also showed the higher level of ESP scoring. The half-runs which were expected to give high scores were compared with the half-runs expected to give low scores.

The comparison did not show a significant difference: alpha level during the half-run was not useful in predicting the ESP scoring level for the half-run. Cadoret's results are not supported by the outcome here, but it should be added that this experiment was not an exact replication of the Cadoret experiment.

Because of the experimenters' interest in a possible relation between alpha *change* and ESP scoring, an unplanned statistical analysis was made to compare runs showing large differences in alpha activity between the two halves of the test run with those showing small differences in alpha activity. Division was made at the median, and only the *amount* of alpha change between run-halves was considered, not the *direction* of change. However, no significant difference in ESP scoring level was found between the large as compared with small alpha-change runs.

Later reflection led to a re-examination of the records in the light of the recent emphasis on the effects upon run-score variance of transient mental states such as mood (2, 3) or attitude toward the ESP task (4, 5).

Mounting evidence of a connection between transient states (mood or attitude) and variation of ESP test scores (i.e., variation above and below the chance average) suggested that the results of the EEG experiment might profitably be analyzed *post hoc* in terms of a possible relation of alpha activity to the variance of test scores. Since this variation in run scores appeared to be related to transient variables like mood and attitude toward the task, perhaps it would also relate to the very transient states of mind reflected in changing EEG activity. The 30 runs showing the largest amount of change in alpha activity between the two halves of the ESP run were compared with the 30 runs showing the smallest amount of change. Comparison was in terms of run-score variance; that is, in terms of how far the run score deviated from chance average regardless of whether the scoring was above or below the chance average level.

The runs with large alpha change showed a marginally significant large run-score variance. In other words, runs in which alpha activity tended to shift considerably between the two halves of the run were apt to give scores that varied considerably from the chance average level. Results as definite as or more definite than those obtained here would occur less than one time in twenty by chance alone.

On the other hand, runs showing small alpha change gave a run-score variance somewhat smaller than that expected by chance, but not to a significant degree.

When the variation of scores in runs with large alpha change was compared with the variation of scores in runs with small alpha change, a difference was found which would be equalled or exceeded only about once in 50 such experiments by chance alone.

The evidence of large run-score variance in the runs showing large change in alpha naturally raises the question as to which kind of marked alpha change is producing the effect. Was the effect predominantly present in the 18 runs that showed a marked *increase* in alpha from the first half to the last half of the run; or was it in the twelve runs that showed a marked *decrease* in alpha from the first to the last half of the run?

The runs where alpha activity increased markedly throughout the run were almost entirely responsible for the effect noted above. These runs showed a run-score variance so great that it or a more extreme variance would occur by chance only once in one hundred such experiments.

By contrast, the runs where alpha decreased markedly throughout the run showed a smaller than theoretical run-score variance, though not significantly smaller.

It appears that a marked increase in alpha rhythm during the second half of the ESP run tends to be associated with a score that varies considerably from the chance average level; however, it says nothing about whether this variation is apt to be in the positive or negative direction.

ALPHA INCREASE, CALL BALANCING, AND ESP

Earlier studies (4, 5) indicated that psychological freedom from the "logical," or "intellectualistic," tendency to call equal numbers of each ESP symbol is associated with large run-score variance. Furthermore, the opposite tendency of balancing calls over all the symbols seems to produce small run-score variance. The tendency to call equal numbers of all the symbols is a kind of mental activity which should tend to block the alpha rhythm, especially in the latter portion of the run where "calculation" becomes more crucial in balancing out calls. Therefore, the ESP runs where subjects showed a marked increase in alpha rhythm throughout the run should be runs where subjects were able to escape the tendency to balance their calls over all the

ESP symbols. For this reason, it was suggested, prior to any examination of the relevant data, that in the runs showing marked increase in alpha rhythm the subjects should show less of a tendency to guess each symbol an equal number of times than in the runs showing marked alpha decrease.

Using an appropriate measure of the subject's tendency to guess the ESP symbols an equal number of times in each run, it was found, as expected, that runs accompanied by marked alpha increase showed less of a tendency toward balanced guessing than did runs with a marked alpha decrease. From a statistical standpoint, the difference is a reasonably reliable one, since a difference this great or greater would occur by chance in only one out of fifty such experiments. Runs where alpha increased strongly from the first to the last half of the run were runs where the subject was able, to some degree, to escape the "logical" tendency to balance his guessing over all the symbols.

DISCUSSION

When the alpha rhythm increased markedly throughout the ESP test run, there was a significantly large run-score variance. Note, however, that the significance of this finding must be qualified somewhat by the fact that the finding was not anticipated prior to the experiment; that is, it is a first indication of this effect and needs confirmation.

When the alpha rhythm increased markedly throughout the ESP run, there was less tendency on the part of the subject to balance his calls. This tendency, when present, can be construed as evidence of an "intellectualistic," or "logical," approach to the ESP task.

Earlier work had, as mentioned above, suggested that sizable deviation in an ESP run, regardless of direction, requires that the subject be spontaneous during the task and that he escape the rather natural tendency to "logically" structure his guessing. The present findings, though only suggestive, lend some strength to this idea. In the present study, ESP runs in which the subjects' EEG records suggest a certain spontaneous orientation toward the task do in fact show considerable run-score variance and do in fact show a psychological freedom in terms of actual calling patterns. Thus the present study complements quite well the earlier work on the effects upon run-score variance of the tendency to balance calling. The present findings must, however, be regarded as only suggestive because analysis of such effects was not planned prior to the experiment.

A major suggestion which emerges from this study is that future work on the relation of EEG and ESP should look not only at the level of alpha activity but should examine EEG changes as well. Perhaps brain processes (changes of "state") are of importance here, as well as relatively steady brain states. This is not really a surprising suggestion in terms of what is known about the function of the brain in relation to alertness, wakefulness, and sleep.

The convergence of this EEG study with the earlier work on balanced calling and run-score variance suggests that experiments would be of value in which the subject's tendency to balance his calling is experimentally manipulated during runs while EEG recordings are made.

LITERATURE CITED

1. Cadoret, R. J. "An Exploratory Experiment: Continuous EEG Recording During Clairvoyant Card Tests." Unpublished manuscript, 1952, abstracted, *Journal of Parapsychology*, 1964, **28**, 226.
2. Rogers, D. P. "Negative and Positive Affect and ESP Run-Score Variance." *Journal of Parapsychology*, 1966, **30**, 151–59.
3. Rogers, D. P. "Negative and Positive Affect and ESP Run-Score Variance—Study II." *Journal of Parapsychology*, 1967, **31**, 290–96.
4. Stanford, R. G. "The Effect of Restriction of Calling Upon Run-Score Variance." *Journal of Parapsychology*, 1966, **30**, 160–71.
5. Stanford, R. G. "A Study of the Cause of Low Run-Score Variance." *Journal of Parapsychology*, 1966, **30**, 236–42.
6. Stevenson, I. "Telepathic Impressions: A Review and Report

of Thirty-five New Cases." *Proceedings of the American Society for Psychical Research*, 1970, **29**.
7. Towe, A. L. and Ruch, T. C. "Association Areas and the Cerebral Cortex in General." In *Neurophysiology*, pp. 464–82. Philadelphia: W. B. Saunders Co., 1963.
8. White, Rhea A. "A Comparison of Old and New Methods of Response to Targets in ESP Experiments." *Journal of the American Society for Psychical Research*, 1964, **58**, 21–56.

MILAN RYZL AND MARIE BALOUNOVA

IBM Cards in ESP Testing

Little research has been reported in which an IBM card has been used to record the subject's trials in an ESP experiment. Such a procedure has definite advantages since it allows immediate and easy scoring by a computer and facilitates subsequent statistical analyses.

An opportunity to use IBM cards to record ESP trials arose when the authors came from Czechoslovakia to the United States bringing some data from previous experiments which they wanted to have analyzed by a computer. The work of transferring the data from record sheets to IBM cards brought the authors in close contact with the computer technique for the first time. This created an atmosphere of excitement and novelty which is often thought to be valuable in an ESP experiment.

The question was: Would it be possible to demonstrate ESP by punching IBM cards on the IBM keypunch (a device similar to an electric typewriter) so that the holes punched by the subjects would match the holes punched on a target card? It was decided to use this method in both clairvoyance and precognition test conditions to see if any difference between them would be shown. A secondary aim was to test whether hypnosis could influence a subject's performance.

Preparation of the target cards: The standard IBM card is made up of 80 columns of numbers from zero to nine. The authors decided that a target card would be prepared with 80 holes punched in it, one in each column, and that they, acting as subjects, would punch IBM cards on the keypunch

---

Presented at the Spring Review Meeting of the Institute for Parapsychology, May 3, 1968.

IBM Cards in ESP Testing 63

Fig. 1. IBM card as clairvoyance target with 80 holes (one in each vertical column) punched. Subjects tried to duplicate this card by ESP.

and try by ESP to punch their cards so that they would correspond to the target card.

The target card for the clairvoyance portion of the experiment (see Figure 1) was prepared by Robert Brier who had agreed to prepare a random series of target numbers for the experiment and to serve as witness. To do this, Brier found an entry point in a book of random numbers following a standard method used at the Institute for Parapsychology. (For a description of this procedure see Appendix B.) This entry point determined the 80 targets which were then punched (by the witness himself) on the IBM card. The punched card was duplicated and one copy kept by the witness as a routine precaution against any changes in it. The original card was then inserted in an opaque cover and sealed in an envelope to be used by the subject as the target.

The target for the precognition arrangement was prepared as follows: MR took a blank IBM card and placed it in an envelope with a transparent window so that the whole card was visible. The blank card was thus a substitute for the target in the clairvoyance test. The actual target, of course, had not yet been determined. It was understood that, after the subjects had punched their trials on their IBM cards, the witness would find an entry point in the table of random numbers and thus determine the sequence of 80 numbers which would then be punched onto the enclosed card. Thus, the subjects were predicting which holes would later be punched on the card.

PROCEDURE

Each column of the IBM card was equivalent to one trial, with a one-in-ten chance of being correct. Each card consisted of 80 trials, and these constituted one run.

Both authors served as subjects in the experiment which consisted of ten sessions in all. Each session involved the use of both the clairvoyance and precognition targets (in the latter case, a blank card). The subject tried to make as many hits as possible by punching one number in each of the 80 columns of an IBM card. He then repeated this procedure nine more times, thus completing ten cards, or ten runs, in each condition per session which he intended to have match the respective target.

The order of clairvoyance vs. precognition trials was that, in sessions 1, 3, 5, 7, and 9, MB began by punching ten cards for the clairvoyance target. MB was then hypnotized by MR and merely given suggestions that she would do well. She then punched another ten cards for the clairvoyance target and, following that, ten cards for the precognition target, both while under hypnosis. MB was then awakened and completed the punching of another ten cards for the precognition target. Thus, in each session, MB punched 40 cards. Next, MR punched ten cards for the clairvoyance target and then ten cards for the precognition target. He was not placed under hypnosis and thus punched only half as many cards as MB.

The authors did not want MB always to be first, nor did they want the clairvoyance runs always to precede the precognition runs. Therefore, the testing orders were alternated. In sessions 2, 4, 6, 8, and 10, the reverse order was used. MR punched ten runs of precognition and ten of clairvoyance. Then MB punched ten runs of precognition while waking, then ten more while under hypnosis. Still hyp-

IBM Cards in ESP Testing

notized, she punched ten clairvoyance runs. Then, in the waking state, she punched ten clairvoyance runs.

In the ten sessions, six different conditions were included (MB hypnotized-precognition, MB hypnotized-clairvoyance, MB waking-precognition, MB waking-clairvoyance, MR waking-precognition, MR waking-clairvoyance). In each condition, 100 cards (8,000 trials) were punched. When all cards were thus punched, the authors duplicated them automatically on the IBM duplication machine. They kept the original cards and gave the copies to the witness together with the envelope containing the clairvoyance target card. Thus, neither the witness nor the subjects, after examining the subjects' punched cards, could have fraudulently created a different target to match the trials.

Finally, to determine the precognition target, the witness found one more entry point in the tables of random numbers in the usual way. This was done under the authors' supervision before the witness had had time to inspect the punched cards he received from the authors. He determined a sequence of 80 numbers, wrote them down with a copy, kept the copy so that the authors could not later punch a different card to match their trials, and gave the original list to the authors. The authors then punched these numbers on the precognition target card, copied it, gave the original to the witness, and kept the copy.

By using this procedure of duplicating trials and targets, both the authors and the witness had their sets of target cards and data cards. Both these sets were scored and analyzed by the computer. This computer processing was performed separately for both sets. As could be expected, analyses gave identical results.

RESULTS

There were only 80 targets in the clairvoyance and 80 targets in the precognition experimental arrangements. Thus, each subject made many trials for each punched hole on the target card. The statistical evaluation method used takes into account the fact that a number of trials were made for each list of targets.

The results of the combined scores of both subjects were not significant, nor was MR's score.

MB, however, scored a total of 184 hits above chance (odds against chance: 1,000 to one). MB scored more hits under hypnosis than in the waking state, and more hits in the precognition runs than in the clairvoyance runs, but neither of these differences was significant.

DISCUSSION

Since only one target card was used for precognition and only one for clairvoyance, it was possible that the significant results were obtained by what is known as the *stacking effect* rather than by ESP. (For a description of the stacking effect, see Appendix D.) To determine if this was the case, a statistical analysis was carried out. If the stacking effect were responsible for the significance, then one might expect some of the 80 targets to have considerably more hits than the remaining targets. Inspection of the distribution of hits (per trial on the card) showed that this was not the case.

The experiment had three objectives: the first was to test the card-punching method of recording trials; the second, to test the effect of hypnosis; and the third, to see if the clairvoyance and precognition techniques would produce different results. The first objective was well attained, although by only one of the two subjects. But MB's high scores showed very well that, for her, the card-punching method was a successful and feasible variation. The second and third objectives showed in each case that, while one of the test conditions (hypnosis vs. waking, and precognition vs. clairvoyance) yielded somewhat higher scores than the other, the difference was not very great. Apparently, MB could demonstrate ESP with or without hypnosis and in either precognition or clairvoyance tests, at least with the novelty of the card-punching technique.

Part II
Mind Over Matter

Preface

Research on psychokinesis (PK) is clearly moving ahead today. Comparing the reports from this two-year period with the one preceding shows as much, and already there are grounds for saying that the next biennium will outdo even this one. PK research now promises to catch up with ESP research. For this reason alone it is an advantage to have the historical outline of the laboratory work on PK as the first paper in the section. The new studies stand out best against this review of earlier work.

Indeed one very much needs to see how firm the foundation is on which PK stands today. These more recent experimenters knew that, and proceeded with the confidence it naturally and rightly gave them. There is probably nothing in the whole of parapsychology even today that presents a sturdier claim on the rational mind than the Quarter Distribution analyses brought out by Dr. Rhine in her review. There one sees, too, the logical development of the PK type of psi research in the experimental evolution of the field of parapsychology. This research on PK is a strong division in itself and yet it is only a part of the larger unity of the total system of psi exchange.

One sees then why it is important to attempt, as Drs. Feather and Rhine did in the help-hinder experiment, to see whether two heads are better than one in a PK test. From their results it does not look as if they are, but it does seem clear that the subject's mood makes a difference to PK performance.

Again one needs history to get the import of W. E. Cox's new venture into the kinds of machinery that PK can influence. As a matter of fact, one really needs the entire chapter Dr. Rhine gives him in her book, *Mind Over Matter*. It will not be surprising if the reader ends the Cox paper with the question: What can PK *not* affect?

At least that is a good question with which to go on from the report on the moving pendulum to that on the living plant monitored by a polygraph. Following up the novel approach, which was reported in *Parapsychology Today*, Dr. Brier makes his second contribution to the development of methods for testing the green-thumb hypothesis—that the mind can directly affect plants. Coming as the paper does, right after the Cox report, it is well that the author himself is prepared for the question as to whether PK may not after all be affecting the machine instead of the plant.

The research of Dr. Barry does not answer that question, but raises many others for the continuing research on living matter as a target for psychokinesis. One of the novel elements in this experiment is the fact that PK was used to *retard* the growth of the fungus (a pathological organism). How appropriate it is then, for a physician to pursue this type of psi application. One thinks of the obvious comparison of Dr. Barry's countryman, Louis Pasteur, whom every schoolboy now calls "great," although few recognized Pasteur's greatness when he was at Dr. Barry's stage in his experiments.

Some mention should be made, perhaps as an aside, of the present fad of "talking with plants," and seeking to record intelligent responses via the polygraph. Too much serious attention has already been given to claims that were tested and found wanting long before they were ill-advisedly publicized—as it was, on doubtfully adequate grounds. These so-called plant-perception claims should not be confused with such experiments as those of Dr. Brier and Dr. Barry.

Even between the lines the reader of these few papers can only dimly perceive that this section leaves us on the threshold of a new epoch in PK research. New methods, new areas of phenomena, new species, and some challenging new concepts are already being born in the current period. They will all, however, be better understood and appreciated in the light of the history and reports in this section.

* * * *

Preface

Dr. Louisa E. Rhine, author of the historical paper, has been for many years a staff member of the Parapsychology Laboratory at Duke and of its successor, The Institute for Parapsychology, and since 1956, co-editor of the *Journal of Parapsychology*. She is the author of numerous articles and three books: *Hidden Channels of the Mind, ESP in Life and Lab*, and more recently of *Mind Over Matter*. Together with her daughter, Dr. Sara R. Feather, who was at the time also on the research staff of the Institute and is now practicing clinical psychology, she conducted the PK experiments with automatic dice-throwing reported in the second paper.

W. E. Cox is a veteran parapsychologist especially devoted to PK research and responsible for a number of innovations in its apparatus and methodology. He is a research associate of the Institute for Parapsychology. Dr. Brier has been introduced in the preface to Part I; Dr. Jean Barry is a physician practicing in Bordeaux, France, and the report given here is his second experiment with PK on plants.

—J.B.R.

LOUISA E. RHINE

PK in the Laboratory: A Survey

The idea that matter can be moved by mind alone has little reality to the average person, although it is an ancient one once considered a mark of the supernatural. Few persons today have had any reason to think that such an effect does occur and much everyday experience to show that it does not. Nevertheless, research on the topic which is known as psychokinesis, or PK, has been going on since 1934. However, few persons outside of the field of parapsychology know about this research, or that the general result of it is to show that such a phenomenon of mind is a reality.

The PK research began at the Duke Laboratory after extrasensory perception (ESP) had been shown to be a mental capacity. The objective of this new research was to see whether a direct effect of mind on material objects could be demonstrated under strictly controlled experimental conditions.

Effects of mind on matter without muscular intermediation had a long background of reported spontaneous occurrences like clocks that stopped at the time of a death. These reports, however, have not been very numerous at any one time, nor were the circumstances of their alleged occurrence usually very convincing. Spontaneous experiences suggesting telepathy and other forms of ESP, before that mental capacity was established, had been both more frequent and much better attested than these that seemed to involve the direct action of mind on matter.

However, the idea that a PK effect might sometimes occur was supported not only by spontaneous cases, but also

---

Dinner Address at the Winter Review Meeting of the Institute for Parapsychology, January 3, 1969.

PK in the Laboratory: A Survey

by reports about so called "physical mediums." Objects were alleged to move without contact in their seance rooms. But whether any of the claims were true had never been established beyond question, and fraud had been proven in numerous instances. Still, the combination of reports of spontaneous and mediumistic occurrences raised enough of a question to justify a systematic study.

This was the situation in early 1934. PK seemed to call for parapsychological investigation, but no technique for testing it had been devised. A laboratory method was required that would yield results which could be evaluated statistically to show whether they were or were not caused by chance.

A young gambler came to J. B. Rhine (JBR) one day, claiming that he could at times cause the dice he threw to come up with the face he wanted. The belief in such an influence on dice is, of course, an ancient and familiar one, but until then had not been thought of as a problem for laboratory research.

The dice-throwing technique as a test for PK appeared to have the necessary qualifications. It could be used in the laboratory, it was quick, easy, inexpensive, and had proved interesting to many different kinds of people through the ages. The results lent themselves readily to statistical evaluation because the basic number of faces or combinations of them to be expected by chance could be easily calculated.

In the first exploratory series of tests, JBR used about 25 different volunteer subjects. A single pair of dice was used throughout, and the target was "high dice," a score of 8 or above. The series gave a highly significant number of hits (+230 on 454 runs of twelve throws each), but this result, of course, could be considered evidence of PK only if the dice were not biased. They were cheap white dice with black spots from the local dime store, quite probably not true. But this possibility was in mind from the start, and if extrachance results were obtained, a way to control for dice bias was to be duly considered.

Of course, precision-made cubes could have been used,

but the decision was instead to build controls into the test plan rather than rely on precision, which in any case might be impaired with usage. So the same dice were used in a series of tests with low dice and sevens as targets. If bias had caused the excess of hits on high-dice combinations, there should be a corresponding deficit of hits on the opposite faces. No such evidence of dice bias was found.

The control thus introduced in this first series of tests was only suggestive, however, because the times and numbers of trials were not equal. But before long the idea of throwing for all targets the same number of times and under the same conditions became standard practice and was eventually adequate to lay the ghost of dice bias.

Another obvious possibility to eliminate was that skilled throwing might account for some of the hits. Accordingly, even before the first series of tests was finished, a small shelf was rigged up which would release the dice to fall by gravity onto a padded surface. Results of tests with this device approximated those thrown by hand.

Techniques were varied in other ways and compared. In many, the dice were shaken and thrown from specially made dice-cups irregularly roughened inside to randomize the dice throws. Others used a mechanical device so constructed that the subject never touched the dice. No evidence of a relationship between the throwing method and scoring appeared. The conclusion was that the more convenient cup-throwing method gave a reasonable control against skilled throwing. It became the method generally used.

These controls against the possibilities of dice bias and skilled throwing brought a high degree of assurance that any significant results achieved could be laid to PK.

From 1934 to 1942, 24 papers by a number of different experimenters accumulated at the Parapsychology Laboratory. Their net effect was to suggest that dice had been influenced by the subject's thought. None had been published, however, and information on the matter thus was restricted mainly to those in contact with the Laboratory.

However, it happened that in 1941 the records of many

PK in the Laboratory: A Survey

ESP experiments were examined to see whether the hits had been evenly distributed over the runs as they could be expected to be by chance. It was found that they were not. Instead, they had favored certain positions, mainly the first ones in runs or sections. This was evidence of something more than chance. The "position effects" so identified were indication of the operation of ESP. They gave that work another line of evidence in addition to that of the total extrachance scores. They were evidence of psychological influences in the data.

With this outcome fresh in mind, in 1942 the 24 PK papers were collected for analysis to see if PK results, too, followed psychological patterns. It was found that 18 of them had been so conducted and the records so kept that an analysis for position effects could be made. These papers, of course, recorded data from experiments made between 1934 and 1942, the eight years during which the research had been conducted. The analysis now made on them concerned a point on which the experimenters at the time were entirely ignorant. They had not been looking for the position of the hits in their data, but only for significant overall deviations from chance.

For the analysis, the pages were divided into their four quarters, and the number of hits in each quarter was tabulated. A strong tendency was discovered for the hits to be bunched together at the start of the runs and sessions instead of being scattered randomly over the record pages. Most hits occurred in the upper left quarter, fewest in the lower right. The difference between these two quarters was highly significant. Taking the experiments individually, all but two showed this decline in scoring rate from the first quarter of the pages to the last.

Finding this evidence hidden in the old record sheets and adding it to that from the overall test results made the case for PK strong enough to warrant publication. Accordingly the first of the papers appeared in the *Journal of Parapsychology* in 1943.

Publication, of course, widened the circle of researchers,

and by the early 1950's more than 50 papers had appeared in print. Among those which did not come from the Laboratory were some from England and one from Germany. Most reported positive results.

In the course of experimentation from 1942 on, different types of target shapes were tested including discs and spheres, and suggestive results were secured. Then, in early 1950, a further change of technique was introduced by W. E. Cox. This involved throwing objects for place targets rather than for die faces, and came to be called the placement technique. Most of the 20 papers published from 1950 to the present report experiments using placement tests. A few miscellaneous projects used microphysical particles and living organisms as targets.

All of the tests reported thus far on dice and similar objects involve the PK effect on objects already in motion. By throwing or releasing the cubes so that they would ordinarily fall in chance patterns by gravity, the effect of the subject's intention has been to alter those patterns to a statistically significant degree. This means that the PK effect has been demonstrated as operating on moving objects. No success has yet been obtained in the laboratory in the attempt to move stationary objects by PK. Some of the tests using living tissue and microphysical particles as targets have shown positive deviations, but these still await confirmation.

THE NATURE OF PK

One of the first questions that arose when significant extrachance scores were obtained in the work on die-face targets was that of the relation of PK to the mass of the target objects involved. Accordingly, a number of tests were made in which the size of the dice used was varied and compared. But within the limits tested, the results were not in proportion to the mass. When different numbers of dice per throw were used, again the results did not show a relation to the mass of the cubes. Whatever the size or number of dice, the scores in general were best with the dice the subjects liked most to work with.

The general result of tests involving size and number of dice was that about six medium-sized dice were preferred in tests in which size or number per throw was not a point at issue. This number of cubes was large enough to be interesting and small enough to handle conveniently and the chance of hits (one in six) convenient to estimate. All of this, of course, had a bearing on the psychological side of PK but did not show a relation to the physical properties of the objects involved. The scope of variations tested, however, was comparatively limited, the largest dice used being little more than an inch on the edge. No systematic search was made for an upper limit beyond which PK cannot operate, nor has there been one since.

Several of the early PK subjects got significantly negative scores when trying for a positive deviation. Lottie Gibson, a subject whose scores were usually above mean chance expectation, obtained a significant negative deviation when given a prolonged test in the dark. Children tested by Betty McMahan in the dark after they had scored positively in the light, scored significantly negative in the light but positively in the dark. In both cases it seemed that the positive scores marked the preferred condition; the negative, the nonpreferred.

The fact that negative deviation (psi-missing) sometimes appeared in PK tests as it had in those for ESP told something important about the nature of PK. First of all, it suggested a relationship between ESP and PK, since both showed this same psychological effect and usually for what seemed like similar causes. Second, psi-missing showed that PK is not a stable ability in the sense of being something a person either has or doesn't have; like ESP, it is a process that can operate in the intended direction under favorable conditions and may still operate under less favorable conditions but in the direction opposite to conscious intention. Something in the unfavorable condition apparently tends to block the intended response which then is directed elsewhere. Since the entire operation goes on at an unconscious mental level, the person cannot either know when this happens or do anything about it. Negative scores are the result.

The differing response of different subjects to working in darkness well illustrates the effect on PK of the subject's attitude toward the test conditions. A number of experiments have shown that the attitude of the experimenter can also affect the results. The work of Laura Dale of the American Society for Psychical Research, for example, seems to show that her subjects' results followed her attitude toward the tests rather than their own. She reported two experiments, using in each some 50 subjects. Since each subject participated in only one session, the attitudes of individual subjects could have had no enduring overall effect. The first experiment produced significant evidence of ESP, but the second did not. The 50 subjects for each experiment, although different persons, were all college students selected similarly; any great difference in PK ability in two such groups as large as these would seem highly unlikely. There was, however, a great change in the experimenter's attitude between the two experiments. In the first, Mrs. Dale was eager and enthusiastic; in the second, intended as a confirmation of the first, she reported that the tests had become a routine burden and downright tiring.

Another evidence of the effect of the attitude of the experimenter was shown in the first Dale experiment in the contrast between the scores of the men and the women subjects. The women's deviations were significant, but the men's were not. The experimenter reported that she felt at ease with women and enjoyed testing them, but that she was constrained and ill at ease with the men for she felt they might be critical of the test. The scores appeared to reflect her attitude.

Other experimenters besides Mrs. Dale have noted that results seem to be influenced by their own attitude toward the experiment, although experimental conditions usually are not such that a sure discrimination can be made between the effect of the attitude of the experimenter and that of the subjects. In fact, even in Mrs. Dale's case, it is not possible

PK in the Laboratory: A Survey

to say whether the result was a direct or indirect effect of her own attitude; it is not clear whether she influenced the dice herself or whether her attitude affected the subjects, who in turn influenced the dice. The question, "Who did it?" is vital in PK research whenever two persons are involved, but whatever the answer, the attitudes of at least one of those present certainly affects the outcome.

From the start of the PK research the question of the relationship of PK to ESP was in mind. From an *a priori* viewpoint it looked as if there should be a relation. Mentally forcing a designated die face to fall uppermost could not be solely a blind physical process; somewhere in the operation there has to be intelligent recognition of the specified number. Evidence of a close relationship soon began to accumulate. Several different experimenters achieved significant scores throwing dice to match "blind" (hidden) targets, which they could only have identified by ESP. This, as well as the findings that both ESP and PK show psi-missing and that both are affected by the attitudes of subjects and experimenters, supported the assumption that ESP and PK are so closely related that, for practical purposes at least, they can be considered different phases of a single mental process.

As the evidence for PK built up, different experimenters began to wonder just how PK influenced the objects. Two hypotheses emerged, one described as loading, the other as kinetic. The loading theory was that an internal shift of balance occurs in the die or other object to change the center of gravity in favor of the desired outcome. The kinetic theory was that the force acts externally to, in effect, push or pull the object at the critical instant. As long as the targets were die faces either theory could be held and no reason could be advanced for excluding the other.

When placement tests were introduced during the 1950's it became possible to make inferences as to which theory was most likely. The placement tests, as already mentioned, involved a change of target type from a die face to the place where the target objects fall. The dice as before were released to fall by gravity, but in placement tests the point of release was centrally above an equally divided surface. The division was marked by a line or wire running the length of the surface in the direction of the fall. The objective was to influence the dice to fall to one side. Tests with placement targets by Cox, G. Cormack and H. Forwald soon produced extrachance scores. They indicated that PK could operate to place the falling objects as well as to produce extrachance face scores. This finding favored the kinetic theory over the loading theory as the *modus operandi*, for the idea of a push to deflect the fall one way or another, seemed simpler and just as effective an explanation as that of a changed center of gravity.

The idea was then introduced of throwing two kinds of dice at once in placement tests, but directing the subject's major attention to only one of the two, the other, however, also being recorded. These experiments, especially some of Cox's, showed that subjects tended to deviate positively on the primary targets and negatively on the secondary, and the difference was often significant. Sometimes the negative scores of the secondary objective were even greater than the positive scores of the first. This kind of effect was one that had also been found in ESP tests when a comparison of two conditions was made, i.e., one positive, one negative result. It had been referred to as the differential effect. It apparently means that psi, operating unconsciously as it does, produces divergent effects when two operations occur in close sequence. If one circumstance leads to psi-hitting, the other apparently tends to block the correct target and produce psi-missing.

Leading from his placement tests with dice, Cox has since been trying to perfect a machine by which a higher percentage of PK hits would be possible than with gross target objects like dice. He tried an experimental device utilizing water droplets, then went on to others of electromechanical nature. The results he has reported show an increase of several percent over the estimated general rate of success with die targets.

Forwald's research on placement PK has been especially

outstanding. An engineer-physicist, his research centered on the physical forces involved in PK. In the course of a dozen or so separate reports, each one being the record of hundreds of die falls, he attempted to measure the physical forces involved in PK. Specifically, he attempted to measure the energy that it must have taken to displace the cubes from chance positions to those observed in his PK test. He is the only experimenter thus far who has worked this out by physical formula. To do this he marked off the surface of the dice table into centimeter squares, measured the distance the cubes fell in the intended direction, subtracted the distance they would be expected to move by chance and obtained the data necessary to compute the energy involved in the motion of the dice.

When Forwald attempted to compare cubes of differing mass, however, he found, as had earlier experimenters, that the results did not follow physical principles, at least not the obvious ones. From a parapsychological viewpoint, it looked as if they were following psychological influences instead. It looked as if his results were affected by such psychological factors as novelty, expectation and desire. In practically all of his measurement experiments, Forwald was his own subject, so that his own attitude and expectations were inextricably involved in the results.

Forwald himself, however, did not easily accept the parapsychological viewpoint but continued to look for a physical constant in the materials of the cubes. Eventually, he was driven to a molecular, or atomic, theory. The atomic theory was not proven either when Forwald ceased to report further results on the question. In spite of a great amount of research, Forwald was still unable to show any basic physical regularity in the PK results. However, in the course of his research, he tested and got results with so many different materials that he showed fairly well that materials as such are not limiting factors. More than that, the long course of his experiments on the question of physical vs. psychological influences suggests that psychological influences overshadow the physical ones, at least within the limits so far tested.

Whether and where an upper limit of physical mass, for instance, can be reached beyond which no psychological influence can take effect, is still to be determined.

THEORIES ABOUT PK

On the basis of already published material on PK research it is now safe to conclude that the PK effect occurs. Not only has its reality been shown, but also something of its nature, but as yet very few theories to explain it have been advanced. The inquiry that led to its discovery did not begin with theoretical considerations but because of spontaneous occurrences that seemed to suggest a mental influence on matter. These reported occurrences were challenging because they seemed to involve a principle that violated the current theory—that physical objects can only be moved by physical causes. The first question, therefore, was whether or not PK actually occured. Theory to explain it was secondary, and for years experimenters were too busy trying to answer the first question to take much time out for concern with the second.

Over the years since the establishment of ESP, a few philosophers have attempted to fit that phenomenon into a theoretical scheme, but none have as yet advanced a theory to cover the combination of ESP and PK. However, both JBR and Robert H. Thouless in the course of their investigations published papers that included tentative hypotheses as to the place of PK in the personality.

As early as 1943, JBR's tentative explanation appeared in a *Journal of Parapsychology* along with the first experimental reports on PK. The establishment of a PK effect meant for him proof that the mind has real force, and so can activate brain action which in turn activates nerves and muscles to produce the movement of physical objects. Thus PK can initiate voluntary muscular activity within the body. According to this hypothesis, the ordinary function of PK is within the organism where it produces certain electrochemical and other changes in the brain which start a chain of physical reaction in the nerves and muscles of the body. The theory does not imply dualism because it regards both mind and brain as aspects of a unitary system.

JBR considered this idea of PK in the organism to be its normal and ordinary function. Spontaneous occurrences and results in the laboratory were instances when the effect was exerted on objects external to the organism and therefore were unusual manifestations of it.

Later, in the light of evidence that psi operations are unconscious and are not limited in time and space like ordinary sensory-motor operations, JBR suggested that psi might well have originated far back in evolution before the sensory-motor system developed. He questioned whether primitive organisms may not have made their contact with their environment by psi, and that the psi function gradually became submerged later as the sensory-motor system developed, consciousness probably developing at the same time. If so, the PK effect would gradually have been more and more confined within the individual's own organism.

Thouless' thinking about the place of PK paralleled JBR's. Thouless saw psi and sensory-motor experience as the organism's alternative means of making contact with the environment, the latter now being the more common and familiar one. But like JBR, he considered that it may not always have been thus. Since psi is essentially unlimited by time and place, the primitive organism operating by psi could have almost universal information. But, after all, the information needed to be restricted in order to be more practicable. Nature therefore responded by developing the sensory-motor system and retaining the PK function as a method of liaison between mind and brain. Like JBR, Thouless regarded PK effects outside of the organism as unusual manifestations of a function normally confined within the organism.

But finding a place for psi in the organism still left the basic psi principle in conflict with current mechanistic theory. Thouless was unable to find a way of reconciling the two. He concluded that a mental force or entity is necessary in order to initiate and influence brain activity. He adopted a Hebrew character, *shin*, as the name of this mental ability and ascribed to it the energetic function of mind that initiates brain activity. He felt that a continuity between *shin* and brain must exist but that it still remains to be discovered. In JBR's formulation, PK supplies that continuity.

Two non-parapsychologists have also considered the place of PK in the scheme of things. J. R. Smythies, an Edinburgh psychiatrist, considers that the ordinary concept of a three-dimensional physical world is not necessarily complete and that psi may operate in a higher dimension than current mechanistic theory recognizes. Professor (later Sir) John Eccles, a neurophysiologist, found in his studies of brain action in relation to the mind reasons for thinking that the initiation of muscular activity lies in the mind and that PK may well be the means by which it is accomplished. This idea, of course, conflicts with the general viewpoint of neurologists and physiologists, who conceive of all physical movement as being initiated by the brain.

Perhaps the most significant common thread running through the ideas of these four individuals is that they all find it impossible to accommodate the fact of psi within the mechanistic framework. Psi calls for a mind-oriented, as distinct from a brain-oriented, theory. No brain-oriented theory has yet been advanced that explains the facts. Psi as a reality must be fitted into the personality, but this apparently cannot be accomplished within the mechanistic system as conceived today. The fact that it cannot means that a considerable shift in present thinking must be made. The "fitting in" calls for reorganization, but the nature of the reorganization will depend on the kind of facts that further PK research reveals. The research to date indicates the general direction, but basic specific questions remain to be answered. Reliable positive deviations have been secured thus far on target material in motion. Apparently, this is the "easiest" point of attack; initiating movement in static systems appears to be much more difficult. However, it may be that the latter is not intrinsically more difficult, but that testing it may require a technique that has not yet been found. At any rate, in the future this area certainly must be "invaded" by reliable research methods.

A compelling reason for achieving results on static objects is that it seems to hold the key to the understanding of the effect of PK on living organisms. This should be important in questions of health and disease. Psychosomatic medicine, still little more than a stepchild of medicine proper, would be greatly affected if the role of PK in it were demonstrated, recognized, and understood.

Even these few considerations show that the PK research of the future will be as exciting as it is important. The present is obviously only the beginning. But at least it is a beginning. Both for its possible place in the more practical affairs of men and for its theoretical implications on the nature of the human being, it is a study that deserves to be pushed to the limit.

Even at the present stage, because of the laboratory evidence, spontaneous occurrences that seem to involve PK become less inexplicable than formerly. A background of principle is supplied of which they can be considered examples. Much more important, however, is the fact that the idea of the relation of mind and body is drastically affected by the change from a brain-oriented to a mind-oriented concept of personality. The nature of man is drastically different if his mind rather than his physical brain is his guiding aspect. In fact, as JBR says, the implications of this viewpoint in contrast to the presently dominant mechanistic one stagger the imagination, as it points again to the viewpoint of the man in the street, and also the man in the pulpit. The discovery of PK seems inevitably to point to this return to the earlier, more intuitive viewpoint regarding the nature of man.

SARA R. FEATHER AND LOUISA E. RHINE

A Help-Hinder Comparison

Evidence that a human subject can influence an object by mental force inevitably raises the question of whether two subjects trying to influence the same object in the same direction can produce a greater effect than one alone. And if two subjects try to influence the same object in opposing ways, will the effect be lessened?

The only published report bearing directly on these questions is of Humphrey's 1947 experiment with an observer who alternated randomly between trying to "help" a subject wish for a given face to turn up on dice the subject was throwing, or to "hinder" by wishing for a different face (2). Significant positive scoring was achieved when both tried for the same face; insignificant positive scoring when each tried for a different face on the same throw. The work strongly suggests that two subjects are more effective when working to the same purpose (helping) than when working to different purposes (hindering).

Humphrey herself suggested the need for procedural refinements in seeking an answer to the help–hinder question. In her experiment, the observer knew whether he was trying for the same or a different face although the subject did not. Since this knowledge might inadvertently alter the observer's attitude or motivation, she suggested that both subjects be kept ignorant of which condition is in effect when the dice are being thrown.

The present study asked the same question as Humphrey's, but included several experimental design modifications. Both subjects were ignorant of which runs were which

---

Presented at the Autumn Review Meeting of the Institute for Parapsychology, September 13, 1968. Complete report in *Journal of Parapsychology*, September 1969.

until the end of a session. An automatic dice machine was provided so that, except for turning the switch at the beginning and end of each run, there was little difference in the roles of the two subjects during the test session, instead of one playing a dominant role.

This report covers two experiments conducted during the summer of 1968. The first was limited to the question of whether two subjects affect a pair of dice differently when they try for the same face than when they try for different faces simultaneously. The second experiment was directed to the question of whether the subject's mood has an additional effect upon the same–different target comparison.

Help–Hinder Experiment

The subjects in both experiments were the authors, SF and her mother, LER, both on the staff of the Institute for Parapsychology. During the test period, LER was writing a book on PK research, which perhaps added to her motivation as a subject.

PROCEDURE

The tests were conducted in a small experimental room with an automatic dice machine in clear view of both subjects. The dice were in a $24 \times 4 \times 4$-inch rectangular plexiglas box rotated by an electric motor. Six triangular plexiglas baffles were fastened on the inside walls, and eleven aluminum baffles protruded from the walls into the cage itself to insure ample rotation of the dice when they fell the 24-inch distance from one end of the cage to the other. If uninterrupted, the motor drove the box through a half-revolution in about four seconds and then rested for four seconds before beginning the next automatic turn. The four-second rest period gave the subjects time to record the die faces, which they did independently of each other after each half-turn of the box.

Two high-precision ⅝-inch red dice with balanced white insets were used for each throw throughout the experiment.

A pool of target orders was prepared in advance, each

listing the six die faces in various orders. The target orders were paired so that three of the die faces would be in matched positions on both the lists in a pair, but the other three faces would be in different positions. (For instance, if one subject had the order 1, 2, 4, 5, 6, 3, the other subject might have 4, 2, 6, 5, 1, 3, giving both subjects the same target in the second, fourth, and sixth position but different targets in the first, third, and fifth positions.)

Each target served for a run of twelve throws. For half of the runs both subjects had the same target so that each of those runs would be scored against a single target. For the other half of the runs, the subjects had different targets, so that on these runs, each subject's runs were scored against her special target. The total number of run scores was thus half again the number of actual runs.

The large number of possible permutations of the six die faces insured that a subject could not tell from his list what the target order on his partner's list might be. In no session were there more than two runs of one type (i.e., same-target or different-target) in succession.

Most of the tests were conducted early in the day. Before each session, LER selected at random a pair of target lists for that session from a large number of lists in paired black envelopes. Without looking at the contents, LER kept the first black envelope and handed the second to SF. Both subjects then moved to positions where a 10-inch circular screen separated them to prevent exchange of visual cues, and each removed her target list from its envelope. Both subjects took special care not to divulge the target order to the other at any time during a session.

After each subject had noted her target for the first run, SF turned the switch to activate the automatic dice machine and allowed it to rotate for twelve turns, or one standard run. At the end of a run, the machine was stopped for a brief interval while each subject consulted her list for her next target. The next run was then initiated in the same manner, and so on until a six-run session was completed.

A Help-Hinder Comparison

There were four such sessions in each series. The experiment included one pilot series and four confirmatory series.

Each subject independently recorded the die faces that came up at each half-revolution of the machine as a double check on the accuracy of the record. At the end of a session, each subject checked her own record sheet for hits, then compared it with the other's to see which trials had had the same and which different targets. SF collected both record sheets, which were independently rechecked by an assistant. In no case was there a discrepancy in recording which could affect the scores.

The experiment comprised five series of four sessions each. There were six runs in a session, and twelve throws in a run.

RESULTS

The total score for the 20 sessions combined (180 run scores, 4,320 trials) was not significant, yielding only 18 hits above mean chance expectation. However, the first, or pilot, series suggested a difference in scoring direction under same- and different-target conditions. There were eleven more hits than chance expectation in the twelve run scores with the same targets, while the 24 run scores for different targets had five hits fewer than chance expectation. However, this direction of difference did not hold up in the four confirmation series; indeed, it was actually reversed to a marginally significant degree, with 18 fewer hits than expected by chance in 48 same-target run scores as compared to 30 hits above chance expectation in the 96 different-target run scores (odds against chance of the difference: 100 to three).

After the final series, the run-score variance (i.e., the fluctuation above and below mean chance expectation for each run) was evaluated for the same- and different-target conditions. (The experimental design had specified one target per run for each subject to allow an adequate basis for just such a variance analysis.)

The evaluation suggested an unforeseen difference in the manner of scoring between the same- and the different-target conditions. The scoring on the same-target runs varied more than would be expected by chance. In other words, the score for each of the same-target runs went both considerably above and considerably below the chance average of four (odds against chance of the fluctuation: 20 to one). In contrast, the scoring in the different-target runs varied somewhat less than would be expected by chance, i.e., those scores were at or near chance expectation. (Odds against chance of the difference between the two conditions: 100 to four.) Most of this difference is attributable to the large variance in the same-target run scores. The difference was found in eight out of the ten comparisons possible in the five series.

Since the variance difference had not been anticipated, a further check of the effect was desirable. Data were available from two other experiments in which this same procedure had been used, each with a total of 108 run scores: the mood experiment, described below, with SF and LER as subjects; and an experiment conducted by SF, with BB and SF as subjects. In the mood experiment, five of the six possible comparisons showed larger run-score variance under the same-target condition than under the different-target condition. The other experiment, although it gave no overall indication of PK, showed larger run-score variance under the same-target condition than under the different-target condition in four of the six possible comparisons.

Seventeen of the 22 comparisons made possible by the records of these three experiments, then, showed larger run-score variance under the same-target condition than under the different-target condition (odds against chance of the difference: 500 to one), which suggests that this is an effect fairly well distributed across different experimental series.

DISCUSSION

Although high-precision dice with balanced insets were used, there was still a possibility that dice bias could have caused the PK run-score fluctuation. This possible alternative to PK as an explanation was checked by comparing the scores with the variance in the runs on each different target face. No target face had turned up significantly more than the others, nor did the run-score variance averages for the six faces differ significantly.

The best assurance against the possibility of dice bias, however, was that the same dice had been used for tests under both experimental conditions and that random selection distributed the six targets fairly evenly within each of these two conditions. For the runs with five of the six faces as targets, the average run-score variance was larger under the same- than under the different-target condition, which reflects the general trend of the results and supports the conclusion that the difference is due to PK, not to dice bias.

The variance results indicate that when the two subjects tried for the same target face they either succeeded very well or missed very badly; whereas when they were trying for different target faces, they had slightly less success or failure per run than would be expected by chance alone. The difference is mainly contributed by above-average fluctuation in the same-target run scores.

Perhaps this result is analogous to two blind people attempting to help each other pick up a bucket of water. If their hands happen to grasp the handle at the same time in the properly spaced positions, they succeed better than either one alone; but if their timing or spacing is off, they are more likely to spill the water than if either alone were lifting the pail.

The results of this experiment failed to confirm Humphrey's finding that the total number of hits under the same-target condition was significantly higher than under the different-target condition. The Humphrey report does not make it possible to determine if her results showed a run-score variance difference comparable to that noted in the present work. However, there are enough procedural differences between the two studies to render inapplicable any conclusions about the failure to replicate Humphrey's results. For one thing, one of her subjects knew which throws had the same-target ("help") and which the different-target ("hinder") condition. For another, one of her subjects played a predominant role by throwing the dice, while the other merely observed and tried to help or hinder.

Unpleasant-Mood Experiment

The objective of this second experiment was to compare the effect of pleasant and unpleasant moods upon PK scores under the same- and different-target conditions.

Early in ESP research experimenters began to suspect that the mood of the subject is likely to affect his scoring rate. The general impression has been that a pleasant mood leads to positive scoring and an unpleasant mood at least to chance level scoring if not to negative scoring (psi-missing). (For a discussion of psi-missing see Appendix C.) A number of ESP studies had been designed to test these assumptions.

One of the first was Nielsen's experiment in which subjects checked items on a mood scale after taking a precognition test by themselves at home (3). Contrary to general expectation, the scores did not vary in relation to pleasant and unpleasant mood so much as in relation to how extreme the mood rating was. Significantly high scoring accompanied subjects' extreme moods, whether pleasant or unpleasant; but the deviation was only moderately positive when the mood was moderately pleasant, and moderately negative when the mood was moderately unpleasant. Perhaps a more important feature of Neilsen's experiment was that the subjects took the tests whenever they chose and were encouraged to include different mood states, so that the study probably sampled a wider range of mood than the typical laboratory experiment with subjects who, though volunteers, are more or less "caught" in the mood they happen to be in when the test is given.

The effect of mood on ESP run-score variance was also studied by Rogers (4,5). In his first experiment, using himself as the subject, the results of the precognition tests he took when he was in a state of "positive affect" differed significantly from those when he was in a state of "negative affect." He defines positive affect as an attitude of interest, enthusiasm and confidence in the test, and negative affect as the reverse. All of his ten negative-state series showed less run-score variance than expected, while eight of the ten positive-state series showed greater variance than expected. A second study with five other people as subjects replicated those findings.

Carpenter undertook a further breakdown of mood and run-score variance using Nielsen's scheme of dividing mood ratings into moderate and extreme types (1). Of particular relevance to the present PK study was his finding that within moderate-mood conditions, the scores of subjects in pleasant moods varied more from chance expectation than those in unpleasant moods.

That mood might similarly affect PK scores has often been assumed, but no experimental test of the assumption has been reported to date. The researches relating mood to ESP scores had set the stage for such a PK experiment, and the authors began it incidentally to the help–hinder experiment in the summer of 1968.

In the course of the pilot help–hinder series, SF had stated on several occasions that she did not feel like experimenting because she was depressed or in an unpleasant mood that day. Testing was then postponed to a more auspicious time, with the incidental result that the help–hinder PK experiment subjects took all of those tests when they were in moods sufficiently pleasant to preclude any mention of mood. The help–hinder experiment, therefore, provided a pleasant-mood experiment, and is so designated in this section of the report.

When the first confirmatory help–hinder series began, it had already occurred to LER that here was an opportunity to test the widely held assumption that unpleasant mood can adversely affect PK scores. Consequently, LER started the unpleasant-mood experiment as a separate study under her own direction, using the days when SF was unwilling to participate in the help–hinder experiment because of her unpleasant feelings. LER handled the record sheets on those days, but in every other way except for mood the procedure was identical with the first experiment.

SF's definition of unpleasant mood was of course quite broad. Occasionally her unpleasant mood included physical symptoms such as headache or sleepiness, but a constant factor was a general feeling of depression that corresponded fairly closely to Rogers' definition of negative affect, i.e., not interested in making the test, not enthusiastic about the test, and not confident of ability to score well at that time.

RESULTS

Three series of PK tests, each providing 36 standard PK run scores for a total of 108 run scores, were conducted under unpleasant-mood conditions. The 108 run scores showed 19 fewer hits than would be expected by chance alone. Analysis of the results showed a slightly positive deviation under the same-target condition (five hits above mean chance expectation in the 36 same-target run scores). SF scored 10 fewer hits and LER 15 fewer hits than chance expectation in the 36 run scores each yielded by the different-target runs.

The hit totals under each condition were compared with those in the four pleasant-mood series which were conducted during the same time interval. One of the two comparisons was statistically significant: the different-target scores varied according to mood in the expected direction; that is, the pleasant-mood scores were positive and the unpleasant negative (odds against chance of the difference: 50 to one). The same-target scores differed in the reverse directions to an insignificant degree.

Comparison of the run-score variance for the two moods revealed no overall significance, but went in a direction similar to that found by Rogers with ESP scores, that is, the pleasant-mood scores varied from chance more widely than the unpleasant. The variance of the different-target scores in the unpleasant-mood experiment was restricted to a highly suggestive extent (odds against chance: 20 to one).

Since the experiment was exploratory, and since there is

no precedent for an appropriate variance measure for PK, the score variance was further analyzed using the session as the unit of comparison. The number of hits or misses under each condition in each session was compared with the expected session total, and the variance was calculated in relation to this expected mean. When the two subjects were trying for the same target for three runs, they provided one three-run session score; when trying for different targets, two three-run session scores. On this basis, the different-target scores of the two mood experiments showed a significant difference (odds against chance of the difference: 100 to one), and the pleasant-mood scores varied more widely than the unpleasant. On the other hand, the same-target scores tended to vary more widely in the unpleasant mood than in the pleasant (odds against chance of the difference: 20 to one).

DISCUSSION

The results supported the main expectation that unpleasant or depressed states of mind would adversely affect PK scores when the subjects were aiming simultaneously at different targets, but not when the subjects were aiming at the same target. The combined same- and different-target scores of the unpleasant-mood tests differed from those of the pleasant-mood tests in the direction of the main expectation, but the difference was not significant.

This general difference is in line with previous ESP findings, but has not been reported in connection with PK before.

Further *post hoc* exploration of the results suggests that the session unit may be a sensitive indicator of mood effect for both same- and different-target scoring. The large variance in the pleasant-mood results of the different-target runs indicates that when the subjects were in a pleasant or neutral mood they were consistent in hitting or in missing throughout the session, but when in an unpleasant mood they were inconsistent from run to run so that the scores tended to cancel each other. An opposite effect was noted when subjects were trying for the same target.

While the above suggests that the 72-trial unit (session) is more sensitive to the effect of mood than the 24-trial (standard run) unit, variance studies are relatively novel in PK research, and it would be advisable to experiment with various trial units in future explorations.

Obviously, the method used in this study to classify moods as pleasant or unpleasant can give only a very gross division and more objective methods must be used in further work. However, it is interesting to note that while the test mood was classified according to the report of only one of the subjects, SF, both subjects contributed about equally to the difference between the pleasant- and unpleasant-mood scores. LER was not aware that SF's mood affected her own mood, yet the relation between them (mother and daughter) must have been close enough so that SF's negative moods induced LER to score similarly on PK tests in this instance.

This study, which is exploratory in many respects, was initiated to pursue the help–hinder PK problem tackled by Humphrey in 1947. It brings out a number of new and related problems which need to be explored along with the main question.

LITERATURE CITED

1. Carpenter, James C. "Two Related Studies on Mood and Precognition Run-Score Variance." *Journal of Parapsychology*, 1968, **32**, 75–89.
2. Humphrey, B. M. "Help–Hinder Comparison in PK Tests." *Journal of Parapsychology*, 1947, **11**, 4–13.
3. Nielsen, Winnifred. "Mental States Associated with Success in Precognition." *Journal of Parapsychology*, 1956, **20**, 96–109.
4. Rogers, David Price. "Negative and Positive Affect and ESP Run-Score Variance—Study I." *Journal of Parapsychology*, 1966, **30**, 151–59.
5. Rogers, David Price. "Negative and Positive Affect and ESP Run-Score Variance—Study II." *Journal of Parapsychology*, 1967, **31**, 290–96.

W. E. COX

PK on a Pendulum System

Most psychokinesis (PK) research has used moving objects to register the PK effect. Dice-throwing came first with specified target faces as the measure of success, and then discs were used. Later there was a shift to placement testing, with cubes or balls released to fall by gravity onto a centrally divided table while the subject tried to influence them mentally to roll to the designated side of the table. An even larger variation came with the introduction of more complex apparatus using electric systems as the PK yardstick.

One of the author's earlier PK testing devices used a clock to record the exact time it took for a series of electric relays to close when given an electric impetus by the subject. The subject's task was to speed up the closing of the relays by PK and then, in reverse, to retard the closing.

A more recent device uses a pendulum connected to an electric system that records its movement. Each pendulum trial has two parts, or halves, as the subject tries to lengthen or shorten the pendulum's swing. In one half-trial the subject tries to make the pendulum swing out as far as possible, and in the other to make it swing out a lesser distance.

Apparatus: An 8-inch wooden pendulum suspended from the top center of a wooden box 12 inches high, 10 inches deep, and 8 inches long, released by a push button, swings through an arc of slightly less than 180°. Near the end point of its swing, the bottom of the pendulum, which is wide and opaque, enters the path of a light beam aimed at an electric-eye sensor. Interruption of the light beam closes a switch connected to an electronic counter. The counter registers

---

Presented at the Spring Review Meeting of the Institute for Parapsychology, May 3, 1968.

the length of time the beam is interrupted. When the pendulum swings wide, it interrupts the light beam for a longer time, and the counter records a higher reading; when the swing is shorter, the pendulum does not travel quite as far into the path of the light beam, the light is cut off for a shorter time, and the counter records a lower reading.

The electronic counter can measure a given process to the accuracy of one ten-thousandth of a second, or a hundred times more exactly than the hundredth-of-a-second accuracy of the standard electric timing clock the author used in the previous work. This counter has nine decade-counting units, three of which are in the form of illuminated vertical sets of digits 0 through 9 (see Figure 1).

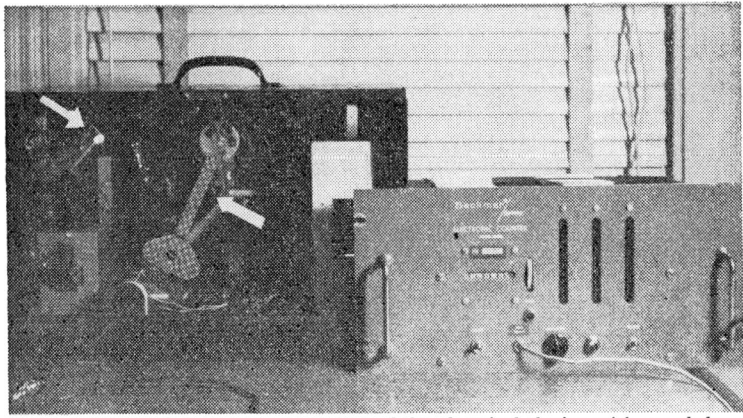

FIG. 1. PK pendulum test apparatus: (left) electrical device with pendulum (arrow) which briefly obscures the light (arrow); (right) electronic counter with three vertical columns. Digits are illuminated in each column to indicate length of time the light was obscured.

PROCEDURE

Each subject was asked to follow a previously prepared random target order taken from a pile of target orders kept facedown for the purpose. The randomness of the target orders was restricted to include only sheets with exactly eight each of the high-low and low-high order. To insure variety, the randomness was further restricted to avoid more than four consecutive targets of one order. For a high-low order, the subject tried to influence the pendulum to swing out farther (high) before returning, and then a moment later to swing out a shorter distance (low), or the reverse for a low-high order. Each trial consisted of one attempt for high and one attempt for low. Each run included sixteen trials (32 half-trials). The objective was to create as large a difference as possible between each pair of high and low readings.

The experimenter sat near the machine. Usually the subject sat several feet behind him so the experimenter would not see the target order before the end of the run since the intention, of course, was to test the subject's PK, not the experimenter's.

Most subjects thought of the counter as the target rather than the pendulum. In fact, in the experimental series, the pendulum box had usually been kept closed, so that the counter was the only target-object in view. Although subjects were told of the pendulum's function, and that the wider a swing, the higher the reading, concentration on the counter served the purpose of directing the subject's attention to the end result rather than to the mechanics of the process.

Some subjects preferred not to watch the counter at all. A few wanted to watch the pendulum itself, and when this was permitted the subject would concentrate on a "fast" (farther) swing instead of a high reading, or a "slow" (shorter) swing instead of a low reading.

The reading was recorded and the counter reset to zero at the end of each half-trial. The limits of the swing could be altered arbitrarily by adjusting the equipment, but the terminal (recorded) part of a full swing lasted about 1,500 ten-thousandths of a second on average. The two recordings per trial were entered on one line of the record page. A reading of 1585-1561, for example, would be a hit if the target order was high-low.

When a run was completed, the target order (F-S or S-F) was entered beside the record of each pair of counter readings. Trials where the readings matched the target order were scored as hits. To complete and check a run of 16 trials took three or four minutes.

RESULTS

In a pilot series of 60 runs of 16 trials each, 53.2% of the trials were hits, whereas only 50%, or 8.0 hits in a run of 16 trials, would be expected to occur by chance. In 40 of these runs the experimenter acted as subject and also did the recording. In his own 40 runs, the experimenter averaged 56% hits. The other subjects averaged only 50% hits. Since the odds against chance of the 53.2% hits averaged for the pilot series are 50 to one, the pilot series was considered encouraging enough to justify a try for confirmation.

Four 16-run series with special groups or individuals as subjects comprised the main experiment. Most of the subjects in the first series were individual visitors to the Institute for Parapsychology invited to participate. They averaged 54.7% hits. Subjects in the second series were 13 high school students visiting the Institute as a group, who averaged 50% or chance. A group of interested university students participated in the third series and averaged 55.9% hits. One subject, PC, a student who had previously scored well on other PK machines, did all the runs in the fourth series and averaged 56.25% hits.

The average for the 64 runs in the four series was 54.5% hits (odds against chance: 200 to one).

DISCUSSION

The average percentage of hits with the pendulum device compares favorably with the averages from tests on other machines constructed by the author which are based on different electro-mechanical principles. It seems reasonable to conclude that PK can affect the swing of a pendulum, but the actual locus of the PK effect is still unknown; that is, the subject's influence may have affected the pendulum or it may have taken effect at some other point in the moving parts of the apparatus (e.g., a relay).

PK on a Pendulum System

Research on the range of usable devices for PK testing can well aim first at improving scoring rates, searching for advantages in convenience, increasing control, and stimulating the subject's interest. Eventually, of course, it will be important to find the specific locus. When that is known, it may help in building apparatus that can take full advantage of the PK potential, and even perhaps to find ways of amplifying the effect.

ROBERT BRIER

PK Effect on a Plant-Polygraph System

Reports of spontaneous happenings apparently due to psychokinesis (PK) cite a wide range of targets. Rhine's paper on spontaneous PK (6) lists a variety of physical effects reportedly associated with human crises which possibly could have involved PK. Among the phenomena instanced are stopped clocks, falling pictures, shattered glass, lights that turn on and off, doors that open and close, and other physical occurrences coincident in time with crises significant for the individuals who reported them. Since these effects on material objects were usually suspected of relating to the human event only because of coincident timing, the suggestions they offer regarding the occurrence of PK must be considered tentative, and, of course, the question of accuracy in reporting makes it still more difficult to draw conclusions. If there is a genuine relationship, however, the range of effects caused by PK must be very great.

In contrast, the range of significant PK effects identified under experimental conditions is comparatively limited. In the early PK work at the Duke University Parapsychology Laboratory, dice throwing was the most common procedure. Significant extrachance scores were achieved when the target was a given die face or combination of faces, and also when the task was to make a rolling cube come to rest in one or another designated target area.

In later PK experimentation W. E. Cox, among others, introduced target innovations. Much of Cox's work has involved attempts to influence complex electrical systems such as clock mechanisms, mercury switches, and electrical relays

---

Presented in part at the Spring Review Meeting of the Institute for Parapsychology, April 30, 1967, and in part at the Spring Review Meeting, May 3, 1969. Complete report in *Journal of Parapsychology*, September 1969.

(1). The subjects in these tests attempted to accelerate or retard a mechanism so constructed that any PK effect would be measured by the hands of a clocklike device. Although extrachance scores were obtained, it is still not clear what part of the system was affected by PK, and consequently impossible to say just what the target actually was or where or how PK operated. In these experiments as in all the dice research, the PK effect was directed at moving objects, but only at inanimate ones.

A few experimental attempts have been made, however, to influence living systems by PK. One of the first was Richmond's experiment with paramecia (5) which demonstrated a positive effect and suggested that PK could have been involved.

The Vasses experimented with plants and reported positive results (7, 8), although the publications are not sufficiently detailed to allow for adequate evaluation of the work. Grad carried out more extensive work on plant growth, reporting significant results on the germination and growth of seedlings in response to human influence (3, 4).

Cleve Backster, a polygraph expert, recently claimed he had obtained evidence by means of polygraph recordings that plants perceive human thoughts. Although Backster's claim seemed unsupported by empirical evidence, the idea of using a polygraph to seek evidence of PK effects on living tissue seemed worthwhile and was adapted for the research reported here.

The primary objective was to look for a relation between a subject's concentrated attempt to affect the life processes of a plant by PK and variation in activity of the plant tissue as measured by the polygraph.

Pilot Experiment

After preliminary tests to determine the best experimental design, two philodendron plants were selected for use as targets. The two philodendron plants were rather small (approximately 8 inches high and 5 inches wide) and were chosen

FIG. 1. Living PK targets: two philodendron plants (with other plants in the same pot) shielded by glass and separated by opaque screen.

to closely resemble each other in size and shape. They stood on a small table in the experimental room separated from each other by an opaque 24 x 18-inch screen. By turning his head, the subject, who sat about five feet away, could easily direct his eyes to one or the other plant. The one on the left side of the screen was labeled A, the other B. A small light bulb in front of the screen between the two plants served to signal the subject to start or stop concentrating. (See Figure 1).

The polygraph and light bulb switch were in an adjoining room so that the experimenter could not see the subject, in order to preclude exchange of visual cues to the target order. Electrodes attached to each plant passed through an aperture in the wall to connect to the polygraph. Two polygraph pens were used, one to record the activity of each plant (see Figure 2).

PROCEDURE

The subject was shown a sample target sheet containing his instructions. After he understood what he was to do, the experimenter gave him several sealed envelopes containing target order sheets, either AB or BA, made up in advance by a second experimenter so that the experimenter would not know which target order the subject selected. The AB target sheet read as follows:

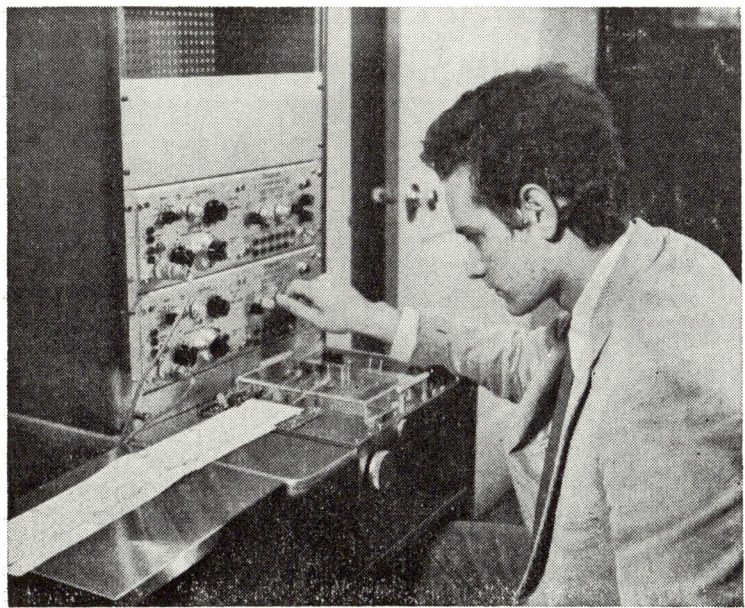

Fig. 2. Experimenter monitoring polygraph as it records the electrical activity of two plants.

When the bulb goes on, please concentrate and try to increase the activity in plant A. (30 sec.)
When the bulb goes off, relax. (30 sec.)
When the bulb goes on for the second time, concentrate and try to increase the activity in plant B. (30 sec.)
When the bulb goes out, please place this sheet in the black envelope.

BA target order instructions were altered appropriately.

METHOD OF EVALUATION

After ten subjects had been tested, the experimenter, still without knowledge of the target order, evaluated all ten charts to see if he could identify the target order followed by each subject. Figure 3 is a somewhat simplified drawing of an imaginary chart. The top and bottom jagged lines presumably represent the electrical activity of plants A and B

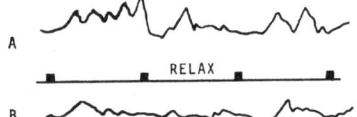

FIG. 3. Electrical activity chart of two target plants.

respectively. The middle line is an indicator of events and delineates the two experimental periods with relaxation period between.

A fine wire, 1 cm long was used as a standard for measuring the peaks. If the tip of a jag in the line was more than 1 cm from the middle line, the jag was counted as a peak.

For statistical evaluation of the data in Figure 3, the five peaks for A during the first period were cross-added to three peaks for B during the second period as a measure of the evidence of the AB target order. The one peak for B during the first period and the two peaks for A during the second period were cross-added for evidence of the BA target order. In the illustration there are 6 (5 + 1) peaks for the AB order and 3 (1 + 2) for the BA order. Thus this record indicates that the actual target was AB.

RESULTS

The above method of evaluating the subject's ten charts led to identification of the actual target orders in nine of the ten cases (odds against chance: 50 to one).

After the charts were evaluated by the experimenter, a second judge was asked to make an independent evaluation. In eight out of nine charts, the second judge's evaluation agreed with the experimenter's. The second judge could not come to a decision on the tenth chart, and a third judge was asked to evaluate this chart. Her evaluation accorded with the experimenter's. Thus, nine out of ten evaluations were in the same direction as the experimenter's, and of these, eight were hits.

A more complicated statistical evaluation gave results on the same order of significance. This method showed

PK Effect on a Plant-Polygraph System 107

that of the 246 peaks recorded during the experiment, 143 occurred during an activity period and 103 during a control period. By chance, 123 peaks would have been expected in each.

DISCUSSION

These evaluations should be viewed as only crude first steps toward an adequate evaluation method. An important problem is that such statistical analysis assumes each peak to be statistically independent of all others. This may not be a correct assumption since whatever might cause the plant to become active, might cause many peaks to appear, not just one. Thus, if, during a single 30-second period, the plant grew active and showed seven peaks, all seven might have a common cause, whether parapsychological or not, and might more appropriately be treated as one unit rather than seven independent units. When the second evaluator applied this method, the result was not significant. This, however was because the second evaluator counted fewer peaks than the experimenter, an indication that although the method of measuring peaks was designed to be objective, it left room for judgmental differences.

In any event, the results of the preliminary and pilot tests seemed to warrant full scale investigation of the possibility that PK affects living tissues.

Experimental Series 1

The experimental design was modified to include two experimenters as an added safeguard, each experimenter to be "blind" to the part of the operation conducted by the other.

PROCEDURE

The target order and typed instructions were prepared and sealed in envelopes by a third person who gave them to the second experimenter. The first experimenter brought the subject to the second experimenter, who shuffled the envelopes and gave one to the subject, instructing him not to allow the first experimenter to see the target. When the trial was over, the subject still held the target order sheet, while the first experimenter checked the peaks on the chart and returned the chart to the second experimenter. Thus, the subject never handled the chart and the experimenter never handled the target sheet. The subject then gave his target sheet to the second experimenter, and at this point the first experimenter told both the second experimenter and the subject in each others' presence which target order the record sheet indicated. The result was thus arrived at by a "double blind" procedure.

In other respects the procedure was the same as that used in the pilot experiment.

As in the pilot series an attempt was made to select subjects who could be expected to do well. When appointments were made with subjects the experimenter had not met, the experimenter chatted briefly with them first. If a subject mentioned that he felt he had no ability or did poorly with plants, or if the experimenter suspected he would score negatively, he was given a "courtesy series" test which was not included in the results. (Two such subjects appeared; both scored negatively.)

Again, ten subjects were tested (besides the two in the courtesy series).

RESULTS

Six of the ten charts indicated the correct target order; four did not. Although in the expected direction, this was not, of course, a significant result. The overall peak count, although also positive, was also not significant.

Experimental Series 2

The high percentage of success in the pilot experiment (90%) and in Series 1 (60%) was encouraging, but with so few trials, did not carry much statistical significance. Therefore Experimental Series 2 was designed to test each subject twice in order to accumulate more data.

PROCEDURE

When the subject picked up his sealed instructions from the second experimenter, he received two envelopes. The target orders in these envelopes had been shuffled, so could be AB and AB, BA and BA, BA and AB, or AB and BA, all with equal probability. The subject opened one envelope, followed the instructions, and was then given a minute to rest. After the minute of rest, he opened the second envelope and followed those instructions. The experimenter then evaluated the charts for both trials and returned with the subject to the second experimenter as before.

RESULTS

In all, there were 20 trials, two by each of ten subjects. Of these 20 trials, 13 were hits. Although the results were in the expected direction, the number of trials was still small and the trend not strong enough to yield statistical significance. The overall peak count was also in the expected direction but not significant.

The experimenters then decided to apply another method of evaluation which, it was believed, would identify subjects who might be psi-missers so that the data of all subjects could be used in the evaluation. By this method each subject's first trial was taken as a prediction of his second trial. Since a psi-misser might be expected to miss on both trials, a miss was predicted for the next trial whenever the first trial was a miss. If the second trial in this case did turn out to be a miss, it would favor the hypothesis that the subject actually was influencing the plant, but negatively. Conversely, if the subject made a hit on his first trial, a hit was predicted on the second. When the data of Series 2 were analyzed in this way, the first trial successfully predicted the second trial in seven of the ten cases, which of course was not a significant value, though in the expected direction.

In addition to cross-addition scoring, the overall peak count was also checked by this new method. For those subjects who scored above chance on the first trial, the greater number of peaks was expected to indicate what the target order was. For those subjects who missed on the first trial, the smaller number of peaks was expected to indicate the target. In all, there were 165 peaks on the subjects' ten second trials. By chance, one would expect half (82.5) to be in accordance with the predictions (hits). Actually, 96 were hits, (odds against chance: 50 to one).

Experimental Series 3

A further change in design was made to speed the accumulation of data. The method of measuring peaks used in the preceding experiments requires much practice and time to apply. Also, it is not completely objective, as shown in the pilot experiment when a second evaluator disagreed with the experimenter's evaluation in one out of ten cases. A new method of evaluation was therefore adopted.

PROCEDURE

Some changes were also made in procedure. A clear sheet of glass was placed between the plants and the subject to shield the plants from the subject's breathing and similar effects. Also, a different pair of rooms was used, which made it possible for the experimenter to call to the subject when a trial was to begin instead of using the electric light signal. (This was not an intended change, but one necessitated by extraneous circumstances.)

The most important change was inspired by a report from two anonymous French scientists of their work with mice (see pp. 17–27 of this volume). The mice, free to jump from one side of a cage to the other, could use precognition to avoid an electric shock randomly administered in one side of the cage or the other. Much of their behavior could be attributed to normal causes; for a mouse which received a shock in one side of the cage to jump to the other side would be normal behavior. When a mouse deviated from such "mechanical" behavior, the experimenters concluded that sometimes the deviation might be due to psi; that is, that the mouse's motivation for the jump might be precognition of where the next random shock would occur.

PK Effect on a Plant-Polygraph System

Applying analogous reasoning to the plant situation focused attention on the trials during which the plant's activity changed its normal trend, for example, when the chart indicated that a general upward movement had suddenly been interrupted by a downward trend. The question was: did PK cause the change? Consequently, in this series the subjects were not asked to try to increase the activity of the plant but to "increase the current flowing through the leaf." (Actually resistance of the leaf was what the polygraph monitored.)

After receiving one target (AB or BA) from the second experimenter, each subject was directed to use this same target order in four attempts at influencing the two plants. In each trial a 30-second try at one plant was followed by a 30-second rest and a 30-second attempt to influence the other plant. After a subject completed four attempts, the experimenter evaluated the charts, and then he and the subject returned the target and chart, as before, to the second experimenter.

Figures 4-7 diagram the method of evaluation and the criterion of what constituted a usable trial.

An upward movement of the pen of the polygraph showed that the resistance of the leaf of a plant had decreased. The four graphs (or their reverse images) illustrate all possible combinations of upward and downward movements of the polygraph.

The unchanging upward slope of the line in Figure 4, indicates that resistance of the leaf of plant B did not change

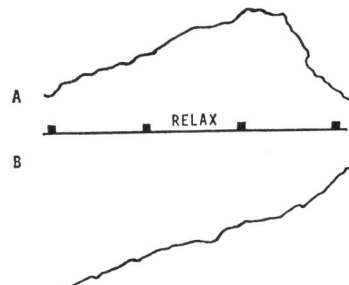

FIG. 4. Chart indicating AB target order for plant A.

noticeably between the two periods of concentration. In plant A, however, the slope changed from upward in the first concentration period to downward in the second concentration period. This indicated an AB target order since the resistance of A decreased during the first concentration period and increased during the second. Figure 5 is the rare instance where the charts for both A and B indicate the same target order. In A the resistance decreased and then increased; in B, increased and then decreased. Both slopes in the same direction (Figure 6) give no indication of the target order. In Figure 7, although there is a change from one concentration period to the other in both plants, the conflicting evidence does not point to a target order; plant A indicates an AB order, plant B, a BA order. It should be noted that in each graph the slopes of all four areas are either upward or downward.

Occasionally one of the four areas of a chart had neither an upward nor downward slope, but only a horizontal line. Such a line might mean that the plant was inactive or it might mean mechanical failure in the polygraph. If in any of the four areas there was no difference in the height of the tracing when the beginning was compared with the end, this area was ignored in determining the target order. Thus only areas which included slopes either up or down were considered.

The general criterion for what constituted a usable trial was: If the current decreased or increased in at least two

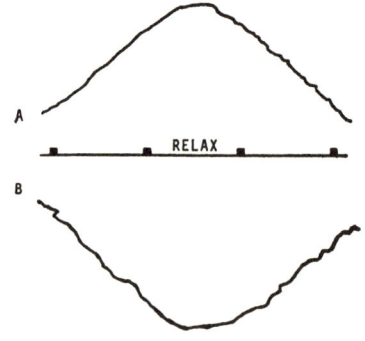

FIG. 5. Chart indicating AB target order for both plants.

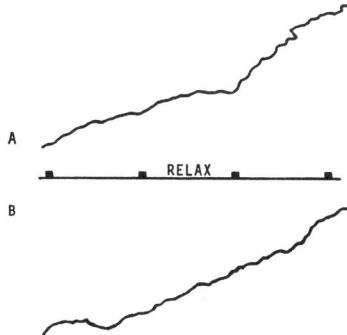

Fig. 6. Chart indicating no target order for either plant.

periods, and if the majority of these periods indicated the same target order, then the trial was considered usable.

Two analyses were intended: First, analysis of overall hits to see if the deviation was large enough to be significant; second, analysis to determine if those subjects who had more than one usable trial were consistent in their results—that is, were the second, third, and fourth trials in the same scoring direction (positive or negative) as the first?

RESULTS

Ten subjects took part. In all there were 20 usable trials, and of these, 13 were hits—a deviation of +3, which is not significant. Of the ten subjects, six had more hits than misses, a result quite in line with the earlier experiments. When the first trial for each subject was used as an indicator of the remaining trials for that subject, there were seven hits and three misses, which again is positive but not significant.

Experimental Series 4

PROCEDURE

The ten subjects tested in this series were asked to make five trials instead of four. Each subject was given five separate target envelopes instead of one. The target orders were randomly determined, so that a subject could have had a different target order for each trial, or five identical target orders, or a combination of these. The concentration and

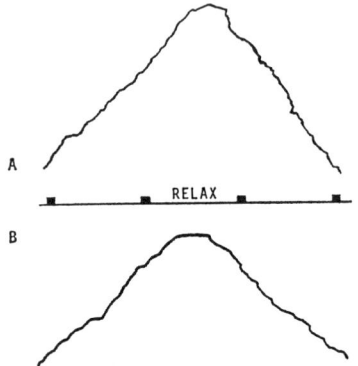

Fig. 7. Chart indicating conflicting evidence of target order for both plants.

relaxation periods were shortened to 15 seconds, one trial taking 45 rather than 90 seconds in order to reduce fatigue and boredom on the part of the subject.

RESULTS

Of the 22 trials this experiment yielded, 14 were hits and eight were misses. This was in the expected direction, but the deviation is not beyond the chance level.

Of the ten people tested, three had an equal number of hits and misses. Of the seven remaining, five had more hits than misses. Again, while in the expected direction, the result was not significant.

The charts were analyzed to see if the first of each subject's trials accurately indicated the scoring direction of the remaining trials. The first trial provided an accurate prediction for six of the 13 subsequent trials—not a significant result.

Experimental Series 5

PROCEDURE

The new method used in Experimental Series 3 and 4 facilitated evaluation of the data. Since the method produced results generally trending in the same direction, an additional series was scheduled to see if additional data would confirm the trend. This time 20 subjects were tested by the method used in Experimental Series 4.

RESULTS

The series yielded a total of 32 usable trials. Of these, 20 were hits, a deviation of +4, which is in line with the earlier trend but not significant in itself. A majority of the subjects showed this effect, a trend in line with the expectational though not to a significant extent. Of the 16 subjects who had either more hits than misses or more misses than hits, ten had more hits.

Overall Results

The research project included seven independent series of tests: the preliminary series, the pilot study, and experimental series 1–5. The experimental series comprise an attempt to confirm the effect found in the first two series. The results of the pilot and each of series 1–5 were positive (odds against chance: 20 to one).

Since it is best not to combine the results of experiments which utilize basically different methods, only the results of the last three experiments are combined for final presentation.

In all, there were 74 usable trials, of which 47 were hits. This is a deviation of +10 (odds against chance: more than 100 to one).

The experimenter made a total of 512 decisions as to whether a slope on the charts was upward or downward. A second experimenter without knowledge of the experimenter's decisions, independently evaluated all 512 decisions from the charts. When her evaluation of a trial disagreed with the experimenter's, the chart was given to a third evaluator whose independent evaluation broke the tie. The final result was 509 agreements with the experimenter's judgment and three disagreements, or more than 99% agreement, which indicates that the method of evaluation is a relatively objective one.

General Discussion

The primary purpose of this research was to seek evidence of a PK effect on living tissues, and in this some progress was made, especially in methods. These are of value in the continuing investigation. Positive effects were noted and PK seemed the plausible cause. The experiment leaves open the question of whether the subject's PK was affecting not the plant but the polygraph. The problem of locating precisely where the PK effect occurs is often met in PK research, and no solution is yet in sight. Any final conclusions on this point must therefore await additional research.

The secondary purpose was to work out satisfactory test procedures, and here again success was only partial. The method of evaluation that was developed, based on whether the line traced by the polygraph pen was lower or higher at the end of a period of concentration than at the beginning, seems to offer greater reliability than the peak-count method used at the start. The high level of agreement between the experimenter and the second evaluator indicates that the method is usefully objective. However, improvements in the method of gathering data are badly needed. The amount of data reported is disproportionately small for the considerable effort over a three-year period covered by the report. Appreciable progress in research on the effects of PK on biological systems will depend on more efficient experimental design.

LITERATURE CITED

1. Cox, W. E. "The Effect of PK on Electromechanical Systems." *Journal of Parapsychology*, 1965, **29**, 165–75.
2. Duval, Pierre, and Montredon, Evelyn. "ESP Experiments with Mice." *Journal of Parapsychology*, 1968, **32**, 153–66. (See also pp. 17–27 in this volume.)
3. Grad, B. "A Telekinetic Effect on Plant Growth, I." *International Journal of Parapsychology*, 1963, **5**, 117–33.
4. Grad, B. "A Telekinetic Effect on Plant Growth, II." *International Journal of Parapsychology*, 1964, **6**, 473–98.
5. Richmond, N. "Two Series of PK Tests on Paramecia." *Journal of the Society for Psychical Research*, 1952, **36**, 577–88.

6. Rhine, L. E. "Spontaneous Physical Effects and the Psi Process." *Journal of Parapsychology*, 1963, **27**, 84–122.
7. Vasse, Dr. and Mme. P. "Influence de la Pensée sur la Croissance des Plantes." *Review Métapsychique*, Nouvelle Serie, 1948, **2**, 87–94.
8. Vasse, P. "Expériences de Germination de Plantes: Méthode du Professeur J. B. Rhine de Duke." *Review Métapsychique*, Nouvelle Serie, 1950, **12**, 223–25.

JEAN BARRY

Retarding Fungus Growth by PK

The effect of psychokinesis (PK) on inanimate matter has been demonstrated in a great many experiments over the past 35 years (3), but only recently and to a much more limited extent have the effects of PK on living matter been investigated. This report covers a laboratory test of PK on a living organism. The experiment was conducted in an agronomy laboratory where excellent technical services and equipment were available, enabling the experimenter to maintain optimal conditions of operation and control.

One experiment with living organisms was reported in 1963 by Grad (2). A person who claimed to be a healer attempted to influence the growth rate of seedlings. The healer mentally treated some plant nutrient solution. Test plants were watered with treated solution; controls, with untreated. Assistants who did not know which seedlings were being tested measured the growth at the end of the experiment. Grad obtained positive results; his test seedlings grew more than the controls.

Brier is conducting a related experiment (1) using electrical recording apparatus attached to plants to measure subjects' mental influence on the plants. Subjects try to control a test plant's resistance to electric current psychokinetically. Brier's preliminary experiment gave positive results; for his subsequent findings, see paper on pp. 102–117.

In an earlier experiment under controlled laboratory conditions, the present author tested the ability of human subjects to inhibit the growth of two fungal plant parasites, *Stereum purpureum* and *Rhizoctonia solani,* by volitional

---

Presented in absentia at the Winter Review Meeting of the Institute for Parapsychology, December 29, 1967. Complete report in the *Journal of Parapsychology*, December 1968.

concentration. The results were positive; the treated cultures grew less than the untreated cultures. The effect was most marked on the mycelium of cultures of *Rhizoctonia solani*, a fungus that causes many plant diseases known as "Rhizoctone Brun."

PROCEDURE

The fungus was cultivated in 10 cm petri dishes in the laboratory. An inoculating loop was inserted in the center of the dishes at 5:30 P.M. the day before each test session, and the dishes were then placed in an incubator kept at 21°C which had intermittent lighting during 12 hours out of 24.

The experimental conditions were extremely closely controlled, and in each session all possible precautions were taken to ensure that all the petri dishes were subjected to the same conditions. The genetic purity of the fungus, composition of the culture medium, and relative humidity, temperature and lighting in the surrounding environment were carefully regulated to make sure that the only variable factor which could influence the growth of the fungus differentially was the psychokinetic one.

Test sessions took place in a little room adjoining the incubator. There at 8:30 A.M. the day after the dishes were inoculated, each subject was assigned five experimental dishes and five controls. All ten of the dishes were brought to the subject directly from the incubator. Subjects were asked to concentrate on trying to retard growth in the experimental dishes, and to disregard the controls. The controls were kept in the test room for the same length of time, subject to the same environmental conditions. In general, an assistant who took no other part in the experiment handled the various manipulations. Each subject sat approximately 1.5 meters from the dishes and stayed there for 15 minutes as determined by a timer but was free to concentrate in whatever way he saw fit.

The results were measured by the routine procedure for such biological measurements. At the moment when the first mycelium filaments verged on touching the rim of the dish in any one of the ten culture dishes, all ten dishes were immediately measured by someone who did not know the aim of the experiment and who did not know which were the control dishes. The boundaries of the colonies were outlined on uniform sheets of thin paper; the outlines were cut out and weighed in milligrams under conditions of constant temperature and humidity.

The weights of the five experimental cut-outs from each trial were totaled and compared with the total weight of the five corresponding control cut-outs. No attempt was made to evaluate relative degrees of growth, but if the experimental total was less than the control, the trial was considered a hit; if more, a miss.

Nine experimental sessions were completed. Ten different subjects participated, the number of subjects in each session varying from three to six. In the sixth session, one subject, Bu, completed two trials (with a different set of dishes for each trial), once in the presence of the others (Bu^1), as was usual, and later alone (Bu^2). In the seventh session, a pair of subjects concentrated on one set of dishes at the same time. In the eighth session, a different pair tried this procedure.

RESULTS

Of 39 trials, 33 deviated positively, three deviated negatively, and three were equal or tied. In the 36 trials which showed a difference between experimental and control growth, there were 15 more hits than would be expected by chance (odds against chance: more than 1,000 to one).

Only two subjects, S and B, took part in all nine sessions. For both S and B, eight of nine trials were positive and one was tied. The other subjects participated in from one to seven sessions. One subject, G, made one tie and two of the three negative trials as well as three positive trials. A pair, Bu + R, made the other negative trial.

Of the eleven subjects or combinations of subjects (Bu^1 and Bu^2 is of course only one subject), ten scored above chance, and only one scored below chance (odds against such consistency in subject scoring: more than 100 to one).

Thus the results are significant both on totals and on subject consistency, strongly suggesting that the subjects exerted an influence on the fungus growth.

The above figures represent the combined total growth in the five test dishes used for each trial in comparison with the total growth in the five corresponding control dishes. They do not give the consistency of the subject's influence on each individual test dish. That is, a trial could have included a test dish with hardly any growth at all and other dishes with only slightly more growth than in the corresponding control dishes and still be counted as a hit. Each of the 195 test dishes was therefore compared with its corresponding control. One test dish had the same amount of growth as its control. Of the 194 test dishes which differed from their controls, 151 had less growth than their controls (odds against chance: more than 1,000 to one). The rate in some sessions was particularly high. In session six, for example, 29 of 30 test dishes had less fungus growth than their corresponding controls (odds against chance: more than 1,000 to one).

DISCUSSION

In view of these results, the hypothesis that thought can hinder the growth of these destructive fungi seems well confirmed. The implications of these findings challenge even the imagination. They should be followed up with all possible dispatch.

LITERATURE CITED

1. Brier, Robert. "PK on a Bio-Electrical System." In *Parapsychology Today*. Edited by J. B. Rhine and Robert Brier. New York: Citadel Press, 1968.
2. Grad, Bernard. "A Telekinetic Effect on Plant Growth. I." *International Journal of Parapsychology*, 1963, 5, 117–133.
3. Rhine, Louisa E. *Mind Over Matter: The Story of PK*. New York: Macmillan Company, 1970.

Part III
Factors in Psi Test Performance

Preface

What makes psi ability work? The question has several aspects. Psi works not only in varying strengths but in different forms and directions. Accordingly, one may ask what controls the amount of psi effect, that is, whether the total score or deviation from chance is large or small; or one may ask whether the deviation took a positive or a negative direction from the chance mean. Thus the question of what influences the psi process can be examined under at least two clearcut headings: efficiency and direction. There are other less common ways psi can register its effect (for example, the position effects described in Appendix A) but these need not concern us here.

With regard to direction, the same total amount of psi effect may show itself on either the plus or the minus side of the expected chance average. It may even jump back and forth from one side to the other and cancel its effects unless tested for run score *variance* (see Appendix E). However, in an experiment comparing performance on two types of tests, the results may show a positive deviation (psi-hitting) on one type and a negative one (psi-missing; see Appendix C) on the other, and thus produce what is known as the psi differential effect (PDE). This effect can easily be measured by the standard methods (critical ratio of the difference) and has been one of the most useful discoveries ever made about how psi operates. The PDE works as it does because it is so easy for psi to switch from hitting to missing; the subject is not conscious enough of how his ability operates to control its direction, although it may conceivably become controllable. But enough is known about these plus–minus shifts to indicate that they are psychologically determined on an unconscious level, and many factors that cause them are known. In fact it is just such work as this section and the next presents that reveals what these factors are. It is steadily converting mystery about the psi process to order and understanding.

The first paper in this section brings out these two aspects of the psi effect in a clear and beautiful way. The experiment provides three conditions. Two of these conditions—comparison of location of runs on the record page and distinction between the two persons who checked data—had to do with the amount of ability; they determined where the ESP took place and where it did not. In this instance, one run and one checker got it all. The third factor, however, divided the results produced by the first two factors into two parts, directing half of the psi effect into positive deviations and the other half into negative. But while this third factor depended on the subjects' correctly precognizing also which checker would check a given run, actually the conscious guessing as to which checker would check a given run tended to differentiate the psi effect into two equal but opposite deviations, the rightly guessed runs getting the positive scoring.

Why should this occur? Why should the mere matter of guessing right or wrong about the checker split the ESP effect (quite unconsciously, of course) into two different directions of deviation? An answer to this central question would put the science of parapsychology ahead more than anything else at this time, for it would enable experimenters to eliminate the elusive shift to psi-missing. However such results at least provide further clues to the factors that exert this influence over psi. Getting these results, as has been done, under the almost ideal conditions of a doubleblind precognition experiment and then getting them well confirmed, as these are, is progress at its best.

* * * *

The second paper deals with "response bias"—the tendency to call certain target symbols too often and thereby undercall others. This is another of the factors that significantly split ESP data into positive and negative deviations. The idea back of this research was that the particular targets a subject guesses most sparingly are likely to give a higher scoring rate and thus yield positive deviations. The equally interesting thing about this is that when he overcalls one or more targets his scoring rate does not merely stop at chance on these targets; it produces negative deviations.

In general, any preferential attitude of a subject toward the psi test has been found to affect his scoring rate favorably in contrast to a negative attitude. Whether this attitude has to do with the subject's "belief in psi," his feeling toward the person giving the test, or toward the targets used in the test, seems not to matter greatly. Probably the most extensively investigated attitude in relation to ESP testing is the well known "sheep–goat" differentiation of test subjects begun by Dr. Gertrude Schmeidler. Subjects were separated into two groups: sheep, those favorable to the idea of ESP; and goats, those inclined to reject it. Two of the papers that follow explore a closely related question—whether the subjects who have had ESP experiences perform differently from others on ESP tests. In the first of these, the Jones–Feather paper, the questionnaire inquired about a range of five specific types of experience, and this breadth of coverage was the basis of separation. As it turned out, the best show of ESP activity came from the subjects who had had more variety of personal experiences.

In the Moss–Gengerelli research, those who gave the strongest ESP performance were in general those who registered both a belief in ESP and actual spontaneous experience of ESP. As often occurs in research, however, the main purpose was overshadowed by an incidental discovery—that a still better separation of the high versus the low scorers could be made by dividing the subjects on the basis of their association with the arts.

* * * *

One of the questions most often asked about psi ability is whether the sexes show any differences in it. The more or less general reply has become that there is no evidence to show that either sex performs better than the other under equally adequate test conditions. It is true, as Dr. Louisa E. Rhine points out in her book, *Hidden Channels of the Mind*, that many more women than men *report* spontaneous experiences. Also, many research reports mention sex differences in scoring rate under particular conditions, and Dr. John Freeman has found in his classroom tests of precognition that boys and girls react differently to certain types and arrangements of the same targets. Dr. Brier's report on the extensive precognition test given to junior high school students in different parts of the United States shows that when the data were grouped according to sex they yielded significant evidence of psi. It is perhaps remarkable that anything of reliable nature was found in so impersonal a mass test, but some basic biological differentiation seems to have operated as a secondary determinant persistently enough to justify a conclusion that ESP occurred.

* * * *

Ideally an experimenter may hope to be able to turn to account what he learns about the conditions that influence psi performance. To some extent this is being done in a few researches by selecting subjects, test conditions, and types of procedures as they have been found to favor good performance. Little systematic attention has been paid, however, to the opportunity a speaker often has to test the influence of his remarks on his audience. Dr. L. E. Rhine's paper on testing small audiences before and after ESP talks describes and illustrates a feasible method. Her experience indicates that factors influencing psi test performance can to some extent be manipulated by the speaker. It is a step ahead to produce effective attitudes—that is, ahead of merely measuring them.

Of the authors in this section, Drs. Feather, Brier, Stanford and Rhine have already been introduced. Joyce Jones was research assistant to Dr. Feather at the Institute for Parapsychology when this work was done. Dr. Thelma Moss is assistant professor of psychology at the Neuropsychiatric Institute, University of California at Los Angeles. Dr. J. A. Gengerelli is professor of psychology at the same university.

—J.B.R.

SARA R. FEATHER AND ROBERT BRIER

The Effect of the Checker on Precognition

ESP's apparent independence of space and time gives rise to many bizarre possibilities of just what may be influencing the subjects. What, for example, influences an individual who is trying to predict the future random order of a set of targets? In this research we investigated the possibility that such a subject could be reacting differentially (presumably by precognition) to the person or persons who would later check his test.

Some evidence pointing to this possibility had already been found at the Institute for Parapsychology. In one case, a member of the research staff administering a group precognition test had planned to check his data by the usual procedure, but to facilitate the work, he gave half of the data to an assistant. The assistant checked those data against targets provided by the random numbers immediately following those used by the experimenter. As it turned out, the results checked by the assistant showed above-chance scoring, those checked by the experimenter showed below-chance scoring, and the difference was statistically significant. Since there was no other obvious difference in the conditions affecting the two groups of subjects, the suggestion was made that the scoring difference could have been due to the fact that different people had checked the data.

A second indication came when another experimenter collected some precognition data from a lecture group. An assistant helped check the data, and once again there was a significant and unexpected scoring difference in the data checked by each of the two people. In this case, the data

---

Presented at the Spring Review Meeting of the Institute for Parapsychology, May 3, 1968. Complete report in *Journal of Parapsychology*, September 1968.

scored by the experimenter himself gave results in accord with the experimental hypothesis, while those checked by the assistant were clearly in the reverse direction.

The unanticipated and significant difference found in these two instances was enough to raise the question of whether it can make any difference to the subject if one person or another will be chosen later to check his test.

The present experiments were designed to investigate in a more direct way if the person who checks precognition tests may himself be a significant variable affecting the scores of the subjects; and if so, whether the effect is due to a subject's conscious expectation of who will check his test or to unconscious precognition on his part.

Pilot Experiment I

One of the authors, SF, tested a group of subjects who were taking a lecture course in parapsychology at the local YWCA in November 1967. Following the scheduled evening program, the members were asked to participate in a test to find out whether they would score differently on runs which would be checked by the lecturer, SF, and runs which would be checked by another member of the Institute staff. The other checker was deliberately not identified, although at the time of the experiment, SF had already decided to ask RB to serve as the second checker.

PROCEDURE

Subjects were asked to complete a total of four standard 25-call precognition runs, each call to predict which of the five ESP symbols would be correct according to a random target order to be determined later. They were told that two of these runs would be checked by the experimenter and two by another person, and that the decision as to which runs would be checked by whom would be made later by a random procedure. In addition, subjects were to record their predictions of the runs that would be checked by SF by writing her initials at the bottom of those two runs. The

The Effect of the Checker on Precognition

results thus could be analyzed for the effect of both conscious expectation and precognition of the checker which is, of course, on the unconscious level.

The next day, the record sheets were alphabetized, and a random number table entry point obtained by the standard procedure. Another random procedure was followed to determine which two of each subject's four runs would be checked by SF and which two by RB. SF used the numbers following the entry point to provide targets for the runs she checked, and RB used the following numbers for the runs he checked.

RESULTS

The 92 runs completed by the 23 subjects yielded 44 fewer hits than would be expected by chance alone (odds against chance: 50 to one), which justifies the conclusion that precognition had occurred in the experiment. The runs checked by RB gave 33 below, and those by SF 11 below, the expected chance average. However, the finding of main interest concerns trends in the 46 runs checked by the experimenter, SF. The data scored by RB showed no discernible trends.

The subjects had accurately predicted that SF would do the checking for 19 of the 46 runs checked by SF, and the score for these 19 runs was positive with eight more hits than chance expectation; but for the 27 runs which the subjects had erroneously predicted would be checked by someone else but which SF actually did check, the score was negative with 19 fewer hits than chance expectation (odds against chance of the difference: 20 to one).

Pilot Experiment II

In February 1968, SF tested a similar group of 32 students who were also taking a course in parapsychology at the local YWCA. The test procedure was identical to that of the first experiment except that 10-call runs were used for the precognition test instead of the standard 25-call runs.

RESULTS

This second pilot experiment yielded overall results very similar to those of the first pilot, although the total was insignificantly negative with a deviation of −16 hits in 51.2 runs. (The fractional number of runs is the result of rearranging the 10-call runs into the standard 25-call form.) SF checked 25.6 runs which yielded a +3 total; RB, on the same number of runs, had a total of −19, again an insignificant difference but in the expected direction.

In the data checked by the experimenter, SF, once again, there was differential scoring according to the subjects' expectations. There were seven hits above mean chance expectation in the twelve runs subjects had correctly predicted SF would check, and four hits below chance on the 13.6 runs they had incorrectly predicted someone else would check (odds against chance of the difference: more than 30 to one).

The results support the suggestion that subjects' conscious predictions of who will check their data makes a difference in whether they hit or avoid the target on the trials which will eventually be scored by the experimenter.

The pilot studies raised a further point. The differences noted in the data that were checked by the experimenter contrast sharply with the absence of any such differences in the data checked by some other person. The contrast suggests that it is not only the subject's expectation of who will check his data, but also who does check it eventually, that is important. If it were only the subject's conscious expectations that affected his scoring, there should be equal differences between the scores for the comparable groups of runs in the data checked by a second person. The fact that there were no such differences in these data suggests that both the subject's expectations and the checker are important to some degree. It also suggests that a subject's expectation that the experimenter will be the checker tends to lead him to score positively when that expectation will be, in fact, fulfilled, and negatively when it will not be fulfilled.

Confirmation Experiment

A repetition of the two pilot experiments was conducted by the second author, RB, when he lectured to a parapsychology class at the New School for Social Research in New York City in April 1968. There was enough similarity between the New School students and the two earlier groups in general motivation and background knowledge of ESP to make the class a suitable test group. Results were expected to show the same trends as those in the pilot experiment.

PROCEDURE

The same test procedure was employed with RB now the experimenter who asked his subjects to predict the two runs which he would be scoring. He informed the subjects that the remaining two of their four runs would be checked by someone else at the Institute for Parapsychology. He did not identify the second person, but had already arranged that SF would be the other checker.

RESULTS

The overall score for the 140 runs gave 19 more hits than mean chance expectation. The experimenter checked 70 runs and found a deviation of −5, while SF, in an equal number of runs, found a deviation of +24. The difference was not significant, nor was it in the expected direction. Again, the data checked by the second checker (SF) showed no discernible trends.

The most interesting results were again from the 70 runs checked by the experimenter, in this case RB. Of the 70 runs RB checked, the 31 which the subjects had correctly predicted he would check gave a deviation of +15, and the 39 runs which the subjects had incorrectly predicted someone else would check gave a deviation of −20 (chance odds against the difference: more than 50 to one).

Because these results confirmed the earlier finding of an ESP differential effect related to who checked the data and who the subjects expected would check the data, it was legitimate to examine the results more closely for clues as to how or where this scoring effect on the runs which the experimenter would check might be localized. The data of the pilot experiments was therefore analyzed according to the position of runs on the score sheets. (For a description of position effect, see Appendix A.)

The scoring was found to be concentrated in the first of the four runs on sheets checked by the experimenter. The direction of the effect apparently depended on whether a subject had predicted correctly that the experimenter would check that run or incorrectly that someone else would do so. In the experimenter-checked runs in the two pilot series, there were 18.2 "first" runs. Of these first runs, there were 6.6 which the subjects had correctly predicted SF would check, and these 6.6 runs gave a deviation of +15. In contrast, the 11.6 first runs which the subjects incorrectly predicted someone else would check, gave a deviation of −17. The difference of 32 hits is very significant (odds against chance: 10,000 to one).

Examination of the data from the confirmation series also indicated that the effect was strongest on the 21 first runs checked by the experimenter. The seven first runs which subjects correctly predicted RB would check gave a deviation of +12, while the 14 first runs which they incorrectly predicted someone else would check gave a deviation of −8. The difference of 20 hits is significant (odds against chance: 100 to one).

General Discussion

The results of these experiments show three distinct effects: the position effect, the effect of the checker, and the effect of the subjects' guess as to who the checker will be.

The position effect shows in the concentration of the significant scoring in the first runs on the record sheets, which accords with findings of many other psi researchers.

But in these experiments the position effect did not appear in all the first runs; it was confined to the set of first runs which the experimenter himself eventually checked, regardless of who the subject consciously expected would check them.

However, the *direction* of the significant scoring was apparently dictated by the subjects' conscious expectations about the checker. The scoring went above chance in the set of first runs which subjects had correctly guessed the experimenter would check, but below chance in those which they had incorrectly guessed an assistant would check.

This is a complex result. The run position and the subjects' preference for the experimenter as checker apparently determine the *amount* of ESP performance, while the subjects' conscious guesses about the checker's identity influenced the *direction* of deviation of ESP scoring, determining whether the subjects psi-hit or psi-missed.

These phenomena raise some interesting theoretical questions. Are we to assume that even before the targets or the identity of the future checker are determined, the identity of the checker affects a subject's ESP responses as he makes them? And how does a subject discriminate between his own correct and incorrect impressions of which runs the experimenter will and which he will not check?

These questions lead back to the basic question: What does the subject precognize? Is it only the symbols that will be entered on the sheet later, or is it also the person who will enter the symbols? If the person must be included, then the range of variables which may affect precognitive scoring is considerably wider than has been assumed in the researchers to date.

REX G. STANFORD

Response Bias and ESP Test Performance

An experiment was designed to test the hypothesis that bias against a particular response increases the probability that this response, when made, will be an accurate, or psi-mediated, response.

Extrasensory perception might be termed "an ability without a modality." Extrasensory information may emerge into consciousness in any of a variety of possible ways. A problem for the parapsychologist is that these ways are so diverse and that they are in no sense unique to psi material. ESP information may become manifest as a fleeting thought or association, as a vague feeling or hunch, as a visual image (hallucination), as an apparently somatic symptom, or by other means (4, pp. 78–100; 5). It bears repeating that none of these kinds of events is unique to psi material. It is in this sense that ESP can be said to have no modality of its own. Unlike visual or auditory perception, for example, ESP is not characterized in consciousness by any cues peculiar to itself. This must be part of what is implied by saying that the function of ESP is unconscious.

How, then, it is possible for psi-mediated material to get acted on as veridical? How can it be recognized as information about the objective world, or even get noticed in the "stream of consciousness?" Put in another way, how is it possible to discriminate the signal from the noise?

In at least some portion of the spontaneous cases, a tentative answer can be given to these queries. Psi-mediated thoughts, feelings, and sensations appear to draw the experiencing person's attention because they are inappropriate

---

Presented at the Autumn Review Meeting of the Institute for Parapsychology, September 1, 1967. Complete report in *Journal of Parapsychology*, December 1967.

in their context. Something the person is experiencing does not "belong" with the "normal" thoughts, feelings, or sensations appropriate to the situation. The perceiver may infer, if he believes in psi or "intuition," that something "out there," beyond the reach of his senses, is responsible.

It is not unusual for an event which is inappropriate in its context to capture attention; this is a feature of ordinary perceptual psychology.

If this line of reasoning is correct, then a feeling or thought—e.g., "something terrible has happened to John"—may or may not be noticed or acted upon depending on its relative appropriateness in the context. If a person often thinks of something terrible happening to John—e.g., if John has a dangerous job—such a thought will probably be dismissed as a passing worry. But if John is unlikely to be in danger ordinarily, a person is more likely to recognize and act upon psi-mediated information about peril to John, everything else being equal. If the perceiver is not normally concerned about John, the "signal" will likely be attended to because it is distinctive or inappropriate in its context, but if the perceiver normally worries about John, such discrimination of "signal" and "noise" will be difficult. Also, when many "false alarms" occur such thoughts may come to be ignored.

Granted the existence of psi, it might even be said that a thought is more likely to be accurate in psi-mediated situations where the normal probability of that thought's occurrence is low rather than high.

The laboratory ESP test situation may, at times, be analogous. Certain ESP test responses have a relatively low probability of occurrence. In a matching test, for example, responses are made relatively seldom on the far right-hand and far left-hand key cards. Are such low-probability responses more accurate than responses which tend to occur more often? Are seldom made responses more likely to be accurate than frequently made ones?

If so, then as the predisposition to make a particular ESP-test response decreases, the likelihood that the response, when made, will be accurate increases. Assuming the function of ESP in the test situation, it might be said that the extra "push" of psi is needed to trigger a response which goes against a bias. The subject is not necessarily more "sensitive" on these responses; it may be that his negative response bias simply reduces the number of false alarms for that particular kind of response. This concept ties in with recent sensory psychology work on signal detection theory which separates the question of sensory sensitivity from the effects of criterion shifts (response bias changes) upon performance (7, pp. 3–57). No exact analogy is claimed, however, between this recent sensory work and what happens with ESP; not enough is yet known to warrant such a claim.

The question raised here requires an empirical answer. Are responses against which there is relatively strong bias more accurate in the ESP test situation? The earlier parapsychological literature, as well as some of the more recent work, provides considerable data to support such a hypothesis. Indeed, in all of my explorations, I found remarkably few results that were *not* in the direction anticipated by this line of reasoning. The following examples fairly represent the data surveyed.

Both of the Martin-Stribic clairvoyance experiments (1, 2) show an essentially inverse relation between call frequency for a given symbol and the success of calls on that symbol. In order to avoid possible statistical artifacts due to overcalling of symbols, I compared the success rate of responses made with approximate chance frequency with the success rate of the responses made least frequently in the two experiments. There were approximately 10,000 trials on the more frequently called symbols, 8,000 on the less frequently called symbols. Success was, as expected, greater with the infrequently called symbols. The odds against a difference this size or larger occurring by chance alone are 50 to one.

Ryzl and Pratt noted a similar effect in working with Stepanek as their subject (6). Stepanek tended to call white less often than green when the target was one of the two. Of

Stepanek's 1,193 green calls, 54.8% were correct, but 59.4% of his white calls were correct. The odds against a difference this great or greater occurring by chance alone are 20 to one.

Pratt's recent report on an extensive analysis of calling patterns and ESP scoring (3) appears to fit in very well with the hypothesis under consideration here. He found that in many series, Mrs. Stewart tended to avoid calling the same symbol twice in a row, which is equivalent to saying that she had a response bias against calling the symbol that had just been called. The present hypothesis would lead us to expect a high rate of success for calls repeating the preceding call, in those series showing evidence of this bias. These second members of double calls were compared for success with the second numbers of two-call sequences from the same series which were not doubles and were not undercalled. As expected, the success rate of the second members of double calls was remarkable; the difference in scoring rate was in the anticipated direction and was so great that the odds against a result at least this extreme happening by chance are less than one in fifty billion.

In a recent and as yet unpublished study, Dr. John A. Freeman asked subjects to use ESP in choosing one of five columns across the page. His subjects showed marked preferences for responding in certain columns. A comparison of columns which were selected less than a fifth of the time with columns selected more often than that showed high positive average scoring on infrequently marked columns and considerable below-chance average scoring on frequently marked columns. The difference in scoring levels between the two call frequency conditions is in the expected direction and is statistically reliable. The odds against the occurrence of a difference at least this extreme by chance alone are 500 to one.

The above examples illustrate four very different kinds of ESP-test situations—symbol call frequency biases, binary choice response bias, sequential biases, and call-column preferences. In all these situations, subjects showed a tendency toward greater accuracy in the undercalled responses. This suggests that whenever a given response is relatively improbable, ESP success on that response will be relatively great as compared with the responses made more frequently. Response bias seems to function as a kind of filtering process such that the responses biased against are less often called for non-ESP reasons.

This experiment was aimed at obtaining the effect exemplified in the above experiments. The design included no experimental manipulation to affect the subject's degree of response bias, but encouraged the subject to vary his response frequency at his own discretion, an arrangement psychologically closer to the more standard test situations in which the effect was initially observed.

PROCEDURE

This work was carried out in Winston-Salem, N.C., in the summer of 1967 while the author was on the staff of the Institute for Parapsychology. Twenty-eight subjects, students of high-school age who were enrolled in a special summer education program, were tested in small groups at the school. They had volunteered to participate in an "ESP radar test" which they had heard about earlier in the day.

Subjects were told that ESP could be used rather like radar to locate objects or to identify objective events, and that this form of ESP, called clairvoyance, has been well established.

They were then given a one-page ESP test form picturing a pair of mock radar screens each four inches in diameter. Each screen was divided into 36 sectors (see Figure 1). Each subject was also given a sealed, opaque envelope containing a sheet with an identical pair of radar screens on which the actual targets had been marked with a red felt marker. There was no more than one target in any one sector. The target sectors had been determined on the basis of a random number table, with an average of 18 targets per screen, so there was a one-half probability that a given sector had a target in it. Target envelopes were numbered, and subjects recorded this number on their record sheets. Sub-

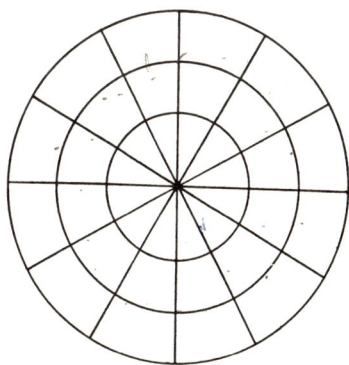

Fig. 1. "Radar screen" target form used in ESP testing.

jects were told how to orient the envelope so that the hidden screens would correspond to Screens 1 and 2 on their record sheets.

Subjects were asked to use their clairvoyance to mark on their test forms where the hidden red targets were, first on Screen 1, then on Screen 2. They were told that each hidden screen had roughly 12–18 targets. (This allowed the subjects to "bias" themselves by choosing how many target identification responses they wished to make.) The experimenter explained that they had only to locate the sectors containing the targets, that it was not necessary for the position of their response within the sector to coincide exactly with that of the hidden target. The experimenter stressed that sectors should be chosen as accurately as possible, that placing marks wildly all over the screen would not help them to get a score better than chance average.

Subjects were told that the person with the best total score in each group would win a packet of ESP testing materials and a booklet describing ESP testing procedures, and that scores and a statement of who had won the prize would be posted 30 minutes after the end of the test.

In scoring the tests, only target identification responses were counted as trials. The test screens were divided into two groups, those with relatively few target identification responses and those with a relatively large number. The division point was chosen to make the number of calls in each group as nearly equal as possible. This division point, which was decided upon prior to any examination of the relevant data, identified as low-frequency the screens with 16 or fewer responses, and as high-frequency the screens with 17 or more responses.

RESULTS

The 465 trials on the low-frequency screens had significantly more hits than would be expected on a chance (average) basis. The odds against the occurrence of results at least this positive by chance alone are 2,000 to one. The 412 trials on the high-frequency screens had suggestively, but not quite significantly, fewer hits than could be expected on a chance (average) basis. The difference in scoring rate on the high- and low-frequency screens was highly significant; the odds against a difference this great or greater occurring by chance alone are 20,000 to one.

The effect of call frequency on scoring was so consistent over all the screens that the odds against consistency this great or greater occurring by chance alone are 1,000 to one.

It might be asked if the effect reported above was due to individual differences—whether subjects who call with a high frequency do poorly and those with a low frequency do well. The evidence, however, runs counter to this interpretation. Twelve of the subjects contributed *both* high- and low-frequency screens. A within-subject analysis of scoring and call frequency based on these twelve subjects yielded a very significant difference in the expected direction.

If a reliable negative correlation had been found between the number of target identification responses and the actual number of targets, this would have provided a spurious source of the call frequency-success relationship, but the data show no such reliable correlation.

DISCUSSION

The results accord with the experimental hypothesis that bias against a particular response increases the probability that this response, when made, will be an accurate, or psi-mediated, response. However, suggestive as the current results and the evidence from the literature cited earlier may seem, definite conclusions must await further research.

Experiments have been planned which will systematically subject each subject to varying degrees of a treatment designed to produce bias against a particular response. This would control the source and degree of bias.

How general the relation of response bias to success may be is not known. If a person actively dislikes a certain symbol, for example, will he nevertheless do well on the few times he calls the symbol? What would happen if electric shock or another aversive stimulation were used to produce bias? Questions like these are innumerable and serve to emphasize the fact that in the data cited earlier, as in the current experiment, the source of the bias is relatively unconscious.

The present experiment provided a simplified ESP test situation which gave the subject considerable latitude for self-biasing. The results gave evidence of the anticipated effect of response bias upon success. If the research continues to support this hypothesis, the understanding of performance characteristics in ESP testing may be brought closer to our growing understanding of detection performance in sensory situations in which there is minimal discriminability of signal from noise and for which modern psychophysics treats response bias changes (response criterion shifts) separately from sensory sensitivity.

Some specifically parapsychological problems may be relevant to the kind of result reported here. Perhaps a new approach can be made to research on the possible relation between a feeling of conviction and success in making ESP responses. Perhaps also new insight will be provided into the problem of using physiological indicators to pinpoint extrasensorially mediated responses as opposed to merely accurate responses. The question of response bias and success, like any meaningful question in science, leads beyond itself.

LITERATURE CITED

1. Martin, Dorothy R., and Stribic, Frances P. "Studies in Extrasensory Perception: I. An Analysis of 25,000 Trials." *Journal of Parapsychology*, 1938, **2**, 23–30.
2. Martin, Dorothy R., and Stribic, Frances P. "Studies in Extrasensory Perception: II. An Analysis of a Second Series of 25,000 Trials." *Journal of Parapsychology*, 1938, **2**, 287–95.
3. Pratt, J. G. "Computer Studies of the ESP Process in Card Guessing: II. Did Memory Habits Limit Mrs. Stewart's ESP Success?" *Journal of the American Society for Psychical Research*, 1967, **61**, 182–202.
4. Rhine, J. B., and Pratt, J. G. *Parapsychology: Frontier Science of the Mind*. Springfield: Thomas, 1957.
5. Rhine, Louisa E. "Hallucinatory Experiences and Psychosomatic Psi." *Journal of Parapsychology*, 1967, **31**, 111–34.
6. Ryzl, M., and Pratt, J. G. "A Further Confirmation of Stabilized ESP Performance in a Selected Subject." *Journal of Parapsychology*, 1963, **27**, 73–83.
7. Swets, J. A., Tanner, W. P., Jr., and Birdsall, T. G. "Decision Processes in Perception." Chap. 1 in *Signal Detection and Recognition in Human Observers*. New York: Wiley & Sons, 1964.

JOYCE N. JONES and SARA R. FEATHER

Psi Experiences and Test Performance

Spontaneous ESP occurrences are commonplace for many people, while others may not have even a single recognizable psi experience in a lifetime. This observation leads to several questions: Do people in the first category actually have more ESP ability than those in the second? And, if so, do the people who spontaneously experience a similar kind of ESP phenomenon perform similarly or differently in ESP tests?

The authors were interested in investigating a possible relationship between certain types of spontaneous psi experiences and ESP test scoring. For example, do the people who report having experienced psi phenomena in the form of dreams score higher than those whose experiences have been of the intuitive type? In order to test the hypothesis that there is such a relationship, some way had to be found of dividing subjects according to the type of ESP they had experienced spontaneously. A questionnaire seemed to offer a means of developing an index.

Numerous research questionnaires inquiring into attitudes toward ESP have contained queries about spontaneous psi experience, but no effort to relate the way an individual scores on an ESP test to a particular type of previous psi experience has been reported. In his 12-item questionnaire to elicit the attitudes of his subjects toward ESP, Bhadra included six questions dealing with personally experienced psi phenomena (1). Answers to these six questions were eliminated when he analyzed his data because the answer to the seventh question summarized the subject's attitude. This

---

Presented at the Spring Review Meeting of the Institute for Parapsychology, May 2, 1969. Complete report in *Journal of Parapsychology*, December 1969.

seventh answer was the only one Bhadra used for his experiment, but the discarded first questions served as a basis for the Psi Experience Questionnaire designed by the present senior author, JJ, at the Institute for Parapsychology.

PROCEDURE

The Psi Experience Questionnaire (PEQ) was designed primarily for use with high school students, but was used with other groups as well. It consists of five questions, the first four pertaining to specific instances of spontaneous ESP. The fifth question also concerns psi ability but less directly (see Figure 1).

Name _____

Sex _____ Class _____

1. Have you ever had a hunch that something you had lost was in a particular, but very unlikely, place--and in fact, it was?
   Yes   No

2. Have you ever had a dream that later came true?
   Yes   No

3. Have you ever had a hunch that a particular person would have a serious illness or accident and later it actually happened as you anticipated?
   Yes   No

4. Did you ever know in advance that you were going to receive a phone call from a particular person on a particular day when you really had no way of knowing this?
   Yes   No

5. Do you consider yourself lucky in whatever you do?
   Yes   No

FIG. 1. Psi Experience Questionnaire (PEQ).

In most of the reported series, the experimenter spoke briefly to the group of subjects on ESP giving examples of laboratory tests and spontaneous cases of various types, and then gave the subjects an ESP test. The subjects were then told that the experimenter wanted to determine how widespread spontaneous ESP was among high school students (or whatever group was being tested), and copies of the questionnaire were handed out. The subjects were asked to answer yes to a question only if they felt sure they had had an appropriate experience. This procedure was varied only in the preliminary series (when the questionnaire preceded the ESP test), and the second confirmation (when a letter replaced the talk).

Preliminary Series

The PEQ was first used in 1968 by JJ at one of the Idea Symposiums at a Durham, N.C., high school. Two groups of high school students totalling 51 subjects were asked to fill out the questionnaire and take a precognition test consisting of two short runs of ten trials each. After the ESP tests were analyzed at the Institute for Parapsychology, the results were studied in relation to questionnaire responses. The overall scoring was at chance, and no significant relationship was found between scoring level and any of the five questions about spontaneous occurrences. The original hypothesis was not supported.

The authors considered that this preliminary series may not have been a fair test of the questionnaire since there had been only ten ESP trials per run instead of the standard 25; perhaps ten was insufficient for detecting subtle ESP effects.

Pilot Series

The PEQ was given a second trial by the second experimenter, SF, with a group of 40 members of a young women's club as subjects. This time, the standard-length run was used, each subject carrying out two 25-trial clairvoyance test runs.

Again, no positive correlation was found between spontaneous ESP experience and ESP scoring. However, a *post hoc* analysis showed a subject variance differential when the results were categorized according to *how many* experiences had been reported. The "High PEQ" group (those who answered yes to three or more of the five questions) showed greater subject variance than expected by chance, while the "Low PEQ" group (those who answered yes to fewer than three questions) showed below-chance variance. In other words, the scores of the High PEQ subjects fluctuated more, and the Low PEQ subjects less, than expected by chance (odds against chance of the difference: 100 to one).

This *post hoc* finding was interesting enough to warrant further pilot work to test the new hypothesis that there is a relationship between frequency (rather than type) of previous psi experiences and ESP test results. The question was whether people who reported frequent spontaneous psi experiences (High PEQ subjects) would show greater variance in scoring than those who seldom or never reported experiencing psi phenomena (Low PEQ subjects), and whether there would be a significant difference between the two categories.

Three more groups were tested in the pilot series. SF gave a group of 31 high school subjects a clairvoyance test. A third experimenter, CS, gave a group of 15 high school subjects a clairvoyance type of test. SF gave a group of 20 psychiatric nurses a precognition type of test.

The results showed subject variance in the expected direction in two of these three groups. Re-examination of results of JJ's preliminary work showed that in those two series also, the High PEQ subjects showed a larger variance than the Low PEQ group.

Pooled results from the four pilot groups in which the standard 25-trial run was used and the two series using the 10-trial run suggested that subjects who reported more ESP experiences in their private lives tended to score either higher or lower than chance (i.e., their scores tended to vary more) than subjects who reported few or no ESP experiences (odds against chance of the difference: 20 to one).

Confirmation I

An opportunity to seek confirmation of this suggestion arose when JJ was asked to lecture on ESP to three groups of tenth-grade students at a high school in eastern North Carolina.

PROCEDURE

The 53 subjects were asked to complete two 25-trial runs each by entering the ESP symbols on the form in the order they guessed would match targets which had already been determined. This was a test of clairvoyance since the standard procedure for finding an entry point into a table of random numbers to determine the targets had already been carried out when the subjects made their calls.

The subjects were then asked to fill out the questionnaire, and urged to answer yes to a question only if sure they had had such an experience.

RESULTS

The overall scoring was only slightly positive, but a breakdown into groups according to the questionnaire gave support to the pilot finding: the High PEQ group showed high subject variance; the Low PEQ group showed low subject variance (odds against chance of the difference: 50 to one).

Confirmation II

Two groups of junior high school students were participating in a national ESP contest sponsored by the Institute for Parapsychology. These 400 students had already scored high on a preliminary ESP test published in *Read* magazine, a publication distributed to schools throughout the United States. Dr. Robert Brier, who was conducting the contest, agreed to include the present experiment in the semifinals of the national contest.

The contest was being conducted through the mail, which meant the experimenters would not be able to give the talk to help orient these subjects to the task of guessing ESP symbols. Therefore this experiment was considered an extension of PEQ use into a new domain; results in the expected direction would help to validate the reliability of the PEQ. Instead of the talk, subjects were requested by letter to complete two runs of a clairvoyance ESP test and then to fill out the questionnaire "as part of a survey," checking yes only if they felt it was really true for them.

RESULTS

Four hundred questionnaires and ESP tests were mailed in two series of 200 each. A total of 276 were returned to the Institute during the specified time by 151 High PEQ subjects and 125 Low PEQ subjects. Analysis of the combined results of the two series showed subject variance in the expected direction for the High and Low PEQ groups, but the difference was not significant.

General Discussion

The main finding in these experiments, that High PEQ subjects show more variance in their overall scoring than Low PEQ subjects, was noted over a fairly wide range of subjects and situations—in an adult women's club, in a group of student nurses, in several senior high school groups or classes, and finally, among a large junior high school population scattered across the country which was reached by letter. As expected, the groups that met with the experimenter and heard a talk on ESP demonstrated the effect more strongly; but even when the test was distributed by mail, the difference, though less marked, persisted.

One of the more reliable findings in the history of parapsychological research is the well known sheep-goat effect, found by Schmeidler and others, relating the subject's attitude toward ESP with his direction of scoring on an ESP test. It is hard to say to what extent the present questionnaire may be tapping the same kind of difference between subjects. There may be some similarity, but the primary finding here is a difference in score variance rather than a difference in scoring direction. Clearly, there are many more believers in ESP than a High PEQ response would pick out —after all, one can believe without personal experience—but those whose own experiences have convinced them may believe in a somewhat different way than the others. Many questions could be asked about just what the questionnaire is measuring and, now that a case for its usefulness has been made, this search is a legitimate next step.

LITERATURE CITED

1. Bhadra, B. H. "The Relationship of Test Scores to Belief in ESP." *Journal of Parapsychology,* 1966, **30,** 1-17.

THELMA S. MOSS AND J. A. GENGERELLI

The Effect of Belief on ESP Success

Hundreds of spontaneous cases involving telepathy have been documented by the American Society for Psychical Research. Careful study of these cases indicates a pattern in the way communication occurred; the person sending the message (transmitter) was usually in a highly charged emotional situation, while the person receiving the message (receiver) was frequently relaxed, sometimes even asleep, so that the message came through in the form of a dream.

The authors attempted to create this type of situation in a recent laboratory experiment by isolating transmitters in a soundproof room where they were bombarded with "emotional episodes" involving sound and images. After each episode, the transmitter recorded his reactions in one room, and the receiver recorded his "free associations" in another. Results showed that judges could match the transmitter-receiver teams significantly better than could be expected by chance, although only rarely were the free associations of the receiver an accurate reproduction of what the transmitter had experienced.

That experiment raised two questions. Would the recievers in such a study be able to choose correctly between two contrasting pictures on the basis of their free associations? And would there be a significant difference in results that correlated with subjects' beliefs about the occurrence of ESP? The experimental design described above was adapted to test for these conditions.

Presented in absentia at the Winter Review Meeting of the Institute for Parapsychology, December 29, 1967. Complete report in *Journal of Parapsychology*, June 1968.

The Effect of Belief on ESP Success

PROCEDURE

One hundred and forty-four volunteers participated in the study, 82 women and 62 men, ranging in age from 14 to 65. Among them were 38 artists of one kind or another, 19 businessmen, 28 students, 24 housewives, 20 psychologists or psychiatrists, 5 professional sensitives, and 10 with various other occupations. All participants were told that the study involved ESP, but no further information was given until the start of an experimental session. Subjects worked in pairs. The 72 transmitter-receiver teams were divided into three groups of 24 teams each:

ESP group: those who believed in ESP and thought they had had ESP experiences.

ESP-? group: those who believed in ESP to greater or lesser degree, but who did not believe they had the faculty.

Non-ESP group: those who were convinced that ESP does not occur.

Two rooms 20 feet apart were used (see Figure 1). Room B contained an Acousticon Isolation Booth (Booth) where the transmitter sat in a comfortable chair, facing a screen ("E" screen). Slides were projected from outside the booth

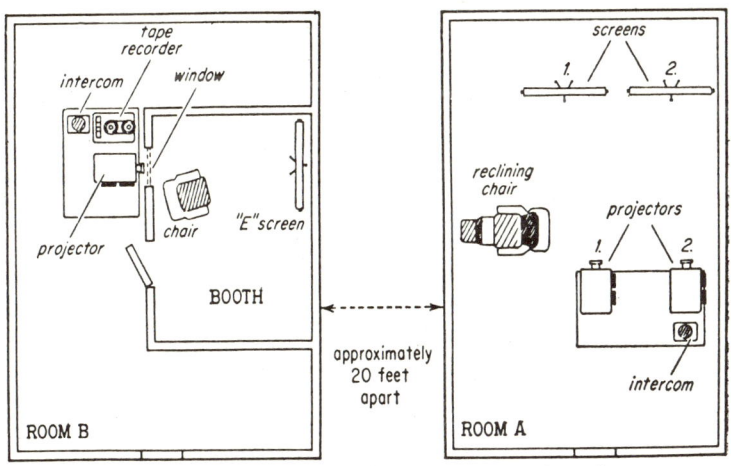

FIG. 1. Arrangement of experimental rooms and equipment.

onto the screen. The transmitter wore a headset over which he heard sound tracks played on a stereo recorder (Tape Recorder). The same six episodes of slides with sound tracks were used throughout the experiment.

The receiver sat in Room A in a large reclining chair which he could tilt back to a comfortable angle. On a table directly behind the chair were two projectors (Projectors 1 and 2), wired so that two slides could be projected simultaneously onto the standing screens (Screen 1 and 2) on the receiver's right and about 10 feet away where the receiver could see both slides.

A buzzer intercom system for the projectionists to signal the beginning and end of each trial was the only communication between the two rooms.

Six "episodes" were devised to create an emotional impact on the transmitter. Each included several colored slides accompanied by appropriate sounds (music, voices, animal roars, etc.). The episodes were grouped into three pairs of contrasting emotional tone.

FIG. 2. Slides used to elicit contrasting emotions.

A
MADONNA AND CHILD

Several famous paintings of the Virgin and Child (Botticelli, Bellini, DaVinci, etc.) from medieval simplicity to late, lush Renaissance art. Music: an orchestral rendition of "Silent Night." Expected reactions: peace, serenity, reverence, etc.

A'
VAN GOGH

Several self-portraits of the artist, from his early representational style to the chaotic impressions of his late mad years. Music: Ravel's "La Valse," punctuated by a man's voice saying "Van Gogh!" with increasing intensity. Expected reactions: wildness, madness, chaos, etc.

B
SPACE

Slides showing rocket and astronauts walking in space. Music: a selection from Holst's "The Planets," distorted to create a weird effect. Expected reactions: excitement, curiosity, wonder, etc.

B'
DRUNK

Slides, starting with a huge glass and small man, evolving into a large, drunk man with small wine glass on his head. Music: "Danke Schoen," distorted to create a drunken effect. Expected reactions: fun, amusement, dizziness, etc.

C
TIGER

Slides of voracious beasts: boa constrictor, eagle, lion, tiger with bloody mouth devouring prey. Music: Antill's "Corroboree," with wild animal screams. Expected reactions: fright, "flight," anxiety, etc.

C'
TREE

A series of Mondrian paintings, starting with abstracts, evolving into a colorful, graceful tree. Accompaniment: a voice saying, "I think . . . I think that . . ." gradually proceeding to ". . . I shall never see . . . a poem lovely as a *tree*, a tree, a TREE!" Expected reactions: expectancy, discovery, etc.

Three episodes were displayed to the transmitter in sequence at each session, but each session included only one episode from each pair of episodes. There are 48 different sequences of combinations of three nonpaired episodes; A, B′, C; or B, C′, A, etc. Each possible sequence was entered on a separate card. Before each session a colleague selected a card at random to determine the combination and sequence for that session.

After a team had been shown both rooms, the transmitter went into the isolation booth in Room B and was given a headset to adjust. After closing the transmitter inside the booth, one projectionist remained outside the booth while showing the episodes, but could speak to the transmitter via microphone. The other projectionist took the receiver into Room A and seated him in the reclining chair tilted back to a nearly prone position. The receiver was then given these instructions:

> Your partner has been given a headset over which he will hear various sounds: music, voices, noises of some kind. At the same time he hears the sounds, he will be shown a series of slides which, hopefully, will have an emotional impact on him. There will be three such episodes, each lasting about a minute. Your job is to relax and "receive" impressions of what your partner is experiencing. If you have any kind of feelings, thoughts, images—any sort of free associations—please speak them into the microphone. When you've finished giving your impressions, I'll show you a pair of slides, one of which was actually shown to your partner. Please choose the one that corresponds best with your impressions. If you have no impressions, I'll ask you simply to guess which one you think is correct. Any questions? If not, I'll signal them to begin the first episode.

It should be emphasized that a different sequence was followed in presenting the three episodes to each transmitter. Either slide of the pair which was then shown to the receiver could be the correct one, depending upon which episode of the pair had been selected. For example, the receiver always saw the *Van Gogh* slide paired with the *Madonna and Child* slide (contrasting Van Gogh's madness with the serenity of the Madonna) whenever either the *Van Gogh* or *Madonna* episode had been shown to the transmitter, and this episode and pair might be first, second or third in the sequence for a given session as determined by the card drawn before each session. This procedure minimized the possibility of leakage. Even if a transmitter from a previous session wanted to give a future receiver a clue he would not know what temporal order might be followed in the later session, or which episode of each contrasting pair might be chosen.

RESULTS

Quantitative: Receivers identified only 2.7% of all their responses as "pure guess." All receivers made one choice or the other at the end of each episode.

The number of correct choices for each receiver could be three out of three, two out of three, one out of three, or none. Chance alone would yield an average of 1.5 correct guesses per session. Analysis by appropriate statistical methods showed that neither the Non-ESP group nor the ESP-? group did any better than chance, but all the ESP group scored well above chance. Of the 24 ESP-group receivers, 19 made either two or three correct choices (odds against chance: more than 300 to one).

The finding that was perhaps of greatest interest had not been anticipated in the original design: during the experiment it was noted that the artists were outperforming the others, even the professional sensitives. After the experiment had been completed, the records of the 72 teams therefore were redivided into groups of both-artists, one-an-artist, and neither-an-artist.

The artists were writers, musicians, actors and others engaged in professions that demand creativity. Of the twelve teams of both-artists, eleven had scored either two or three correct choices; and of the 14 teams in the one-an-artist group, 13 had either two or three correct (odds against chance of the combined result: 200,000 to one).

Another possibility occurred to the experimenters that had not been anticipated, the possibility that rapport between transmitter and receiver might be a factor in ESP. Fourteen of the teams were composed of members who had never seen each other before the experimental session. The results of this non-rapport group were matched against the grouped results of 14 teams made up of mother-and-son, brother-and-sister, twins, etc., combinations. Analysis did not show any difference in performance between these two groups.

Qualitative: A surprising number of free associations were volunteered, even by the Non-ESP group receivers who did not believe in ESP phenomena. These responses ranged from a few strikingly accurate descriptions of the episode to responses which seemed pure fantasy. Many of the free associations between these extremes show the distortions, condensations and symbolic representations typically described in psychoanalytic theory as "primary process" material. The primary process is a primitive type of thinking which dispenses with logic. It operates mainly through visual imagery and is not subject to voluntary control. Despite distortions, receivers were often able to choose correctly on the basis of these kinds of impressions. Below are examples transcribed verbatim from the tapes of "accurate," "primary process," and "pure fantasy" responses given by various receivers:

ACCURATE

(While the Drunk episode was shown in the next room) "This one had a champagne feeling. Champagne Waltz. That's all. [Request for slides] The man with the champagne glass on his head! [Laughs] Definitely."

(While the Madonna episode was shown in the next room) "I get the image of a child. Children. Now it's a cradle rocking. And inside there's a baby with swaddling clothes. [Request for slides] Well . . . [Laughs] . . . it would have to be the Madonna and Child, if my images made any sense."

PRIMARY PROCESS

(While the Space episode was shown in the next room) "I have the feeling of darkness, a huge darkness, pushing up against my eyes. That's all. [Request for slides] I pick the astronaut, because I had the feeling of darkness pushing up at my eyes, closing them."

(While the Madonna episode was shown in the next room) "A feeling of calmness . . . serenity . . . elegance . . . very slow elegance . . . lavishness. Sort of a *My Fair Lady* bit. [Request for slides] The Madonna and Child. I could hear the music of *My Fair Lady*. [Laughs] Strange, isn't it?"

(While the Van Gogh episode was shown in the next room) "I feel some sort of excitement. And a feeling of rhythmical music. I seem to see a sun thing. Occasionally a light disc. [Request for slides] Van Gogh. Because I felt the music, and saw the colors like a sunburst."

PURE FANTASY

(While the Drunk episode was shown in the next room) "Well . . . I saw some rolling hills, black . . . but it looks more like smoke coming from a burning building, flaming. The whole place is on fire now. Firemen rushing in with hoses. Lots of water. Changes to the sea . . . sunset at sea . . . same color as the fire. Daffodils. Spring. [Request for slides] The spaceman . . . I don't know why."

(While the Madonna episode was shown in the next room) "A feeling of gaiety, fast movement, rock-and-roll, go-go, Watusi, that kind of thing. Noisy, lots of action . . . and a feeling of franticness. [Request for slides] Van Gogh."

DISCUSSION

The primary process material, despite the distortions that characterize such impressions, was similar enough to the actual episodes for receivers to make correct choices in several instances. This phenomenon has been reported in other areas of ESP investigation, as well as in possibly related areas. A previous study by the authors included several examples of similar primary process responses accurately matched by judges (1). Psychoanalysts have reported "presumptively telepathic dreams" of patients in therapy which also exhibit primary process distortion. A more recent report on a series of laboratory studies of telepathic dreams by

Ullman and Krippner provided protocols of tape-recorded dreams abounding with primary process material which were significantly matched by judges (2). Several subliminal stimulating studies have also found primary-process distortion a prominent feature.

The question arises: Is there a special kind of person who is most likely to exhibit ESP ability? This study found that receivers in artistic professions performed better than other receivers. Previous work suggests that artistic or creative people do, in fact, seem more able to retrieve primary process material. One study found that art students remembered dreams and reported them more vividly than engineering students, while another described people with artistic talent as more open to subliminal perception, adding that the ability to "relax, be passive, and let the imagery appear" is important for successful artistic performance.

Whether the artist is, indeed, more open to telepathic effects as indicated by this study, and whether that means more psi ability or simply more ability to demonstrate it under laboratory conditions, are questions that can be answered only by another study in which the performance of artists is compared with that of a control group. Such a study is now in progress.

LITERATURE CITED

1. Moss, Thelma, and J. A. Gengerelli, "Telepathy and Emotional Stimuli: A Controlled Experiment." *Journal of Abnormal Psychology*, 1967, 72, 341–48.
2. Ullman, M., S. Krippner, and S. Feldstein, "Experimentally Induced Telepathic Dreams: Two Studies Using EEG-REM Monitoring Technique." *International Journal of Neuropsychiatry*, 1966, 2, 420–38.

ROBERT BRIER

Sex Differences in Mass School Tests

ESP tests have often been given to large groups of people through radio, television, correspondence and the press with the objective of collecting a large mass of data in a single experiment. In general, however, such tests have not yielded much evidence of ESP. Total deviations among groups of unselected subjects are almost invariably within the area of chance. Also, tests handled by correspondence, where the stimulation and motivation that may come from personal contact is lacking, have only rarely provided evidence of ESP.

The earlier mass tests via radio, television, and the press usually involved the clairvoyance technique. For those tests, of course, the targets would have already been selected by random procedures at the time the test was administered. Those who responded were asked to return their guesses to the experimenter for checking against the actual target order. There were, of course, variations, but this was the usual basic technique.

In most of these tests, the number of trials per person was too small and the number of people trying to guess the same set of targets too great for the usual methods of measuring success to be applied. Furthermore, the use of one target series for many guessers introduced the possibility of a stacking effect by which group preferences for a given target may exaggerate the scores. (For a description of the stacking effect see Appendix D.) The mere possibility of stacking plays havoc with statistical appraisal of test results but since so many would be taking part, and since the experimenters had no way of knowing in advance how many

---

Presented at the Spring Review Meeting of the Institute for Parapsychology, May 4, 1968. Complete report in *Journal of Parapsychology*, June 1969.

would participate, it was not feasible to provide each participant with predetermined individual targets of his own.

However, the kind of test now used for precognition makes the testing of large groups more feasible. In such tests a separate target series can later be selected for each subject who fills out a test form.

The first mass correspondence test carried out by this method was one given in 1961 by Rhine in co-operation with the Canadian Broadcasting Company and *Maclean's Magazine* (4), and it is perhaps the most comparable of all to the research to be reported here. Thirty thousand subjects participated in the 1961 experiment. Each subject made ten calls by punching an IBM card in the magazine and mailed the card back to CBC, where a computer generated a separate set of targets for each card and checked the scores. The main result was a significant negative deviation.

The work reported here was another mass test, the test form distributed by way of the January 1, 1968, issue of *Read*, a popular magazine for junior high school English classes. The chief reason for working with *Read* was the excellent opportunity it offered to inform students about parapsychology and the types of phenomena studied by parapsychologists. The fact that the subjects would be junior high school students rather than adults added a promising new factor. There was also some hope that the method described below might produce evidence of ESP in some way, even though past experience discouraged any expectation that a large group of unselected subjects would exhibit an overall significant deviation.

More than a hundred thousand students filled in and returned the test form to the Institute for Parapsychology. Such a huge response was not expected, but the massive volume of data offered an exceptional opportunity to learn if ESP could be detected in a large number of calls accumulated in so impersonal a manner. The volume of the data also presented special problems in checking and analyzing so that the plan of treatment had to be reorganized, but this provided further opportunities to try out new approaches.

Sex Differences in Mass School Tests

First of all, the data could now be divided categorically into groups for various specific kinds of analyses. The test could, in fact, be treated like several experimental projects in one.

Since this was a test for precognition, each subject had to have a different set of targets chosen after the record sheets were turned in, a time-consuming process. Therefore the data were adequate on the side of statistics at least, since each subject had a different target order. Also, of course, the test was perfectly safe from the possibility of sensory cues or cheating.

Because the magazine promised the students their scores, the tests had to be checked and reports returned to the schools as soon as possible.

PROCEDURE

The article in *Read* dealt with psi on a general level. At the end, the text told students they could test their own ESP by filling out the record sheet printed in the magazine. The record sheet was a version of the booklet tests with words and ESP symbols as targets used by Freeman (1, 2, 3). The sheet had five 20-trial columns. Each column had four segments: one segment of five ESP symbols, one of five words, another of five ESP symbols, and another of five words (see Figure 1). Since significant deviations could not be expected in the overall data from so large a number of unselected subjects, the test and record sheet were designed to provide as many and varied opportunities for comparison as possible.

To provide still another basis of separation, subjects were asked to indicate their sex along with their names at the top of the record sheet. This was because Freeman (see report, p. 192) and others had found a slight but persistent difference in the way boys and girls respond to test situations of certain kinds. The sex difference could also be used in conjunction with the other bases for separation in the test score sheets i.e., differences between the sexes could be examined in relation to differences in score distribution and in scoring by segments. With the well-known tendency for

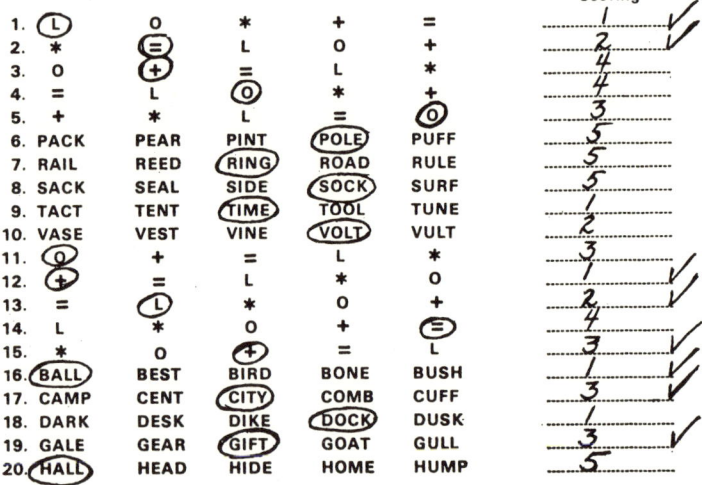

FIG. 1. Precognition test featured in *Read*, a magazine for junior high-school students.

psi-missing and psi-hitting to occur and together disguise ESP effects, differentiation by sex offered an opportunity to find out if the other variables affected the scoring of the two sexes differently.

A special for-teachers-only supplement to the magazine instructed teachers to have each student fill out his record sheet by circling whichever one of the five symbols or words in each row he guessed to be the right one. The record sheets of the entire class were sent to the Institute for Parapsychology to be scored, and the results for each class were to be reported to the teacher.

Scoring procedure: To select the individual target orders, an entry point to a table of random numbers was found by the standard procedure used at the Institute for Parapsychology. (For a description of this procedure see Appendix B.) A number from 1 to 5 as determined by the random number table was written in each of the 20 spaces at the right of each record sheet. This number designated which of the five words or symbols in the row to the left was the target; if the number was 4, for instance, the word or symbol fourth from the left was the target. When all 20 numbers had been entered on a record sheet, each hit was checked. Finally the scores for each of the four segments of the run (two segments of words, two of symbols) were written at the bottom of the sheet together with the total score. A list of the names, segment scores and total scores of all the students in each class was sent back to the teacher.

Within one month after the article appeared, the Institute had received test forms from more than thirty thousand students with more coming at the rate of about a thousand a day. To defer scoring until all data arrived, as is standard procedure for precognition experiments, presented several practical problems. For one thing, it would obviously be impossible to score and return the results to the students before the school year ended. For another, the first step, alphabetizing the students' papers, would be difficult with such a large number.

Dividing the data into smaller, more manageable units would reduce these difficulties, and would minimize the possibility of a maximal error in alphabetizing and checking. (Since the order of the targets for each subject's calls was based on an entry point in a table of random numbers, each student's record sheet required 20 numbers from the random table. If one number from the table was used twice by error, the numbers for all subsequent students would in one sense be "wrong." What was intended was that the first student receive targets 1-20; the second student, targets 21-40, etc. If the experiment were treated as one unit and the targets determined by one entry point into the table of random numbers, and if an error were made early in the experiment, the remaining record sheets would be scored "in error." Dividing the experiment into smaller units limited the effect of such an error.)

After it was decided to divide the returns into manageable units each envelope containing tests that came from an individual teacher was placed in a carton which would hold from 3,000 to 12,000 individual record sheets, and each carton was considered a separate unit or experiment. Each unit was first alphabetized according to state, city, school, and teacher, and finally by the names of students in each class. Then the record sheets in each carton were inventoried to show the number of classes and the number of students in each class, to insure against losing data during the checking process.

Statistical analyses: Since data from such large numbers of unselected subjects working under far from ideal test conditions could be expected to show only slight tendencies, a very general kind of evaluation was needed to explore for the presence of ESP. There were no specific expectations of low scoring, variance effects, etc., but there was some expectation of finding differences in ways of scoring by boys vs. girls. The chi-square goodness-of-fit test is a relatively sensitive indicator of ESP; it tells whether the distribution of scoring is the same as, or different from, that produced by chance. If there is anything unusual about the actual distribution of scores, this test will indicate it. Although sensitive, it is used infrequently because it is valid only when there is a large number of scores. With the mass of data produced by this experiment, it was the ideal statistic to use.

Analysis began when it was believed that approximately half of the data had been checked (actually it turned out to be less than half). Each unit (carton) of data was to be analyzed independently, so that if a significant effect were found in one unit, the other units could be analyzed for confirmation. At this point, enough data were on hand for two independent units, each large enough (approximately 12,000 in one group, 8,000 in the other) for the chi-square goodness-of-fit test. One unit had been checked at the Institute for Parapsychology, the other by outside scorers work-

Sex Differences in Mass School Tests 167

ing under Institute supervision. The test sheets of boys and girls in each unit were analyzed separately, in line with the original intentions. The rate of scoring with words vs. symbols and in each of the four test segments were also analyzed separately.

RESULTS

An ESP experiment, even one involving a great many individuals, does not produce scores exactly at chance even if only chance is operating; a certain distribution of scores is to be expected. In this experiment, the score to be expected most often by chance is 4. However, one also expects many scores of 3 and 5, fewer scores of 2 and 6, and even fewer of the remaining numbers. Looking first at the data checked at the Institute, the distribution of the boys' scores was found to be very close to what would be expected by chance alone. The various possible scores appeared in the proportions one would expect if ESP were not operating. However, the distribution of the girls' scores was quite different (odds against chance of such a distribution: 1,000 to one). The most unusual feature of this distribution was that it included far fewer scores of 0 and 4 than one would expect.

With this significant finding, it was decided to check the other unit for the same effect. Analysis of the second unit of 7,632 papers showed that again the boys' scores were distributed about as would be expected by chance, and again the girls' scores were distributed in a pattern quite different from the one that would be expected if only chance were operating (odds against chance: again more than 1,000 to one).

Once again, the girls' scores included few zeros, but this time twos and fives were also fewer than chance expectation, which contributed considerably to the significance of the results. The number of fours in this case was within the chance range.

In both units of data, there were fewer zeros, fours, and fives in the girls' scores than one would expect by chance, and more of the remaining scores.

One of the specific effects sought in the experiment was the words vs. symbols differential. This effect did not appear to a significant degree. However, the finding that the girls' score distribution differed from the chance curve and that the boys' score distribution did not, offered good enough evidence of ESP to warrant further examination of the data for other less general, more subtle effects. One trend emerged almost immediately when the scoring in the four different segments were compared: when the single *class* was taken as the unit of analysis, the boys' segment scores showed a slight tendency to deviate above and below chance far more frequently than the girls'. This effect, though slight per class, was consistent to a significant degree.

The first batch of data to be examined came from 31 classes. In 22 of them, the boys' totals for the four segments (i.e., all the hits made by the boys of the class in the first five trials of all five columns on the sheet, second five trials, etc.) deviated from chance more than the girls' totals for each of the four segments. These totals deviated by being above chance in some cases and below chance in others, but the boys' numbers of hits in each of the four segments were consistently farther from chance than were the girls' (odds against chance of the difference: more than 30 to one). This finding was encouraging, and therefore the remainder of the records available at that time were analyzed to see if they confirmed the effect. The 31 classes in the first batch of data thus became in effect a pilot study.

The records of 493 classes were analyzed to see if the boys' segment score totals in each class fluctuated more than those of the girls. Of the 493 classes, one would expect only 246.5 to show this effect if ESP were not operating. Actually, in 274 classes the boys' segment score totals deviated from chance more than the girls' (odds against chance of the difference in deviation: more than 100 to one).

Several other suggestive peculiarities appeared when the job of analyzing began; for example, boys in predominantly female classes scored differently from boys in predominantly male classes; scoring differences varied according to age factor, etc. However, only a relatively small portion of the data has so far been analyzed for confirmation of these suggestive findings.

DISCUSSION

In spite of the fact that the data of this experiment were obtained by a mass correspondence test, which is usually considered an unpromising technique, statistically significant indications of ESP were found. Since the project involved a far greater number of subjects than any test yet tried, the reason for success probably lies in the opportunities for comparison that were built into the design, particularly the comparison of differences between the sexes in ways of responding.

The question has been asked over the years whether large divisions of the human race such as national or ethnic groups differ in their response to ESP tests in general, but to the extent such questions have been tested, no reliable differences have been found. Now, however, it appears that there may be a generalized sex-based difference in ways of scoring. The extrachance scoring patterns in this test on junior high school children indicates that this sex difference may be the most pronounced difference of all, or at least the most all-pervading.

The totals, understandably enough, were at the chance level, but the girls showed peculiarities in score frequencies that the boys did not show. Even though the reason for the difference is obscure, the fact that it showed up in a test of such a large number of otherwise unselected subjects of both sexes suggests that, at least under the conditions of this test, it is widespread.

Similar conclusions can be reached about the finding that the boys' scores fluctuated more than the girls' within the run (by segments). This too appears to be a sex-based difference not presently explainable but widespread.

These results strongly support the idea that the sexes differ in their ESP responses. The difference is not necessarily in psi ability, but at least there is a difference in the way the sexes respond to the structure of a test.

Since most of the work of Freeman as well as this *Read* test has been with junior high school children, this evidence of a sex differential may depend on age. Groups above or below this age level have not yet been tested for this effect. The present study, of course, adds only the evidence that the difference exists in a wider sample than had been tested before; in the nature of the case it tells nothing about the source of the difference as some of Freeman's tests tend to do.

The experiment was designed mainly to see if evidence of ESP could be obtained. The fact that significant differences were found which can be interpreted as sex-based differences in response patterns, served the major purpose of the undertaking. It is possible that other significant aspects of the data are still hidden in the total mass, but in view of the immense labor of working with such a volume of data—which is a bit like mining operations on thin veins of ore—it seems better economy now to rest content with the contribution that widespread sex-differentiated tendencies in ESP scoring have been found, and turn research energy to richer fields.

LITERATURE CITED

1. Freeman, John A. "Sex Differences and Primary Mental Abilities in a Group Precognition Test." *Journal of Parachology*, 1968, **32**, 176–182.
2. Freeman, John A. "Sex, Target Arrangement and Primary Mental Abilities." *Journal of Parapsychology*, 1967, **31**, 271–79.
3. Freeman, John A. "Sex Differences and Target Arrangement: High School Booklet Tests of Precognition." *Journal of Parapsychology*, 1966, **30**, 227–235.
4. Rhine, J. B. "The Precognition of Computer Numbers in a Public Test." *Journal of Parapsychology*, 1962, **26**, 244–251.

LOUISA E. RHINE

Testing Before and After Talks on ESP

An ESP test procedure is needed for use with small general audiences when formal control conditions are out of the question. The people who come to hear a talk on parapsychology are usually more or less curious about their own ESP ability but have little idea of how the research is conducted. An excellent way for the speaker to illustrate his explanation is to give an actual test, but if he is a parapsychologist, he knows the limitations of the conditions, and the unlikelihood that any test he could give in the time and circumstances at his disposal could have any research value.

Some inventive mind will no doubt eventually devise tests that could be both meaningful to the audience and of value to the researcher. For the audience, the test should be simple, quick, and interesting, and the results should be immediately available. For the parapsychologist, it must be one that can be administered and scored quickly, that will provide reliable data, and that offers a possibility of yielding statistically significant results. However, until such a device is available, the parapsychologist giving a talk must either give up the idea of getting anything more valuable from the test than a good illustration, or improvise as best he can to try for useful information.

My own improvisations on two recent occasions led to some ideas for adapting procedure that other parapsychologists may perhaps find useful.

First Occasion

Shortly before I was scheduled to speak to the student psychology club at a South Carolina college, I was asked

---

Presented at the Winter Review Meeting of the Institute for Parapsychology, December 29, 1967. Complete report in *Journal of Parapsychology*, March 1968.

to include ESP tests with the talk. Since there was no way to provide proper test controls, I had not planned to give a test and had brought no testing materials with me. However, I found a commercial ESP game that included a five-symbol, 25-card deck made up in imitation of the standard ESP test cards and a pad of small record sheets with five ten-space columns for answers.

In order to give even a quick 10-trial test to a group and keep the members interested by letting them know their scores immediately, I had to let them check their own lists. However, I introduced the test by explaining that, while everyone probably has ESP ability, such a short test taken under such conditions could at best provide only a token indication of ESP ability. I hoped this introduction would reduce any proclivity to "pad" results. Since I could not give each subject a separate target list, one set of targets had to do for all. Multiple calls on the same target of course open the door to the possibility of a "stacking effect." (For a description of the stacking effect, see Appendix D.) However, the situation was frankly impromptu, and the objective only to get results which would have interesting aspects; it was not the time or place for trying to establish or prove anything.

As every experimenter knows, the pooled scores of a group of unselected subjects are not likely to show a significant deviation unless some method can be provided of separating high- and low-scoring tendencies. It occurred to me on the spur of the moment that I could give the test twice, once early in the talk when only the general terms and types of psi had been introduced, and then again at the end, after the experimental evidence had been reviewed and some spontaneous cases described to illustrate how psi ability may function in ordinary life.

I had planned to emphasize precognition in the talk and to make the point that, however unlikely it may seem at first approach, precognition appears just as frequently in reports of spontaneous experiences as ESP of present events (clairvoyance). I therefore wanted to demonstrate precogni-

Testing Before and After Talks on ESP

tion as well as clairvoyance. If I were to get the results to the subjects without delay, the target list would have to be obtained on the spot by merely shuffling the deck of cards by hand as soon as the guesses had been recorded. This, of course, would contravene yet another rule of reliable testing, the rule governing the manner of selecting precognition targets, but since this was not an attempt to *prove* precognition as such, the concession was made.

At the beginning of the talk, I asked the subjects to write yes or no at the top of their record sheets to indicate whether or not they "believed in ESP." This was mainly because the head of the psychology department and one of the professors were present, and I happened to know that both were skeptical of ESP. The atmosphere seemed quite restrained and formal for a student group, and I thought it would at least be interesting to know how many of them were "goats" (skeptics) and how many "sheep" (believers).

The subjects then quickly made one 10-trial clairvoyance run, trying to guess the order of symbols in a little 10-card pack (two each of the five symbols selected from the deck) that was in view face down on the table at the front of the room. When the subjects had finished, another 10-card pack similarly selected was laid beside the first, and the subjects were asked to fill out the second column to represent the order they guessed the symbols in that pack would have after it was shuffled. When this task was completed, the order of the clairvoyance deck was read aloud, and the subjects checked their lists for hits. Then the other deck was shuffled while they watched, its order read aloud, and again they checked their record sheets for successes. The entire process was carried out with dispatch.

In the half-hour talk that followed, I described experimental results that had been achieved in both clairvoyance and precognition research and also spontaneous cases of each. My objective was to let the group know what types of psi ability have been established and that all types are probably about equally widespread in life situations. The subjects seemed to follow the cases with especially close attention, and at the end, a relaxation of tension was noticeable; they moved about in their seats a bit and seemed more at ease than they had at the start. Then the same experimental procedures as before were followed for a second 10-card run of clairvoyance and another of precognition.

RESULTS

There were 47 subjects, each contributing four 10-card runs. When the trials were converted to regulation 25-card runs for easier comparison with other work, there was a total of 75.2 runs, with only ten hits above the number expected from pure chance. But the first 37.6 runs, the "before" section, had 15 hits below chance and the second 37.6 runs, the "after" section, had 25 hits above. The difference between the scores of the two sections was 40 (odds against chance of the difference: 100 to one). Two corrections had to be made; one for the stacking effect already mentioned, and the other for the fact that I could not say beforehand whether I expected the trend to be positive or negative. When both corrections are made, the odds drop to only about 25 to one. However, even these odds suggest fairly strongly that the situation had changed sufficiently by the end of the talk for the difference to be reflected in the trend of scoring. The change in atmosphere between the two sets of trials was so pronounced that even after I corrected for uncertainty about direction, the direction of the change was in line with expectation.

There is, however, a more dependable way of checking up on a comparison of this type. A measure called a "consistency test" can be used for appraising the degree to which the result was contributed by the group. Of the 47 subjects there were ten whose scores were the same in the two sections. Of the 37 whose scores changed, 26 raised their percentage of hits in the second test (odds against chance of this number of subjects improving their scoring: 100 to one). This finding showed that the attitude of the majority of subjects actually had changed. Incidentally, there were more goats than sheep among those who improved their scoring rate on the second test, but the difference in numbers was not significant.

Second Occasion

On the following night, a very different kind of group, a coffee club, asked for an impromptu talk. Most of the members of this group were also college-age young people, but while the psychology club was an academically scheduled organization, the coffee club was neither organized nor academic, but was entirely informal. One of the local churches had lent a large, old-style residence to a group of young VISTA volunteers for use as a center where young people could congregate socially. Plans for a regular schedule of amateur artistic and other activities included a weekly talk by any available outside speaker, and my talk was to be the first. When I arrived, the paint on the walls, which some of those present had put there that afternoon, was not yet dry. The atmosphere that evening was very warm, friendly, and expectant, but quite unregulated and spontaneous. Interest in ESP was vociferously expressed before the meeting began. Even so, and although I had brought the ESP game along, I felt it was hopeless to try to give a test by candlelight to people overcrowded on a sofa and sitting on the floor as these were. But they wanted it, and so I proceeded in the same way as before.

Even before the talk was finished, however, individuals in this group started asking questions and trying to tell about their own experiences. This was no captive audience, but a lively and spontaneous one, and sitting on the floor did not encourage them to stay quiet. At any rate, I had to call their attention back to the second round of tests, which by then came as something of an anticlimax.

RESULTS

There were only 17 subjects in this group. All but three answered yes to the "belief in ESP" question on the answer sheet. There was a total deviation of +18 in the group's scores on the 27.2 regulation 25-card runs. In the "before" runs where the other group had gone below chance, this group had 23 hits above chance in 13.6 runs, but this group's deviation on the 13.6-run "after" section was 5 below chance (odds abainst the difference after corrections: about 50 to one).

Although in the opposite direction, the shift was again consistent enough to be reliable. Of the twelve subjects whose scores changed, all but two gave higher scores before than after the talk (odds against this consistency: about 50 to one). This group's change from before to after was thus fairly significant, although in the reverse direction from that of the psychology club.

It should be added that in these two experiments there was no marked difference in the results from the two types of tests. The scores on the clairvoyance tests showed about the same kind of shift from the first to the second round of tests as did the scores on the precognition tests.

DISCUSSION

Since in both groups a change in scoring trend occurred between the two rounds of tests, the first question is whether the results obtained under such improvised conditions are reliable. While the conditions were certainly far from ideal, there are a number of reasons why the results can be taken seriously enough to warrant presenting suggestions for other tests given in similar circumstances. In the first place, examination of the record sheets of both groups by a staff member of the Institute for Parapsychology revealed no signs of erasures to suggest padded scores, and in fact, the speed of the tests alone would have made changes difficult. The results were cross-checked at the Institute to see if the stacking effect could have augmented the results. For this cross-check, the targets of the two experiments were exchanged, and the new set of unintended hits were used as a control. The hits from these cross-checkings were nonsignificant, which meant the stacking effect must have been comparatively slight if it was present at all. Nevertheless, the statistical correction for possible stacking was applied, as stated above.

While the method of getting precognition targets by merely shuffling a deck does not meet experimental standards for excluding other types of psi, it was adequate here since the only object was to get precognition test scores that were as valid as the clairvoyance test scores—as indeed they proved to be.

The main consideration, however, is that the difference in the scores obtained under the "before" and "after" conditions, rather than a simple deviation, was the significant feature. It would be easy to attribute a deviation to a spurious cause, but a significant group difference between two parts of an experiment is not likely to be spuriously obtained, and certainly not one that in a meaningful way goes in opposite directions in two groups.

There is no way around the fact that the direction of the difference did change, and the change coincided with an apparent psychological shift in each group. There was a sharp contrast in the mental attitudes of the members of the two groups toward ESP and toward the test. The psychology club was a fairly restrained audience—one which at least had had no *positive* build-up for a talk on ESP but which "loosened up" only after hearing the talk. The other group had obviously been building up, perhaps for any talk by anyone who would give one, but especially for this first program for which they had had to plan and to hasten preparations. Whatever the attitude of these young people toward ESP in other situations, by the time the meeting began they were certainly interested and enthusiastic. And of course, a kind of selection could have acted too, so that sheep were more likely to be present than goats. At any rate, the group change from "before" to "after" was obvious in both groups.

The first group's shift from a negative to a positive scoring rate apparently represented a shift from a negative to a positive attitude toward ESP. But the second group's shift from a positive to a negative scoring rate probably represented a shift not from a positive to a negative attitude toward ESP, but from an interested, enthusiastic eagerness to take a novel kind of test to the letdown accompanying repetition when novelty has worn off and when attention has largely shifted away from the task.

My suggestion for experimenters faced with this kind of situation is to use a quick, short run with immediate check-up. At least with subjects the age of these or younger, the more a test resembles a game with an immediate pay-off, the better the chances of success. A few short, fast-moving runs are more likely to interest a general audience than formal ways of testing, and so should yield higher scoring levels.

It may also be of some advantage to play up the idea that each individual is testing himself. The before-and-after idea is also worth considering, especially when the choice of other contrasting conditions is limited. Even so, the two conditions can be expected to show different results only if the initial attitude of the audience is rather pronounced in some way which can be expected to change during the talk.

As a practical matter, a prospective speaker who wants to adopt any of the above suggestions should equip himself with a supply of small, short-run record sheets that can be quickly distributed and checked at once; and if possible, should arrange for two contrasting situations so that high- and low-scoring tendencies can be anticipated in advance and legitimately separated. It is a handicap to have to justify the separation at a later point. Science has learned much from spontaneous situations; the search for a way to take better advantage of opportunities to test a general audience may well prove worthwhile.

Part IV
Main Lines of Continuity

Preface

The three psychologists whose work constitutes this section have shown impressive continuity of progress along essential lines of research. Inasmuch as the reports all deal with conditions, correlates or factors that influence test performance, they could all, of course, have been included in the preceding section. They stand out, however, in the extent to which they have each followed a systematic line of pursuit from one experiment to the next. To the intrinsic value of their contributions they add the dimension of stable programming that is so important to a scientific field.

The first author, Dr. Buzby, here presents continuation of his work that earlier won the McDougall Award. He has been using a combination of psychological methods—a questionnaire and various established mental tests—in his program to identify the set of attitudes and cognitive traits that best enable a subject to demonstrate psi. The first Buzby paper reports on precognition tests alone. Along with the Draw-A-Man test, Buzby used the Embedded Figures test, which is designed to discover how the subject perceives his external world. To these tests was added a questionnaire aimed at measuring the depth of the subject's involvement with ESP. Dr. Buzby's experiments are well controlled and adequately confirmed, but it is still too early for him to say what the differentiation means. That is the way of research—the fact and its confirmation come first—but he is still going ahead with this program on into the ninth decade of his life.

The second Buzby report shows that the Draw-A-Man test may provide a differential clue to the way the subject will perform on tests of precognition and clairvoyance. Here, too, the report shows continuity of the author's earlier results. Eventually, to some reflective worker, the accumulation of these findings will bring insight into the state of mind most favorable to psi operation. For the present, the main virtue of Dr. Buzby's findings is just this year-to-year persistence of complex but orderly relations of psi to related psychological measurements.

* * * *

Even more strikingly persistent has been the research program of Dr. Freeman in his work with school children using booklet tests of precognition. In these tests with different arrangements of target symbols and words (or pictures), Dr. Freeman has accumulated an extensive collection of findings of almost repetitive character showing differences between boys and girls in scoring directions when target symbols or words are arranged with five of the *same* symbol (or word) in a row as compared with five *different* symbols (or words) in a row. However, these same-different target arrangements, along with the differences in response of the sexes, have left the puzzling question of *why*. Why should the sexes behave so differently when their education was so similar? What has the difference remotely to do with sex anyhow?

Now Dr. Freeman reports the dawning of his discovery that it has something to do with certain types of differential mental abilities of the two sexes as these types of intelligence are measured in standard tests. This report is a turning point, and subsequent work already shows that his program is leading to further advances.

Dr. Freeman's second paper reports continuation of another line of his research, also in precognition, that likewise has to do with the conditions affecting psi. In this case the difference lies not in sex but in the subject's disposition as shown by his reaction of liking or disliking the target words in a list on which the tests are based. The subtle aspect of this discovery lies in the fact that some element of personality which merely inclines an individual to a general tendency to like or dislike can so completely reverse the direction of his scoring from psi-hitting to psi-missing, even on the words he likes, if his responses characterize him as a disliker,

Preface

and vice versa. The persistence or generality of this delicate unconscious tendency becomes impressive as it continues to show up. To find anything so elusive that still remains so lawful is typical of psi as a science.

* * * *

The work of Dr. Carpenter on moods in relation to precognition represents another continuing line of successful research on a single general plan. He has been searching for the psi-mood relation, and the best way to exploit it for eventual control of psi. The author has already recognized the possibilities of his method in psi application, and has reported work headed in that direction.

* * * *

Dr. Buzby is professor emeritus of psychology at Beaver College and is attached to the Parapsychology Laboratory of St. Joseph's College, both in Philadelphia.

Dr. Freeman is Research Associate of the Institute for Parapsychology and professor of psychology at Campbell College in Buies Creek, North Carolina.

Dr. Carpenter is clinical assistant professor in the psychology department of the University of North Carolina, and serves on the Psychology Service staff of the John Umstead State Hospital near Durham, North Carolina.

—J.B.R.

DALLAS E. BUZBY

Some Psychological Variables in Psi Tests

I. Precognition Variance with Two Mental Tests

This pilot study and confirmation were designed to examine the relation between performance on precognition tests and psychological variables as defined by a questionnaire on interest in ESP. The study used the questionnaire in combination with the Embedded Figures Test of ability to perceive ideas independently of context and the Draw-A-Man Test of human body concepts.

The author has been testing undergraduate students for both clairvoyance and precognition at St. Joseph's College in Philadelphia for the past several years, using a questionnaire and a psychological test to determine whether certain psychological states are correlated with ESP scoring. Two such correlations have been reported in two papers presented at previous meetings of the Institute for Parapsychology (1).

The questionnaire indicates whether a student's interest in ESP is "vital" or "casual." In nearly every case, the questionnaire was filled out prior to any ESP testing. The first finding was that the vital-interest group showed significant precognition test score fluctuations above and below the mean; the casual-interest group did not.

The Embedded Figures Test (EFT) (2) indicates the subject's manner of perceiving the external world, separating "analytic" perceivers from "global" perceivers. The subject endeavors to perceive a simple figure embedded in a complex design. The more analytical person tends to do

---

Presented in absentia at the Autumn Review meeting of the Institute for Parapsychology, September 2, 1967. Complete report in *Journal of Parapsychology*, March 1968.

this easily because he experiences his surroundings analytically and sees objects as discrete from backgrounds. The more field-dependent, or global, perceiver has more difficulty because he tends to see the prevailing field of context as a whole instead. The second finding was that the precognition scores of the global perceivers varied from chance scores considerably more than those of the analytic perceivers.

Another finding in the 1964-65 precognition data was briefly mentioned as being worth further discussion if the same effect were found a second time. This effect involved still another psychological test, the Draw-A-Man Test, which indicates the subject's tendency to perceive the human body in either a naive or a sophisticated way. The present paper covers the part of the 1964-65 pilot work involving this third psychological test and the later confirmatory study.

PROCEDURE

In the pilot test, the subject completed five precognition runs in one session and five clairvoyance runs in a following session, both using standard ESP cards. Efforts to duplicate the pilot test situation in all respects for the confirmation study were not entirely successful. The pilot testing was carried out in a small room or office, while the confirmation testing was done in a classroom. The clairvoyance tests in the confirmation series had to be given immediately after the precognition tests, all in one session. Since the finding that is of major interest occurred in the precognition data as in previous years, it is reported here. The findings of the clairvoyance data are presented in the paper that follows.
(II)

The administration of the precognition tests was the same for both the pilot and the later confirmation test. The target order for the first precognition run was determined immediately after the run. The experimenter threw three dice to get a three-digit entry into a table of random numbers, and the numbers were translated into ESP symbols according to a standard code. The subject's calls were compared with this target order. The subject then called Runs

2 and 3, and two further target selections were arrived at and the comparisons made. This procedure was repeated for Runs 4 and 5. Tests were scored in the presence of the subject. The use of three stopping points for checking in each subject's five runs presumably added to the subject's interest and facilitated testing.

For the Draw-A-Man Test, subjects were given a sheet of 8½ × 11-in. white paper and asked to draw a man, or a male figure. Dr. and Mrs. Carroll Nash of the Biology Department of St. Joseph's College and the experimenter independently rated the drawings, using a five-point scale. Subjects were divided according to the combined ratings into groups with high and low degrees of body-image sophistication.

Those below the median on the EFT were regarded as analytical perceivers and those above, as global perceivers. The psychological tests in the pilot work done in 1964-65 were administered by the author; those in the confirmation experiment in 1966-67, mainly by a student assistant.

RESULTS

There were 64 subjects in the pilot study who had a vital or casual interest in ESP and could also be classified as either analytical or global perceivers on the basis of their EFT scores. However, four of these had not taken the Draw-A-Man Test. When the drawings of the remaining 60 subjects were rated by the judges in 1965-66, the data from four more subjects were dropped because they were at the median separating those with high and low body-image sophistication, leaving data from 56 subjects for analysis.

Visual inspection of the Draw-A-Man data for the 56 subjects (though for none of the other groups) showed what appeared to be a correlation between precognition scores and degree of body-image sophistication. Consequently, for statistical analysis, the subjects were divided into four categories according to their performance on the EFT and Draw-A-Man Test:

1. Analytical perceiver with low body-image sophistication;
2. Analytical perceiver with high body-image sophistication;
3. Global perceiver with low body-image sophistication;
4. Global perceiver with high body-image sophistication.

Neither the pooled results nor those of any of the four groups yielded significant overall totals. However, the variance method of evaluation suggested that ESP was operating in one section of the data.

If only chance were operating, the expected average score for the five runs of precognition would be 25. Results in the five-run precognition totals for Groups 1, 2, and 3 tended to remain close to this chance figure, but the totals for the subjects in Group 4 (those who had difficulty in isolating the embedded figure and drew rather sophisticated figures) fluctuated considerably both above and below 25. Some Group 4 subjects had totals of 12, 14, etc., and others, 28, 30, etc., but relatively few in this category had totals of 25 or close to 25. The amount of fluctuation in the combined scores in Group 4 differed from that in Groups 1-3 combined (odds against chance: more than 20 to one). The difference indicated that ESP was operating in Group 4, sometimes to hit and sometimes to miss.

When subjects with a vital interest in ESP were excluded, the difference in variance appeared even more marked; that is, when only those with casual interest were considered, variance in the scores of the global perceivers with high body-image sophistication exceeded variance in scores of the other categories (odds against chance: 200 to one).

The 1966-67 precognition tests were planned as confirmation for this finding, which was suggested by the 1964-65 *post hoc* analysis.

CONFIRMATION

Discarding the scores of subjects at the median on the psychological tests and the scores of those whose interest in

ESP was not in either the vital or the casual category, plus difficulties encountered during the confirmation testing in 1966-67, left data from only 24 subjects. This number of subjects, although small compared to the numbers in the pilot test, gave similar results, the scores for 20 of the 24 subjects being in the expected direction. The totals of three out of the four global/high body-image sophistication subjects fluctuated considerably; and 17 of the 20 in the other three categories of subjects showed little tendency toward fluctuation. The fluctuation in the combined scores of those in Group 4 differed from that in the combined scores of the other three groups (odds against chance: more than 20 to one).

Analysis to see if the effect would again be stronger when subjects vitally interested in ESP were excluded from the analysis reduced the number of subjects to only 14. The variance in the casual-interest Group 4 subjects' scores again differed from the variance in the other groups' scores (odds against chance: more than 20 to one). Twelve of the 14 subjects scored as expected, again indicating a consistent effect but at the same level as before the exclusion.

Tests made in 1967-68 did not yield significant results when the scores of global perceivers with high body-image sophistication were compared to all others'. However, analysis using a different criterion on the Draw-A-Man Test gave results that were positive and in line with the earlier findings.

In the earlier work, data were omitted for those subjects whose drawings were rated at the median separating high body-image sophistication and low. Including the data of these subjects in the high body-image sophistication group in the 1967-68 work gave a significant difference in variance between this group and all others. When the data from previous years were evaluated using this new criterion, the variance differential remained significant. Thus it appears that this new method of analysis may better differentiate between subjects with high variance and those with low variance.

DISCUSSION

A relationship between precognition performance and ESP interest as identified by the vital-casual questionnaire has been established in earlier studies. The advantages of combining the Embedded Figures Test with the questionnaire to clarify this relationship has also been shown. The studies reported here indicate that the addition of still a third measure, the Draw-A-Man Test, leads to even clearer definition of the relationship with ESP, and show a meaningful relationship between the scoring tendencies of groups with various psychological tendencies. What this finding may mean in terms of the personality characteristics of the global/high body-image sophistication subjects is still to be explored.

Fortunately, use of these test devices in the search for correlations between psychological and parapsychological test measures need not wait for a fuller understanding of what is being measured. Merely finding a combination of test batteries that correlates with ESP reliably enough to obtain a degree of continuity is an advance. The question is whether this continuity of effect can be obtained by a different experimenter, a question that should be put to test.

II. ESP Type-Differences and D.A.M. Test

In a pilot study in 1964-65 and in a confirmation study in 1966-67, subjects were tested for both clairvoyance and precognition in the same experiment. Since only the precognition results were of interest for the major purpose of the experiment, the clairvoyance scores were disregarded in the first analyses. Both studies and the first analyses are reported above.

Looking back over the 1964-65 data after the second study, the author noted what appeared to be a trend in the clairvoyance results. Those subjects who had drawn rela-

---

Presented in absentia at the Winter Review Meeting of the Institute for Parapsychology, December 29, 1967. Complete report in *Journal of Parapsychology*, December 1968.

JOHN A. FREEMAN

Factors Affecting Success in Precognition

I. Types of Intelligence and Psi Scores

Experiments with a ten-page booklet designed by the author have repeatedly shown that boys and girls respond differently to tests based on choices among ESP targets of different types and arrangements. Intelligence testing has demonstrated repeatedly that boys consistently tend to score higher on tests of spatial relations, and girls higher on tests of verbal reasoning. The work reported here was an attempt to find a relationship between these two sets of observations, specifically to see if selected intelligence tests can distinguish between subjects on the basis of how they will respond on particular ESP tests.

The sex-based differences in response patterns on intelligence tests led to the expectation that girls who score high on spatial tests (i.e., score on an intelligence test like boys) would also respond like the boys on ESP tests; and that boys who score high on verbal tests (i.e., score on an intelligence test like girls) will also respond like the girls on ESP tests.

The expectation was that a subject's scoring on intelligence tests would provide a clue to the type of ESP trial on which he was likely to score above chance (psi-hit) and the type on which he would probably score below chance (psi-miss). (For an explanation of psi-missing, see Appendix C.)

APPARATUS

The experimental equipment was a booklet which pre-

Presented at the Review Meetings of the Institute for Parapsychology, September 2 (Autumn), 1967, and May 3 (Spring), 1968. Complete report in the *Journal of Parapsychology*, December 1967 and September 1968.

John A. Freeman 193

sents rows of symbols and rows of words. Each row includes five items. Some rows show one word or symbol repeated five times, others have five different words or five different symbols (Figure 1). The booklet also has two pages of letters of the alphabet, but since preliminary testing had shown no consistency in results on these pages, they were not used in the present work.

	Page 5					Scoring		Page 6					Scoring
41.	L	O	*	+	▪	_____	51.	▪	▪	▪	▪	▪	_____
42.	*	▪	L	O	+	_____	52.	*	*	*	*	*	_____
43.	O	+	▪	L	*	_____	53.	O	O	O	O	O	_____
44.	▪	L	O	*	+	_____	54.	L	L	L	L	L	_____
45.	+	*	L	▪	O	_____	55.	+	+	+	+	+	_____
46.	PACK	PEAR	PINT	POLE	PUFF	_____	56.	POEM	POEM	POEM	POEM	POEM	_____
47.	RAIL	REED	RING	ROAD	RULE	_____	57.	RACE	RACE	RACE	RACE	RACE	_____
48.	SACK	SEAL	SIDE	SOCK	SURF	_____	58.	SING	SING	SING	SING	SING	_____
49.	TACT	TENT	TIME	TOOL	TUNE	_____	59.	TEST	TEST	TEST	TEST	TEST	_____
50.	VASE	VEST	VINE	VOLT	VULT	_____	60.	VICE	VICE	VICE	VICE	VICE	_____

FIG. 1. On the left-hand page, the subjects choose from different symbols and different words; on the right-hand page, from same symbols and same words.

In previous experiments with the booklet, the girls' scoring was above mean chance expectation on rows of different symbols and same words, and below chance on rows of same symbols and different words; the boys' performance, the reverse.

Two subtests from Thurstone's Primary Mental Abilities test (PMA) for grades six through nine were used to test for ability in verbal reasoning ("Verbal") and scientific and mathematical relations ("Spatial").

The Verbal subtest offers a list of key words, each followed by a group of four words which the subject may in some way associate with the key word, but only one of which is a synonym. The subject is asked to pick out this synonym.

The Spatial subtest offers a list of geometrical figures. Opposite each one is a group of five identical figures in different positions, either rotated, reversed, or reversed and rotated. The subject is asked to select the rotated (but not reversed) figures.

Each subtest is administered within a time limit. A key provided by the publisher determines the scores.

PROCEDURE

Two groups of seventh-grade students, a total of 100 students (50 girls, 50 boys), served as subjects. Group I included 68 subjects (41 girls and 27 boys). Group II included 32 subjects (9 girls and 23 boys).

Group I included two accelerated classes; Group II was an average class. The age level in both was about twelve, but the accelerated students in Group I were probably more advanced mentally. There was the further difference that the accelerated students in Group I were nearing the end of the seventh grade when they were tested, while the average students in Group II were tested just as they were beginning the seventh grade.

Each subject made 80 ESP trials: 15 each of "different" symbols and "same" symbols, and 25 each of "different" and "same" words.

The author spoke to each group for about twenty minutes on parapsychology, allowed a brief question-and-answer period, presented the booklet as a group precognition test, administered the ESP test, and then administered the PMA subtests. The booklets were brought back to the Institute for Parapsychology for checking.

The checking procedure for the ESP test was the standard one for group precognition tests. Booklets were first alphabetized according to the last names of the subjects and then numbered consecutively in alphabetical order. Targets were obtained from random number tables by standard precognition test procedure, and a different set of targets was assigned each subject.

The author scored the ESP booklets; a technician, using a scoring stencil furnished by the publisher, scored the PMA tests. After all tests had been scored, the author and technician exchanged results and rechecked.

RESULTS

The data from each group were divided according to ranking on the Verbal subtest into High- and Low-Verbal subgroups, using the median score for each sex in each group as the division point. The data did not indicate any correlation between Verbal subtest rank and ESP test scoring; analysis of the ESP data in relation to Verbal classification was therefore abandoned.

The data from each group were then subdivided according to ranking on the Spatial subtest into High- and Low-Spatial subgroups. Subjects in the High-Spatial subgroups were expected to score above chance ("predicted-positive") on the rows of same symbols and the rows of different words, and to score below chance ("predicted-negative") on the rows of different symbols and rows of same words; the reverse was expected of subjects in Low-Spatial subgroups.

GROUP I

Converting the Group I trials into standard 25-trials runs gave 217.6 runs. In the 108.8 predicted-positive runs, there were 38 hits above chance expectation; in the 108.8 predicted-negative runs, there were 51 hits below chance expectation (odds against the difference: 500 to one).

The Group I Low-Spatial subgroup (20 girls, 14 boys) had three hits above chance in the 54.4 predicted-positive ESP runs and eight hits below chance in the 54.4 predicted-negative runs, not a significant difference.

It was the Group I High-Spatial subgroup (21 girls, 13 boys) that contributed most of the difference in the overall group score. This group's 54.4 predicted-positive runs had 35 hits above chance, and its 54.4 predicted-negative runs had 43 hits below chance (odds against chance of the difference: 10,000 to one).

The Group I results support the experimental hypothesis that the Spatial subtest can differentiate between subjects at the seventh–eighth grade age level to show which will deviate positively and which negatively on an ESP test.

Dividing all the Group I trials according to type of target showed no difference in scoring on words or symbols.

GROUP II

Converting the Group II trials into standard 25-trial runs gave 102.4 runs. In the 51.2 predicted-positive runs, there were two hits above chance expectation; in the 51.2 predicted-negative runs there were 16 hits below chance expectation. The difference is not significant.

The Group II Low-Spatial subgroup (5 girls, 10 boys) had 13 hits above chance in the 24 predicted-positive runs and 11 hits below chance in the 24 predicted-negative runs, again not a significant difference.

The Group II High-Spatial subgroup (4 girls, 13 boys) had 11 hits below chance in the 27.2 predicted-positive runs and 5 hits below chance in the 27.2 predicted-negative runs, not a significant difference. Thus the Group II results fail to support the hypothesis.

However, a significant difference appeared when all the Group II trials were divided according to the type of ESP target. The 19.2 predicted-positive Group II runs of trials where the target was in the form of *symbols* had 18 hits below chance; the 19.2 predicted-negative runs on symbol targets had ten hits above chance (odds against the difference: 50 to one), but in the direction opposite to that expected.

But the 32 predicted-positive runs of trials where the target was in the form of *words* had 20 hits above chance, and the 32 predicted-negative runs on word targets had 26 hits below chance (odds against chance of the difference: 1,000 to three).

Thus the Group II results support the hypothesis insofar

as they indicate a correlation between a subject's ranking on the PMA Spatial subtest and the direction of his scoring on an ESP test when trials are on targets in the form of words as differentiated from trials on targets in the form of symbols.

DISCUSSION

Group I data support the hypothesis of a significant correlation between scoring on the Thurstone Primary Mental Ability Spatial subtest and score direction on an ESP test. Group II data support the hypothesis when the ESP targets are words, but show a marginally significant reversal of the hypothesis when the ESP targets are symbols.

It is possible that the Group II results are attributable to the fact that the Group II students had not reached the same level of mental maturity as those in Group I. Although both groups were in the seventh grade, the accelerated students in Group I had had special classes with enriched programs and, as noted above, were tested towards the end of their seventh school year, whereas Group II, the average students, was tested at the beginning of the seventh-grade year. Intelligence testing has shown that there is a marked increase in spatial concepts during the eighth year of school, or when students reach 13 or 14 years of age. The accelerated group tested near the end of the seventh school year would perhaps have reached the mental maturity of the average eighth-grade student.

The occurrence of psi-missing on some trials suggests that appropriate intelligence tests can be useful as an indication not only of when positive deviations in ESP performance can be expected, but also of where to look for deviations in both directions if the ESP targets are of different kinds or are differently arranged on the page. It is this psi-differential effect that gives meaning to the data; it shows that the subject manifests ESP by consistently hitting some types of targets and consistently missing other types. Confirmation of a correlation between this hitting and missing and a subject's performance on an intelligence test would mean that the relative ability of a subject, at least of one in this age group, to handle verbal–spatial tasks somehow determines the types or arrangements of targets on which he will show psi-hitting and on which he will show psi-missing.

II. Liked vs. Disliked Target Words

One way of detecting extrasensory perception in a group test is to look for significant total deviation in the pooled scores of the group. Other ways are based on the psi-differential effect (PDE). The PDE has been found by comparing the difference in the way various test groups with differing characteristics score on the same test, and by comparing the scores made by the same group when tested under first one and then another condition. The differing group characteristics may be personality traits, attitude toward ESP, or some other determinable variable. The conditions may be varied by changing some aspect of the psychological or physical test environment, the kind of target or the arrangement of target material, etc. (For an example of this use of the PDE, see report on p. 129.)

In these experiments, the PDE was obtained in still another way. All the subjects were tested together under the same conditions; the difference was provided by a word reaction test which created two subgroups by dividing the subjects according to their individual tendencies toward liking and disliking in general. The experimental aim was to see if "Likers" would deviate in one direction on a precognition test, and "Dislikers" in the other direction.

WORD REACTION TEST

The author's word reaction test presents a list of 25 words, each followed by five blank spaces (see Figure 2). The instructions are that if a subject reacts favorably to a word, he is to put an L (for "like") in one of the five spaces

---

Presented at the Autumn Review Meeting of the Institute for Parapsychology, September 2, 1967. Complete report in the *Journal of Parapsychology*, September 1969.

Word Reaction Test

Name......................

Directions: Please read each of the following words to see what association you feel toward them. If your reaction is pleasant put an L (for Like) in one of the blanks following the word; if your reaction is unpleasant put a D (for Dislike) in one of the blanks. The blanks you put your response in will be matched with a random sequence as an ESP test.

1. Magnolia
2. Dog
3. Fight
4. Beauty
5. Vomit
6. Eagle
7. Sting
8. Waltz
9. Fire
10. Communism
11. Pleasure
12. Home
13. Sea
14. Friend
15. Worm
16. Love
17. War
18. Mother
19. Darkness
20. Cupid
21. Prison
22. Spit
23. Gentleman
24. Candy
25. Insane

FIG. 2. Replica of Word Reaction Test.

after that word; if his reaction to the word is unpleasant, a D (for "dislike"). If there are more L's in his 25 answers than the mean number of L's for the group, he is classed as a Liker; if he has more D's than the group's mean number of D's, he is classed as a Disliker.

The blank spaces following the words constitute the precognition test. The subject is asked to enter his L or D in whichever of the five spaces he guesses will be randomly selected later as the target space.

Preliminary Experiment

The results of preliminary studies with Duke Parapsychology Laboratory staff members as subjects showed that Likers tended to deviate positively (scored above chance) in their ESP scores on trials with the words they liked, but negatively (below chance) on trials with the words they disliked; the Dislikers, on the other hand, tended to deviate positively on trials with the words they disliked, negatively with words they liked. The results were not significant but were suggestive enough to warrant further study.

The original hypothesis was therefore amended to accommodate another kind of PDE: in subsequent experiments, each group would be expected to deviate positively on primary responses (L responses for Likers, D responses for Dislikers) and negatively on secondary responses (D responses for Likers, L responses for Dislikers).

Pilot Experiment

The new hypothesis was tested in an experiment with 40 members of a Durham, North Carolina, high-school science club (1).

PROCEDURE

The author gave a 20-minute talk on parapsychology followed by a question-and-answer period, then administered the word reaction test. Subjects were told that their ESP scores would be determined by the position of their responses in the blank spaces following the words; they were asked to guess which one of the blanks after each word would later be selected as the correct one. No mention was made of Likers or Dislikers or of how the data would be analyzed.

The record sheets were taken back to the Institute for Parapsychology where each sheet was copied for independent checking and was assigned an individual set of random targets obtained by the routine method for precognition tests. Record sheets were alphabetized by last name of the subject and numbered, then given targets and checked in that order.

RESULTS

Twenty-three of the 40 subjects were classed as Dislikers; their D answers were therefore their primary responses. The remaining 17 were classed as Likers, whose primary responses were their L answers. Five of the subjects had inadvertently omitted one trial each.

When the data were converted to standard 25-trial runs, the 21.64 runs of primary responses had 22.8 more hits, and the 18.16 runs of secondary responses had 11.8 fewer hits, than would be expected by chance (odds against chance of the difference: more than 100 to one).

Confirmatory Experiment

An invitation to the author to test a group of high-school students who were taking a summer enrichment program at the University of North Carolina at Chapel Hill provided the next opportunity to test the hypothesis. The procedure was the same as in the pilot experiment.

RESULTS

The 20 subjects made 25 trials each. Again, five of the subjects inadvertently omitted one trial each. Ten of the subjects fell into the Liker classification, ten into the Disliker.

When the data were grouped on the basis of performance on primary responses, there were 11.36 runs of primary responses with 7.2 hits above chance and 8.44 runs of secondary responses with 15.2 hits below chance (odds against chance of the difference: more than 100 to one). The results thus supported the hypothesis that the subjects would deviate positively on their primary responses and negatively on their secondary responses.

A consistency check of the data showed that 16 subjects had a higher average on their primary responses than on their secondary; three had a higher average on their secondary responses; and one subject scored at the same rate on both (odds against chance of such consistency: 500 to one). This check indicated that the observed tendency is fairly general.

Although the subjects deviated positively on their primary responses and negatively on their secondary responses, the deviations tended to cancel out, leaving most of the individual scores at or very close to the chance level. Since one expects by chance some fluctuation of scores, one must suspect a nonchance factor when scores cluster too narrowly around the chance level. Fluctuations from chance expectation are measured by analyzing the variance. (For a discussion of variance, see Appendix E.)

Analysis on this basis showed that the variance in these data was significantly lower than would be expected in a random distribution (odds against chance: more than 65 to one), again indicating the lawful operation of an ESP factor related to tendencies to like or dislike.

DISCUSSION

The results obtained with the word reaction test in these experiments indicate that subtle personality factors produce a psi-differential effect. Although the cause or causes of this effect may originate on an unconscious level, the effect can be measured in positive and negative deviations on an ESP test. Specifically, this experiment indicates that the personality factor that leads an individual to be a Liker or a Disliker somehow determines the way his ESP registers. It looks as if the subject is better able to use his ESP to improve his percentage of hits on targets in consonance with his predisposition to like or dislike. When he is responding to word targets which are opposite to his predisposition, he is more likely to avoid the target and thus deviate negatively. This gives rise to the differential effect.

Knowledge of this tendency toward a differential effect is helpful in determining if ESP is operating, but it is also helpful in showing *how* ESP is operating; that is, psi-hitting sometimes, psi-missing other times. Further knowledge of other causes of this effect will help toward a better understanding of the psi process.

LITERATURE CITED

1. Freeman, John. "A Precognition Test with a High-school Science Club." *Journal of Parapsychology*, 1964, **28**, 214–21.

JAMES C. CARPENTER

Mood and Precognition

The possibility that a subject's mood is related to fluctuation in his ESP scores has been suggested by several researchers. Decline of variance (fluctuation above and below the scores expected by chance) as a test proceeds has often been noted. Since subjects who begin a trial in a state of freshness and spontaneity often grow tired or bored and find concentration an effort as the work goes on, the decline may be related to the subject's state of mind.

The possibility of establishing a reliable association between a subject's mood or state of mind and the degree of variance in his ESP scores led to these exploratory studies.

Rogers has tested subjects for "negative affect" and "positive affect" states (4, 5). He defined "negative affect" as lack of interest in the test and lack of both desire for and confidence in success; "positive affect," as the opposite attitudes. Rogers found that small variance (that is, little fluctuation of scores above or below mean chance expectation) was characteristic of the negative-affect runs, and large variance (or both high and low scores that zigzag across the chance level of scoring), of the positive-affect runs.

MOOD SCALE

Nowlis has worked out an adjective check-list technique for eliciting mood reports (3).

The author arbitrarily selected certain of Nowlis' adjectives in this exploratory attempt to build an operational method for measuring the relevant mood variables.

Two clusters of adjectives which seem generally to re-

This research was supported by a grant from the Stone Fund of the Foundation for Research on the Nature of Man. Complete report in the *Journal of Parapsychology*, June 1968 and March 1969.

late to what Rogers described as "positive" and "negative" mood states were chosen (Table 1).

Table 1
ADJECTIVES SCORED FOR MOOD

Positive	Negative
adaptable	close-mouthed
adventurous	disinterested
ambitious	dreamy
amiable	drifting
assertive	drowsy
business-like	dull
cheerful	hesitant
co-operative	indifferent
decisive	lackadaisical
energetic	languid
fearless	lazy
forceful	light-headed
friendly	quiet
genial	retiring
industrious	sluggish
intent	tired
masterful	unsure
satisfied	withdrawn
task-involved	
warm-hearted	

These 38 adjectives were arranged in alphabetical order with a few other, unrelated adjectives added to camouflage the nature of the scale. Brief instructions were printed at the top. The scale was to be scored simply by counting the number of positive and negative items checked, the preponderant set of items determining if the mood would be considered positive or negative. The mood of a subject who might choose equal numbers from each set was to be considered unclassifiable.

Study I

It seemed reasonable to begin without definite predictions and follow with a second, methodologically similar study to confirm the findings, if any.

The primary interest in the initial study was to see if positive and negative moods as determined by the checklists would relate to ESP variance in the directions indicated by earlier studies.

It also seemed appropriate to inquire into the decline of variance within the test session. This effect had been found earlier in 16- to 40-run series and confirmed subsequently in 20-run series. Since the series planned for this experiment were shorter, it would be interesting to see if the decline effect would appear.

PROCEDURE

Twelve subjects participated in the first study. Ten were personal friends of the author; the other two were members of a club to which the author had lectured on ESP.

Precognition was the type of ESP selected for test, so that subjects could take the test at their own convenience, the targets to be determined later.

The tests were self-administered in the subjects' own homes at whatever times they felt inclined to do them. They were asked to pick a time when they could be alone, do all the runs for one session, and also check the mood scale without interruption. After the specified sessions, all material was returned to the experimenter to be checked. Targets were then to be determined by a standard random procedure.

The first two subjects completed five sessions of four runs each, using a standard ESP record blank designed for 25-call runs. Immediately after completing the fourth run they checked a copy of the mood scale which was stapled to the ESP record sheet and numbered the session record to show the order in which it was taken. All five sets of records were returned to the experimenter together.

The material and instructions for the remaining ten subjects were the same, except that they were asked to do five runs per session rather than four. The first two subjects had reported that they had found four runs quick and pleasant to do. It seemed that one more run would probably not cause negative reactions, so the experimenter added a run to increase the data yield.

The design called for checking the score sheets as they were returned, with the proviso that if sets from more than one subject came back the same day, they would be scored in alphabetical order by the subject's name. After the first subject's data were returned, the experimenter found an entry point in a random number table, converted random numbers to targets, and scored the subject's sets of runs in the order in which they had been marked. Subsequent numbers in the random number tables determined the next subject's targets.

Altogether, data from 59 sessions were returned. (One sheet was lost by a subject before it was filled out.) Four of the 59 were discarded before analysis because the subjects had filled out ten runs rather than the specified five.

RESULTS

Pooling all the ESP data without regard to mood for preliminary analysis yielded an insignificant negative deviation of -46 hits in 272 runs. The mood scales showed a roughly normal distribution of mood scores about evenly divided between positive and negative, indicating that the scale as scored did not "pull" artificially for either rating. The experimenter recognized that a simple separation of ratings into positive and negative classes obscured differences in degree of response. For one thing, the simple positive rating did not distinguish between a sheet with as few as eleven positive adjectives checked and one with all positive and no negative items checked.

This difference in intensity of the mood claimed by the subject seemed of potential interest and, as explained below, proved to be an important variable in its own right.

The main analysis looked first for a relation between mood scores and ESP run-score variance, and secondly compared variance in the first with variance in the second halves of sessions.

With score sheets divided into positive and negative

groups, the variation of scores for each run of each group was calculated. There was no difference in run-score variance between the two groups.

It was decided at this point to look for a correlation of variance with extremity of mood as measured by the mood scale. The experimenter was well aware of the dangers of over-analysis of data, but believed these would be obviated by treating any significant findings as hypotheses to be followed up instead of as conclusions.

Mood scores were split at the median, mood scores from 0 to 4 being classed as "moderate," scores of 5 or greater, "extreme."

The moderate-mood sessions showed, to a suggestive degree (odds against chance: 20 to one) the expected relation between variance and direction of mood; that is, moderately positive runs had a larger variance, and moderately negative runs, a smaller variance. The extreme group, on the other hand, showed a trend (not reaching significance) in the opposite direction, with larger variance in the negative runs.

The data were then pooled and analyzed to see if variance declined from the first to the second halves of the sessions. As in the previous work, wherever the number of runs in a session was odd, the middle run was omitted from analysis. The data did show a variance decline as the session progressed. A significantly large variance appeared in the first-half scores, a nonsignificantly small variance in the second-half scores, and the difference between the two variances was significant.

DISCUSSION

The relations suggested by the above analyses were then framed as hypotheses on which to base the second study.

The first line of analysis, relating mood to variance, suggested no direct relationship of the sort originally hoped for. That is, all the positive mood reports taken together showed no strong association with large variance, nor negative mood reports with small variance. There were, however, indications that mood reports in the *moderately* positive group tended to be associated with large variances and those in the *moderately* negative group with small variances. There was also some suggestion that the opposite relation might be found for the extreme ratings.

Because a decline of variance from first to second half of the sessions was found here, as in previous studies involving longer series, it seemed that a decline could be expected to show up again.

Study II

Eleven subjects participated in the second study. Ten were undergraduate volunteers from psychology classes taught by the author or a colleague, and one was an interested graduate student who asked to participate.

PROCEDURE

Instructions and materials were the same as in Study I except that all subjects were asked to complete four five-run sessions instead of five. This change was made in hopes of better sustaining the interest of the subjects and of collecting the data more quickly than in the first study. All subjects were given a numbered packet which contained the ESP sheets and attached mood scales. The packets were collected from ten to 15 days after they were given out. They were scored in order of the numbers on the packets, again using random numbers to determine the targets.

RESULTS

Preliminary analysis of the pooled ESP data yielded a deviation in the opposite direction to that obtained in the first study. In 210 runs, a positive deviation of only 40 hits was obtained, which is not significant.

The distribution of mood scores was approximately normal with positive and negative scores about equally represented, as before.

Without taking account of the extremity of mood ratings, analysis revealed a slight tendency for positive moods to be associated with higher variance than negative moods, but the difference was not significant.

When the sessions were classified in terms of mood extremity, the moderate-mood sessions showed the expected effect to a suggestive extent; that is, the moderately positive group was associated with large variance, and the moderately negative group with small variance. Again the opposite relation was found to a nonsignificant degree for the extremes. Thus the expectation that the moderate and extreme groups would respond differentially in terms of variance in relation to positive and negative moods was confirmed at a suggestive level.

This conclusion gained support when the data of the two categories expected to have high variance (i.e., moderately positive and extremely negative) were pooled and compared with the pooled data of the two categories expected to yield small variance (i.e., moderately negative and extremely positive). The run scores of the group expected to show high variance had a significant amount of fluctuation (odds against chance: more than 100 to one). The run scores of the group expected to show low variance stayed close to chance (odds against chance of such a close adherence to chance level: more than 100 to one). The difference between the two results is also significant (odds against chance of the difference: 100 to one).

Comparing the data from first and second halves of sessions showed no decline in variance.

DISCUSSION

The expectation that a division of run scores by degree of mood rating would be predictive of the direction of the relationship between mood (positive or negative) and variance, was confirmed at a suggestive level. It seems legitimate to say that this relation at least constitutes a good hypothesis for further study.

Failure to confirm the decline-of-variance effect suggested that a series of only five runs is not long enough to produce the effect reliably. While only speculation, this suggestion called attention to the need for further research on the decline effect.

Study III

The experimenter decided that the results of the first two studies warranted another using similar methods and analyzed on the same lines, but designed to yield more data. Added to the design was the Stuart Interest Inventory (SII), a list of interests such as algebra, dramatics, tennis, skiing, lectures, birds, traveling, etc., to be checked by the subject according to likes and dislikes. The purpose was to see if moderate and extreme styles of responding to the mood adjective check list (MACL) might relate to Stuart's "affectable-unaffectable" dichotomy, studied earlier (6). If a relationship were found, it would form a conceptual link between this line of research and Stuart's earlier work.

PROCEDURE

The materials used were the same as before with the addition of the SII. The experimenter met with 58 Ohio State University students in groups of ten or fewer. All the students had volunteered for the study to fulfill a course requirement for experimental participation. The experimenter lectured briefly on ESP, gave some practice general ESP runs, and explained the nature of the intended study.

The students were asked to take the experimental packet only if they were certain they had the time and desire to do the task without fail. Of the initial pool of 58 volunteers, 48 accepted the challenge.

When all the numbered packets were returned, a complicated calculator procedure was used to convert the day's high temperature to an entry point in the Rand Corporation's book of random numbers, and the targets were determined. The packets were then scored in the order in which they had been numbered. Altogether, 192 sessions totaling 960 runs of 25 trials each were completed.

RESULTS

Once again, mood scores were divided at the median and the data sheets further classified in terms of extremity of mood. As in Study II, the main analysis concerned comparison of the pooled predicted-large-variance runs (moderately positive and extremely negative) with the predicted-small-variance runs (moderately negative and extremely positive).

The predicted-high-variance run scores again showed a significant amount of fluctuation (odds against chance: more than 100 to one); the predicted-low-variance run scores showed variance almost exactly at chance expectation, and the difference between the results was significant (odds against chance of the difference: 50 to one).

These data thus reconfirmed the relationship between mood and variance found in Study I and confirmed in Study II.

The interest inventories were scored according to Stuart's original procedure (6). These scores were separated into mid-range and extreme groups to see how many extreme and how many moderate mood ratings each of these groups had produced. If the two scales are related, one would expect the extreme (affectable) SII subjects to produce a preponderance of extreme mood ratings, and the mid-range (unaffectable) SII subjects to produce more moderate mood ratings. High frequencies could be considered a crude indication of the possible relationship between the two measures. As it happens, a slight trend in the predicted direction showed up, but its proportions were far from significant.

Each five-run session was divided as before into a first and second half, omitting the middle run. The variance in the first-half run scores was significant (odds against chance: approximately 100 to one); the variance in the second-half run scores was not significantly different from expectation, and the difference between the variances of the two halves did not reach significance. The expectation of a decline effect was not confirmed in spite of the significantly large first-half variance.

The decline-of-variance effect presented above, although

showing insignificant difference, indicates that the position of the run in the sequence of five may be an important variable in its own right in predicting the size of run-score variance in the current study (as in the initial pilot study), inasmuch as the first half was significantly large and the second half insignificant. This led to re-examination of the mood-variance relation in the two initial studies in terms of run position in hopes of finding a basis for a stronger hypothesis.

For this purpose, all the data from the five-run sets in the first two studies were separated into predicted-large-variance sets (moderately positive and extremely negative) and predicted-small-variance sets (moderately negative and extremely positive). The two groups were then analyzed in terms of run position. If certain run positions could be found to bear the strength of the mood-variance effects most strongly, a narrower, more discriminating and possibly more powerful hypothesis could legitimately be framed for subsequent testing.

The analysis suggested that the bulk of the large-variance scoring in the predicted-large-variance groups came in run positions 1, 2, and 5. Position 3 variance was smaller than expectation, and position 4 only slightly larger. The predicted-small-variance group gave a less clear picture. All five positions yielded rather small variance, none much smaller than the others. Positions 1, 3, and 4 were smallest and were selected, more or less arbitrarily, to match the three positions in the predicted-large-variance groups.

The data of the current study were then analyzed in terms of both mood group and run position.

The predicted-large-variance group was expected to show most variance in positions 1, 2, and 5; the predicted-small-variance group, least variance in positions 1, 3, and 4. The predicted-large-variance runs were in the expected direction, the predicted-small-variance runs were at the chance level, and the difference between the two was significant (odds against chance of the difference: 100 to one). The results indicate that this more complex analysis provides somewhat greater predictive power than the analysis made before the sessions were broken down into separate run positions.

Although the SII had been given in order to test its possible relation to response styles on the MACL, the experimenter was interested in a recent study by Honorton (1) which demonstrated that the test could be used for predicting scoring direction when scored by a method arrived at empirically by Humphrey (2). This seemed a good opportunity to see if the Humphrey scoring might again discriminate above- versus below-chance scoring trends. All the interest inventories were scored by the Humphrey key, with subjects scoring 8 or more expected to score above mean chance expectation and those scoring 7 or less expected to score below chance. The group predicted to score high did so, producing a deviation of 83 hits above chance in 320 runs. The other group showed a trend, less strong, toward below-chance scoring with 38 hits below chance in 600 runs. The difference between the two rates of scoring is significant (odds against chance: more than 3,000 to one). Thus, the SII as scored by Humphrey's key seems to be of value in separating scoring trends in these data.

General Conclusions

These three studies confirmed the mood-variance relation and at least partially supported the decline-of-variance effect. The analyses were more successful in isolating large-variance scoring than in isolating small-variance scoring.

When combined, the two methods of predicting variance —by position of the run and by mood rating—gave a single prediction somewhat more powerful than either separately.

The Stuart Interest Inventory apparently measures something other than the response styles, extreme and moderate, as defined by responses on the mood adjective check list. The SII was of some utility, however, in separating high-scoring trends from the body of the data when scored by Humphrey's key.

This work is part of the search for precise and reliable

predictors of basic psi performance parameters, notably scoring rate and run-score variance.

LITERATURE CITED

1. Honorton, C. H. "A Further Separation of High- and Low-scoring ESP Subjects Through Hypnotic Preparation." *Journal of Parapsychology*, 1966, **30**, 172–183.
2. Humphrey, B. M. "A New Scale for Separating High- and Low-scoring Subjects in ESP Tests." *Journal of Parapsychology*, 1950, **14**, 9–23.
3. Nowlis, V. "Research with the Mood Adjective Check List." In *Affect, Cognition and Personality*. Edited by Tomkins and Izard. New York: Springer, 1965.
4. Rogers, D. P. "Negative and Positive Affect and ESP Run-Score Variance." *Journal of Parapsychology*, 1966, **30**, 151–159.
5. Rogers, D. P. "Negative and Positive Affect and ESP Run-Score Variance—Study II." *Journal of Parapsychology*, 1967, **31**, 290–296.
6. Stuart, C. E. "An Interest Inventory Relation to ESP." *Journal of Parapsychology*, 1946, **10**, 154–161.

Part V
Parapsychology in Perspective

Preface

A branch of science depends so much upon the close fitting together of each unit into the larger structure that there is great need of histories and various kinds of surveys and syntheses of the individual findings.

This volume reaches out in three main directions to assist the reader in developing perspective on psi relations. First there is the history of PK by Dr. L. E. Rhine, already presented in Part II, in which she traces the temporal development of the extramotor branch of parapsychology. Then in the first paper of Part V, Dr. Thouless takes a broad view of the last quarter century of parapsychology as a whole, in a way that very few scholars are qualified to do. He writes not only as a parapsychologist who has participated in most of the various phases of activity that belong to that field, but also as a broadly participating general psychologist as well. His service as president of the British Psychological Society and as president of the Society for Psychical Research afford some indication of the breadth of his interest. Incidentally, a new edition of his book, *Experimental Psychical Research*, is in preparation.

Still another historical angle is followed in my paper on psi and psychology. The main theme running through this sketch of the 75-year period was the seemingly endless controversy between the two fields—psychology and parapsychology. Only a historical review of this relationship could unravel the threads of the controversy and confusion, discover the grounds of conflict, and indicate how best to avoid unnecessary friction.

The paper is more than mere history; the question of the logical relation between parapsychology and general psychology is more than ever today in need of detached objective study and understanding. Few persons in either field who are qualified to consider the two problem areas together would hesitate to recognize the essential *unity* of the broad area of these psychological studies. At the same time, it is quite a different question whether it is desirable to jam all these branches of study into one university department, or even to integrate them into a single professional society. These questions, therefore, need to be raised, as they are, against the background of parapsychology's growing independence as a discipline along with its interdependence as a branch of science.

The search for lateral perspective for parapsychology—mainly through its relation to neighboring sciences—is given fresh consideration in this volume in the discussion of the relation between psi and physics. The author of the paper that brings this question into better focus is Professor Remy Chauvin of the Sorbonne in Paris, a man well known for his studies in a number of special branches of the biological sciences and the author of a number of parapsychological papers as well. His balanced and objective approach to the problem will commend itself to most parapsychologists who, like himself, have actually worked with psi phenomena in those relations to physical conditions that raise new questions and call for an extended perspective. With common agreement that no established physical principle can account for psi phenomena, each one is free to take up from there according to his own preference as to further interpretation. But the question of just how psi does operate is one for the research itself, and the information to answer it is coming bit by bit from experiments.

With relations of parapsychology to psychology and physics as far clarified as these articles can take the matter, readers who are fascinated by the precognition tests with mice will wish there were also a treatment of the place of psi in biology as well. The development of current interest in the psi capacities of other species, and the participation of these other organisms both as subjects and targets in psi experiments, assure a prominent place for biological parapsychology in the book on the succeeding biennium. A major development is on the way at the moment of writing.

But perspectives are gained not only by looking back through history and looking around at the interrelations with other fields. There is for every field a perspective from within, and this inner relationship is important since it involves the people who do the work, their opportunities, problems, organizations, and prospects for the future. The final paper in the book represents a series of judgments by a senior worker in parapsychology who has been associated with its development over a period of more than 40 years. It contains a few key principles that have been useful in the development of at least one center of psi research. The seven ideas selected for review might well have been answers to questions which would likely be asked today by someone approaching the field who wanted to know what seemed most worthwhile from so lengthy a retrospective view.

What are these questions? What kind of people does a psi research center most need and what qualities are most important in them? These would come first. More specifically, how important is their attitude toward the field itself, their grasp of it and their objectivity? On the other hand, what conditions must the field give these people if they are to succeed? How best to inform the public about a field still dependent on educated lay interest, how to enable it to earn its way on its merits, how to select, train and provide opportunity for the workers that do qualify?

No one has all the answers, but since everyone who tries to be a competent contributor to parapsychology will have questions like these to consider, they need to be discussed.

* * * *

But even with these perspectives, and along with all the papers selected for this book, those who can range more widely in their reading and contacts will want still more. The researches which unfortunately cannot be included here can, however, be traced to the original publications through the abstracts either in the *Journal of Parapsychology* or under the heading, "Parapsychology" in *Psychological Abstracts*. There is thus no need to stress the limitations of the effort of this book to bring together the articles that best contribute to a good perspective of parapsychology at this stage. Like any other endeavor, it must stand as the best which those concerned were able, under the circumstances, to provide. Mounting experience and improving cooperation promise that later attempts will be more adequate.

—J.B.R.

ROBERT H. THOULESS

Parapsychology During the Last Quarter of a Century

There are two principal interlinked differences between the directions of interest of parapsychology today and psychical research as it was in its early years; one is a new way of using experimentation, the other is a shift of interest from the problem of whether psi phenomena really occur to that of finding out what can be known about their nature and properties.

It is true that early psychical researchers such as Myers and Gurney did experiments, but they seem to have regarded them primarily as means of confirming the real occurrence of psi phenomena. On the other hand, they expected to elucidate the nature of psi phenomena by more and more careful examination of spontaneous cases. They did not seem to have any idea of the usefulness of the experiment as a method of finding an answer to a question about the nature of the thing investigated.

Perhaps the most important early contribution made by the Parapsychology Laboratory at Duke University was that it led the way in giving experiment this new role. On re-reading J. B. Rhine's first book, *Extra-Sensory Perception* (9) I am amazed at the number of characteristics of psi that were correctly identified during the early years at Duke. The important point is that parapsychology was now based on experiment as its basic method and that experiment was being used, as in other branches of science, as a means of finding out about what was being investigated. This is a

---

Dinner address at the Spring Review Meeting of the Institute for Parapsychology, May, 2, 1969. Complete address in *Journal of Parapsychology*, December 1969.

direction of research that was started well before the period covered by the present survey, but it has continued to influence research during our period, both in the way of confirming the early indications of the nature of psi and in finding out new facts about it.

CONFIRMATION

I should like here to interrupt the narrative to point out the situation with respect to confirmation in parapsychology. This, I think, is often misunderstood. Writers on the subject often deplore the fact that there are no repeatable experiments in parapsychology. It would, of course, be an experimental convenience if parapsychological experiments were more easily repeatable than they are—if, for example, one could specify to a skeptical experimental psychologist exactly how he could carry out an experiment in ESP with the certainty of getting a positive result. It must be agreed that, at present, this cannot be done. But the difficulty is much exaggerated by the statement that no experiment is repeatable. This statement overlooks the fact that the basic parapsychological findings are being constantly confirmed by repetition. None of us would feel much confidence in a psi characteristic reported by one worker, even with a high degree of significance, unless it were confirmed by other experiments. The high degree of significance is primarily an indication that such confirmation will be found. If there is no confirmation we remain unconvinced, however high the original estimate of significance may have been.

NATURAL HISTORY

In the early days of the Duke laboratory, interest had already passed in parapsychological studies from natural history to experimental measurement. Yet natural history also has its part to play in the development of any science. Experimentation can too easily become a laboratory game divorced from problems of the world outside if no notice is taken of these outside problems. Psychic anecdotes have also a part to play in parapsychology, but not as leading a part as they played in such early publications as *Phantasms of the Living* (1886) (2). A more modern statement of the relation between anecdote and experiment was made during the period now under review by J. B. Rhine in an article in the *Journal of Parapsychology* in 1948 (10). This was a suggestion that such anecdotes should be regarded neither as proofs of the reality of psi phenomena nor as means of settling theoretical questions about their nature, but as serving the purpose of suggesting hypotheses which may afterwards be tested by suitably designed experiments. The project of using stories of spontaneous psi phenomena in this way was carried out by Dr. Louisa Rhine in a series of articles in the *Journal of Parapsychology* and in her book, *Hidden Channels of the Mind* (11). A later example of the fruitful use of anecdotal material in a region in which it is difficult to see how experimental methods could be applied is Professor Stevenson's study of cases suggestive of reincarnation (16).

The point is not that the modern experimentalist despises psi anecdotes or fails to recognize their usefulness as aids to parapsychological research, but that his first reaction to a psi anecdote is not to ask either "How can this alleged fact be explained?" or "How can we make sure that this story is true?" but rather "What experiment does this psi story suggest as a means of testing the explanation of whatever it seems to indicate?"

DISCOVERY

Side by side with the turning from anecdote to experiment as the principal instrument for promoting understanding of psi, there has been a turning from the view that the principal task of research is to demonstrate more and more convincingly the reality of the occurrence of psi to that of accepting as the principal task of research the attempt to discover all we can about the nature of psi. This latter task requires experiments of a different kind from those which were used to get more massive evidence of the reality of psi, as in the Pearce–Pratt series of experiments or the Soal–Goldney investigation of Shackleton.

Already in 1942, in an address to the Society for Psychical Research, I said: "Let us now give up the task of trying to prove again to the satisfaction of the skeptical that the psi effect really exists, and try instead to devote ourselves to the task of finding out all we can about it" (17). By that time, however, this step had already been taken by the Duke Parapsychology Laboratory; the publication in 1940 of *Extra-Sensory Perception after Sixty Years* (7) may be regarded as closing the period of multiplying evidence for the occurrence of ESP and as opening the way for concentration on the task of finding out about it and about other psi phenomena.

That parapsychological research workers no longer regard proof of occurrence of psi as a major task does not mean that new evidence for the reality of psi has been absent from the years under consideration. The most impressive of these is no doubt the set of results obtained by Ryzl with his subject Stepanek, who has shown his ability to score positively at a high level of efficiency (7 percent over mean chance expectation) and unquestionable significance ($p = 10^{-9}$) when tested by two independent experimenters in the absence of Ryzl himself (6). Impressive new evidence of the occurrence of ESP has also come during our period from the publication in English of the Russian experiments on telepathic induction of hypnotic states which were started as long ago as 1932 (18). These at any rate make it clear that if one were willing to embrace the fantastic hypothesis that the occurrence of psi is merely a hoax by dishonest experimenters, one would have to accept the fact that the conspiracy extends very widely.

CRITICISM

That strengthening of evidence for the reality of psi phenomena has ceased to be a major concern for those engaged in parapsychological research does not, of course, mean that the existing evidence has been universally accepted. There are still those who regard the reality of psi phenomena as so intrinsically unlikely that they consider the highly improbable hypothesis of experimenter fraud as preferable to the "impossible" explanation of successful results as resulting from psi. The most important critics of this type who have published during the period under review are Dr. G. R. Price (8) and Professor C. E. M. Hansel (3). These critics have a certain usefulness to the research in providing a testing of its foundations, but it is obvious that no accumulation of further evidence as to occurrence of psi can overcome the argument that since psi is impossible it cannot take place and that successful psi results must be explained in some other way, such as experimenter fraud, however improbable this may be. The invitation to carry out further proofs is an irrelevance which must be resisted.

Although the hypothesis of experimenter fraud may satisfy the critic to whom it appears that psi is plainly impossible, there is one person who knows with certainty whether the experimenter has been guilty of fraud, and that is the experimenter himself. There is a large and growing body of individuals to whom such explanations as those of Hansel are not even possible—those who have themselves got positive results and who know that they got them honestly.

One may also consider that it is not important to be able to produce proof of occurrence that will convince all critics, even if such proof were attainable. What is important is that we should have sufficient evidence for the occurrence of psi to make its investigation a live research interest. I do not think it can be reasonably doubted that the evidence we have for the occurrence of psi has passed this point. So it seems we should go on finding out all we can about it, disregarding the fact that some critics think that we are engaged in a hunt for unicorns. If this were the case, it should be revealed by continued research along our present lines. If nothing were there, we should find nothing.

SCIENTIFIC REVOLUTIONS

The conviction that what is important now is to find out more about the nature of ESP has been strengthened by T. S. Kuhn's book, *The Structure of Scientific Revolutions*, published in 1962 (4). Although the author does not mention parapsychology in this book, he gives an illuminating account of the kind of situation in scientific development of which the emergence of the psi phenomena is an example. In an address I gave to the Royal Institution nineteen years ago, I said: "In the fact that we have experimental results that are unexpected and inexplicable, we have in parapsychology a situation favorable to a profitable advance in theory." Kuhn argues that this is characteristic of all the advances in scientific theory which he calls "scientific revolutions."

These revolutions are such turning points in scientific development as the passage from the Ptolemaic cosmology to that of Copernicus, from creationism to Darwin's evolutionary theory of organic development, from Newtonian to relativity dynamics, and so on. In all of these and in many similar cases, expectations based on a generally accepted system of concepts, laws, and experimental techniques have been found in some respects not to be fulfilled. These nonfulfillments of expectation, such as the failure of the Michelson–Morley experiment to detect motion of the earth through the ether, are called by Kuhn "anomalies." He notes that the first reaction of scientists engaged in normal research in their subject is to ignore anomalies in the hope that they will in the end be found to be explicable in terms of the accepted system of concepts. Only when further research confirms the reality of the anomaly and the failure of the accepted system of theoretical explanation to accommodate it, a state of tension arises which leads to a scientific revolution in which the old explanatory system is abandoned and a new one adopted; in Kuhn's terminology the old "paradigm" is replaced by a new one.

All of this is illuminating for the present position of parapsychology and for the recognition of its immediate tasks. The demonstration of the reality of extrasensory perception and of psychokinesis is a demonstration of the presence of a series of anomalies. How little they are expected is shown by the violent reaction of such psychologists as Hansel against them. If the history of science is a reliable guide in this matter, we should expect them to be rejected until a new explanatory system is put forward which will accommodate them; it is not to be expected that rejection will be overcome merely by the accumulation of stronger evidence in favor of their reality.

THE PRESENT TASK

It would, however, be a misunderstanding of the implications of Kuhn's ideas to infer that our task now is to think out a new paradigm. It is not thus that scientific revolutions have taken place in the past. The call is rather to more detailed and more precise research. As we know more about the psi phenomena and as our knowledge becomes more exact, the shape of the future paradigm will gradually become clear. Then an individual like Darwin, Newton, or Einstein will put forward a new explanatory system in terms of which the phenomena of psi will not merely be explained, but will be shown to be such as we should have expected.

Kuhn then seems to give us additional reason for thinking that the last twenty-five years in parapsychology must be judged, not by the amount of additional evidence that has been produced for the real occurrence of psi, but rather by how much more has been found out about psi. If this is agreed, the answer must be, I think, that real progress has been made but that all that has been done remains small in comparison with what remains to be found out before we can claim to have an adequate understanding of how psi fits into our total picture of how things are.

I think it is reasonable to guess that the time for the emergence of a new paradigm that will accommodate psi is likely to be a long way ahead. An obvious difference between parapsychology and the physical sciences is that, in the physical sciences, expectations can be more easily formulated precisely in quantitative terms, and one can more easily make the exact measurements that are necessary to test experimental expectations.

One of the immediate tasks of psi research would seem to be that of finding out methods of getting more reliable psi measurements. This might be by developing more fruitful experimental designs, by devising better ways of selecting experimental subjects, or by discovering ways of training experimental subjects. All of these have, of course, been tried during the last twenty-five years, but without conspicuous success. I think the search should be continued.

In trying to assess how much of the pattern of psi has been revealed during the past twenty-five years, one must try to select a sample of what seems likely to take an assured place in the full pattern, recognizing that one's selection may be warped by one's own bias and by insufficient knowledge. Not all the researches reported in the literature can be regarded as genuine additions to the total pattern. Some of their results may be accidents or misinterpretations. Others may be due to the inherent unpredictability of psi results, which comes from the multiplicity of causes that may affect them. But whatever may be the reason, where there are divergent results, we cannot be sure of what is indicated. We can only feel confident that we have a real part of the pattern when the findings of one worker are sufficiently confirmed by those of others; where there is not adequate confirmation we must reserve judgment.

THE EMERGING PATTERN

I have already commented on the remarkable number of characteristics of psi that were originally discovered in the earliest researches at the Duke laboratory. Apart from the important finding that the experimenter's knowledge of what was the target card was not essential for the percipient's correct response, the important characteristics of psi pointed out at this time were chronological declines (both internally in an experimental session and over a long period), psi-missing, and temporary inhibition by the introduction of witnesses and by change of task. These characteristics of psi have the special interest that they seem not to be isolated bits of the pattern but a set of bits that seem to fit together to make a larger segment. The unifying principle behind them all is that they appear to be phenomena of inhibition. On purely observational and speculative grounds, it has been suggested that ESP is an earlier form of cognition suppressed in the course of evolution by the more efficient and precise perceptual system operated by the sense organs. The ease with which it is inhibited by various experimental conditions lends some support to this idea.

Another feature of psi responses first indicated in the researches reported in this same book was the position effect, of which the internal declines form one aspect. The general effect noticed was that ESP success may differ in different parts of an experimental task. It may, for example, be higher at the end and beginning of a run than in the middle. At this early stage, no particular importance was attached to this finding although it was noted as an oddity of the results; it is not easy to see why ESP should be more effective at the beginning and end of a run. We should not, however, be discouraged by failure to understand the explanation of a finding in parapsychology; if a result seems inexplicable, that fact gives reason for hope that new understanding of the nature of psi will come from the attempt to explain it.

Not all of the new suggestions as to the nature of the psi process came from the Duke laboratory, or even from America. The discovery of displacement came from Whately Carington in Great Britain when he reported that his subjects seemed to be guessing, not, as was intended, the target picture that was exposed in his room on the night of the guess, but the target picture of some other night, often the night following, although the target picture for that night was not, at the time of guessing, drawn or even chosen (1). His evidence was not very strong, and the finding might have been disregarded if it had not been amply confirmed by Soal's discovery that, in his card-guessing experiments, some subjects were guessing the card ahead of the one intended as target (15). This too looks, at first sight, like an evasion of the prescribed psi task.

Further confirmation of displacement has been delayed by the fact that research workers rarely set out their results in a form that makes it apparent whether displacement has taken place or not. It has, however, recently received important confirmation and amplification by Pratt's computer analysis of Mrs. Stewart's results (5). From this it seems that the effect of neighboring targets on the percipient's responses is more widespread than had been supposed and is by no means confined to the card ahead. This again may be noted as an oddity of psi response which will one day receive its explanation.

The next discovery bearing on the problem of the nature of psi is the important group-difference experiment started in 1942 by Dr. Gertrude Schmeidler on the ESP performances of those experimental subjects who do and those who do not believe that ESP is possible (in her terminology, the "sheep" and the "goats"). In experiments carried out between 1945 and 1951, she found that 692 "sheep" scored at an average rate of 0.8 percent above mean chance expectation, whereas 465 "goats" scored 0.3 percent below (14). Although these differences are not large, the number of subjects is enough to make the positive score of the "sheep" and also the difference between "sheep" and "goats" highly significant; the negative score of the "goats" is marginally significant. This study is of special interest because of the number of confirmatory studies that have been made. The main result of these other experiments has been in the direction of confirmation of Dr. Schmeidler's finding of a "sheep–goat" difference, and this research must take a place among the well assured bits of knowledge about the pattern of ESP.

It is less clear exactly what information it gives us about the psi pattern. Many commentators have asked what is the "sheep–goat" factor that causes these two groups to score differently, whether it is the mere fact of the belief of one group and the disbelief of the other or some more basic temperamental difference underlying this difference of opinion. It may also be asked what is the cause–effect relationship between difference in score and difference in belief. It seems to be commonly assumed that the "sheep" score well because they believe in the possibility of ESP. It may, however, be the case that the causation is in the opposite direction and that the "sheep" are those who are predisposed to believe in ESP because they have in their daily life experience of psi-determined knowledge. There is obviously more to be found out about the relationship shown in these experiments.

A number of other researches have been carried out with a similar design, comparing two groups of subjects different in some temperamental quality in order to see whether the two groups differ in their ESP ability. Not all of these have been correctly evaluated by the statistical methods appropriate to a group-difference experiment, and some of the differences reported have been unconfirmed. An essential difficulty in this type of experiment is, however, that of making a comparison between two sets of measurements, both of which are unreliable in the sense of being largely affected by errors of measurement. Psychological measures of temperament, such as those given by the Rorschach test and tests of "creativity," are so unreliable that one is unlikely to be able to obtain a clear indication of relationship with a measurement as much affected by error as is the measurement of psi ability. No doubt some of the reported relationships between psi abilities and qualities of character or temperament are genuine parts of the psi pattern, but the best way of becoming sure of which these are is to make more reliable our measurements of psi ability. This consideration reinforces the desirability of exploring new methods of measuring psi which will give more error-free measurements than we can obtain at present.

During recent years, at least three researches have seemed to point to new bits of the pattern of ESP. These are the researches revealing the differential effect, the variance effect, and the focusing effect. The discovery of the differential effect was the finding that, whereas testing a group of subjects in a single ESP task very commonly led to the disappointing result of no significant overall score, one might modify the experiment by giving them two different tasks and find that they scored positively on one and negatively on the other, with a significant difference between the two sets of scores. One cannot exactly date this discovery; over a long period differences have been reported between results obtained under different conditions, but the realization that this was a fairly reliable way of getting results in psi experiments began to emerge in the 1950s. Its practical importance was seen to be great, bringing parapsychologists a great step nearer to the ideal of having a fully repeatable experimental design.

Another finding that had both practical and theoretical consequences was when, a few years ago, a number of parapsychologists revived an earlier interest in the use of the variance as a measure of how much the runs (or other groups of guesses) differed from mean chance (12). If a subject's guesses are determined purely by chance or by ESP operating uniformly over the period of his guessing, the variance (i.e., the sum of squares of deviations divided by the number of degrees of freedom) will have a predictable theoretical value. If, however, ESP is operating for some runs and not for others, or if it is acting negatively on some runs and positively on others, the score difference from chance will exceed this predicted value of the variance. The calculation of the variance, therefore, may give an indication of the presence of ESP when no indication is given by the deviation of the total score from its expected value.

Such enhanced variance is a practically useful additional tool for the detection of psi. It gives no additional theoretical insight since it is predictable from non-uniform psi performance. What is more difficult to explain is that variance is found sometimes to be significantly less than its expected value; that is, run scores are closer to the mean chance expectation than one would expect in a random distribution. It appears that the subject, if he has shown psi in the early part of a run of guesses, then unconsciously covers his tracks by making an unexpected number of wrong guesses to bring his score near the expected chance total. This indeed is odd, yet somewhat resembles other apparent tendencies to avoid the appearance of psi activity.

Another new glimpse of the pattern of psi was given

when Pratt and Ryzl discovered in 1963 what they termed the "focusing effect" (13). This was an unexpected finding, and as such, it can be welcomed as likely to throw new light on the puzzles we are trying to solve. The essential point was that the subject's response might be determined, not by the nature of the target, but by which particular target card he was guessing. Later it was also shown that the response might be determined by which one of a number of covers enclosed the target card. To show this curious effect it was necessary that the same card be one kind of target or another, and this possibility was a feature of Ryzl's unusual design of experiment. This effect does not seem to me to be well expressed by the term "focusing." It seems to be a form of what Whately Carington called "displacement," only a displacement, not onto a target other than the one intended, but onto a characteristic of the target object other than the one intended.

THE ROAD AHEAD

This is obviously not an exhaustive account of what has been found out about the pattern of psi. Some of the results reported in the journals will in the future receive sufficient confirmation to take their places as assured parts of the pattern; others very likely will not. We cannot predict how the pattern will look at the end of another 25 years. If present trends continue, knowledge of it will be more advanced than it is now, but I should guess that it will be far from complete.

Kuhn refers to research as puzzle-solving activity. I think we orient ourselves best to parapsychological research if we adopt this view of it. Scientific research may, of course, lead to technological advance or some other form of usefulness, but that is not the motivating factor for the research worker. Essentially he finds something that puzzles him and his activity is directed towards solving the puzzle. The aim of parapsychology is to provide solutions of a particularly teasing kind of puzzle. We do not know in what direction we shall be led by the solution of these puzzles; we do not even know whether we shall be led to a better world or to a worse one. The solving of puzzles seems to be an activity good in itself, since understanding is better than not understanding.

Some voices suggest that experimental progress is disappointingly slow and that we should return to the easier victories of the speculative and anecdotal stage of research. Building with bricks and mortar is, however, always a slower process than building castles in the air; it is reasonable to hope that the resulting structure will be more enduring.

LITERATURE CITED

1. Carington, Whately. "Experiments on the Paranormal Cognition of Drawings." *Proceedings of the Society for Psychical Research*, 1941, **46**, 34–151.
2. Gurney, E., Myers, F. W. H., and Podmore, F. *Phantasms of the Living*. London: Trubner, 1886.
3. Hansel, C. E. M. *ESP: A Scientific Evaluation*. New York: Charles Scribner's Sons, 1966.
4. Kuhn, T. S. *The Structure of Scientific Revolutions*. Chicago: University of Chicago Press, 1962.
5. Pratt, J. G. "Computer Studies of the ESP Process in Card Guessing. I. Displacement Effects in Mrs. Gloria Stewart's Data." *Journal of the American Society for Psychical Research*, 1967, **61**, 25–46.
6. Pratt, J. G., and Blom, J. G. "A Confirmatory Experiment with a 'Borrowed' Outstanding ESP Subject." *Journal of the Society for Psychical Research*, 1964, **42**, 381–89.
7. Pratt, J. G., Rhine, J. B., Smith, B. M., Stuart, C. E., and Greenwood, J. A. *Extra-Sensory Perception after Sixty Years*. New York: Henry Holt, 1940.
8. Price, G. R. "Science and the Supernatural." *Science*, 1955, **122**, 359–67.
9. Rhine, J. B. *Extra-Sensory Perception*. Boston: Bruce Humphries, 1935.
10. Rhine, J. B. "The Value of Reports of Spontaneous Psi Experiences." *Journal of Parapsychology*, 1948, **12**, 231–35.
11. Rhine, L. E. *Hidden Channels of the Mind*. New York: William Sloane, 1961.
12. Rogers, D. P., and Carpenter, J. C. "The Decline of Va-

riance of ESP Scores within a Testing Session." *Journal of Parapsychology*, 1966, **30**, 141–50.
13. Ryzl, M., and Pratt, J. G. "The Focusing of ESP upon Particular Targets," *Journal of Parapsychology*, 1963, **27**, 227–41.
14. Schmeidler, G. R., and McConnell, R. A. *ESP and Personality Patterns*. New Haven: Yale University Press, 1958.
15. Soal, S. G. "Fresh Light on Card Guessing—Some New Effects." *Proceedings of the Society for Psychical Research*, 1941, **46**, 152–98.
16. Stevenson, I. *Twenty Cases Suggestive of Reincarnation*. New York: William Byrd Press, Inc., 1966.
17. Thouless, R. H. "The Present Position of Experimental Research into Telepathy and Related Phenomena." *Proceedings of the Society for Psychical Research*, 1942, **47**, 1–19.
18. Vasiliev, L. L. *Experiments in Mental Suggestion*. Church Crookham, (England): ISMI Publications, 1963.

J. B. RHINE

Psi and Psychology: Conflict and Solution

In reviewing the history of psychology since 1892 and doing so from the viewpoint of a parapsychologist I must give main attention to the controversy between these two areas of study, a controversy that has endured more or less continuously throughout the entire 75-year period. The issue could not well be avoided; it is one of the outstanding clashes in the history of science. But I shall review it in the constructive interest of finding an explanation that may lead to a solution. This friendly invitation is an auspicious beginning. I shall divide the period for convenience into four sections of twenty years each and one of fifteen.

FIRST TWENTY YEARS: 1892-1911

The review begins with the historic meeting called in 1892 by G. Stanley Hall, President of Clark University. There twenty-six psychologists met and organized the American Psychological Association (APA), an organization which last year numbered over a thousand times as many members as the original group. The emphasis of the founders naturally was academic and professional, for most of them were from the American university world of psychology. Although a number of them (e.g., William James, Josiah Royce, James Hyslop, and Stanley Hall himself) had already been active in psychical research, there is no record that the subject was even mentioned in the organization of the association.

An invited address given at the Annual Convention of the American Psychological Association in Washington, D.C., September 4, 1967, and the dinner address at the Autumn Review Meeting of the Institute for Parapsychology, September 1, 1967. Complete paper in *Journal of Parapsychology*, June 1968.

While some of the APA founders made no secret of their lively interest, psychical research just did not seem to belong to the schedule of academic psychology as the APA organizers saw it. Psychology in American institutions had already taken shape along lines that did not include psychical research, and even its psychologist friends gave no indication that they expected things to be otherwise.

Interestingly enough, however, at another psychological meeting that same year, psychical research figured rather prominently. The second convention was an international affair, a much larger one, with an attendance of around three hundred—the Second International Congress of Psychology, which met at University College in London for three days in August of 1892. It was also a distinguished assembly; the psychological leaders of the day were there in force—von Helmholtz, Ebbinghaus, Hitzig, and Münsterberg from Germany; Richet, Janet, Binet, and Bernheim from France; and others equally distinguished. Four Americans read papers.

Odd as it may seem today, the man who presided over this notable gathering was none other than the President of the Society for Psychical Research himself, Professor Henry Sidgwick, the Cambridge philosopher. Nor was the choice of Sidgwick accidental. One of the leading events of the London convention was a psychical research report, Sidgwick's own paper, the *Census of Hallucinations*, which the preceding Congress three years before had authorized him to prepare. The paper was a systematic collection and analysis of reported hallucinations coincident with death, experiences suggesting a telepathic basis of exchange. Sidgwick's later report to the Society for Psychical Research gives some impression of the atmosphere of the Congress: "The severe taboo long imposed upon the subjects with which we deal has been tacitly removed," the report said. "We cannot but feel that this forward step has been achieved more rapidly than we had any good ground to expect." Quite evidently, then, psychical research, although ignored at the APA meeting in Worcester, had its day in court at this international gathering of psychologists in London.

REACTIONS AND THE REALITIES

And yet Professor Sidgwick's own view of the international meeting was, as it turned out, more than a little over-optimistic. Nothing really important for parapsychology seems to have come of this day of recognition—nothing at least that shows in the next twenty years of psychological history on either side of the Atlantic. Even subsequent international congresses accorded parapsychology no further recognition.

Let us look for an explanation. Psychology was having a hard time making its own way in the universities in the shadow of better established branches of science. Psychologists needed to work with phenomena that could be nicely measured under controllable conditions with results that could be readily reproduced from one laboratory to another. The individual psychologist, like the psychology profession as a whole, was seeking acceptance; he needed to choose his ground with care and confine himself to research material that was manageable. The case material of psychical research represented by the *Census of Hallucinations* did not, therefore, impress experimental psychologists.

The parapsychologist himself does not claim for his case material sufficient reliability to warrant final conclusions, valuable and even essential though that material is in its rightful place and use. But even the experiments that had been conducted for a decade or more before 1892 would have presented difficulties for the academic psychologist. Professor Charles Richet's experiments with his hypnotized subject, Leonie, illustrate the point. Richet had been testing Leonie for clairvoyant ability using playing cards enclosed in opaque envelopes. The rate of success shown by the subject's guesses was evaluated by means of the mathematics of probability. The methods were in principle generally commendable and the results significant. But when Richet was invited to demonstrate Leonie in England, she failed to reproduce the impressive results she had given in Paris. Whatever Leonie's capacity, it turned out to be more elusive than Richet had supposed. The ability being tested did not lend itself to the easy demonstration which a new academic science in the competitive university world required.

This type of handicap was by no means the only one psychical research had to contend with. Claims of clairvoyance and other such abilities were identified with strange cults (e.g., spiritualism) which were difficult to take seriously, even apart from academic restraint. Clairvoyance was claimed by the spiritualist medium; to investigate it meant association with mediums. While a securely established physicist like Sir William Barrett, a psychiatrist like Pierre Janet, or a philosopher like Henry Sidgwick could openly take part in such investigations, the university psychologist at the turn of the century felt much less free to wander off into this occult hinterland.

A backward glance over this first period reveals one point that seems especially worth making: relations between psychology and the universities on one side and the parapsychology of the societies for psychical research on the other were fairly normal. There were some critics of psychical research among psychologists, and defenders too, much as between any two branches of inquiry, but there was no great display of philosophical antagonism and rejection. One gets the impression that if parapsychology had been ready with easily reproduced test demonstrations of any single one of its phenomena, its entrée into academic psychology would have met no serious opposition. The minds of professional psychologists were still rather widely open; the outlines of psychology had not yet hardened. The abilities under study in psychical research, however, were not such as to lend themselves to an easy approach. Only a few of the more independent men of the period such as James and McDougall could see far enough ahead at that stage to reserve in their charts of human nature a place for such elusive phenomena.

SECOND TWENTY YEARS: 1912-1931

The second twenty years of APA history brought another stage in the history of psychology and a different type of period for psychical research. It was a time of considerable change and upheaval in American psychology, what with the Watsonian rebellion, the landing of McDougall at Harvard Yard, the phenomenal rise of psychotechnologies and specializations, and the infiltration of new European schools and movements. These new ideas and the babel of new jargons they created broke up the relative complacency of the first two decades of the APA. Under such abnormal conditions things could happen to academic departments of psychology that would earlier have been unthinkable.

PSYCHICAL RESEARCH GAINS ADMITTANCE

It was in this period that psychical research began to penetrate psychology departments, and in quite a number of universities both here and abroad. Coover at Stanford University and others conducted experiments with test results good enough, for that period, to justify continued interest. More than half of the reported studies gave adequately significant evidence of either clairvoyance or telepathy, the two types of ESP ability investigated. In most of these experiments the targets were playing cards and the results were relatively easy to evaluate by familiar, acceptable mathematical methods. The test conditions were, on the whole, as good and as well guarded as the experimental psychology of the time was prepared to make them.

And yet, as it turned out, something was seriously wrong, individually and in general. ESP's invasion of the already well established departments of psychology was definitely not a success. Not one of these separate investigations maintained any continuity. The result was that by the end of this twenty-year period during which psychology opened itself up for a time to the claims of psychical research, most psychologists had dropped their ESP research efforts.

DIFFICULTIES ENCOUNTERED

Having achieved greater security, psychology was at least in a somewhat better position than before to investigate psychic phenomena, but psychical research was still not ready for the new opportunities offered. It is true some good work was done, and some minor advances in method were made, but the psychological peculiarities of the ability under test had not been sufficiently recognized. ESP was still lumped with the other mental abilities being tested. Had psi ability actually been comparable, let us say, to memory or learning, parapsychology would presumably have remained in the psychology departments of the university world where it had gained openings. But ESP was not so easily handled.

One unfortunate factor was the extramural pressure exerted to induce acceptance of psychical research, as when popular interest in the claims of spiritualism forced the issue upon a psychology department. Such influence was felt in several ways. Persons of prestige and influence in some cases publicly espoused the spiritualist cause. Money came into the picture as wealthy people interested in spiritualism made gifts to Stanford, Harvard, Clark, Pennsylvania, and other institutions to encourage psychical research. The great project of proving "life after death" seemed compellingly simple to laymen as well as to a number of scholars, and the question was, in principle, incomparably important.

Again, as in the preceding period, the academic culture of the day was evidently still tolerant enough to permit these ventures into psychical research; there was still no significant display of philosophical bias against it. The same science that lauded Darwin for helping to solve the mystery of the origin of man could not easily refuse to examine evidence on the question of his post-mortem destiny.

But all the pressure and support of public interest, even though reinforced with financial help, were not enough to make up for the difficulties inherent in the research itself. On the one side, the societies for psychical research, aided by all these forces, organized interest and helped to focus more attention on psychical research than the available methods and the available research workers could sustain. On the other side, tolerance, though certainly advantageous, was not enough by itself. Research has to succeed if it is to sustain interest, encourage workers, and receive support and approval. When it is too difficult for successful exploration, the problems, however important, fall into neglect. We can see better today that parapsychology was awaiting a combination of special conditions that the period of the first forty years of APA history plainly failed to provide. In the light of present understanding it is hard to see how parapsychology could possibly have succeeded in holding a place in the academic world during this period. It was simply not ready for the demands of the academic arena.

THIRD TWENTY YEARS: 1932-1951

The third section of APA history was a more settled period for psychology in America than the preceding one. It was a time marked by rapid growth in numbers as well as increased diversification of research and more widely extended application. It was, of course, the period that included World War II, which spurred psychological services into involvement in broader areas of human life and action. Debate over schools of psychology declined, giving way to open-minded interest in new developments. It was a comparatively good time to introduce parapsychology, provided a strong and dependable case could be made for it.

PARAPSYCHOLOGY AT DUKE

This third score of years of APA history covers the main part of the development of parapsychology at Duke University. In the fall of 1927, McDougall had already moved there from Harvard, and there too my wife and I had gone, intending to work under him for a time. What followed then has been reported elsewhere and need be outlined here only in so far as it relates to the interaction of parapsychology with psychology.

In 1926 McDougall urged that psychical research be encouraged within the universities. This attitude was shared

Psi and Psychology: Conflict and Solution

by Duke's founding president, Dr. William Preston Few, which made Duke the logical center for such study. In addition, the newness of the University and the liberal tradition it had inherited from Trinity College provided an exceptionally favorable environment of intellectual freedom and adventure which persisted undiminished throughout the seven years of preparation leading up to the first publication of results.

The situation changed, however, in 1934 as soon as the results were published. The first report was my monograph, *Extrasensory Perception*, describing six years of initial experimentation. This small obscurely published volume reported that extrasensory perception had been found in some carefully controlled experimental tests as well as in many freely exploratory series. The strict control maintained over the better tests of clairvoyance was regarded as the more conclusive part of the findings, since the card-guessing techniques used in the tests were not in themselves novel, and the mathematics of probability had been applied according to established procedures. The various types of precautions that had been taken against sensory cues, such as the use of wooden screens and opaque envelopes and, in some experiments, separate rooms and different buildings, emphasized progressive safeguarding on that problem and by now are more or less familiar.

There were, however, some features that were, at the time, a little more unusual; for example, the introduction of a two-experimenter plan which gave the additional assurance of essentially "double-blind" accuracy. Also, the standards of acceptable significance of the results were above those used in other sciences.

The main differences between the Duke results and all the psi research that had preceded them was the six-year continuity of the work and the impression created of a vigorous, on-going program of university psychical research. The world, the university, and the psychology profession had not had to consider the like hitherto. The report made an impact such as parapsychology had never made before.

A sign of the permanence of this intrusion was the establishment of the *Journal of Parapsychology* in 1937. The *Journal* soon became parapsychology's main educational instrument, and in the course of time developed various features to improve its function. One of these was the appointment of two competent mathematicians to the staff to screen all statistical papers before publication. In this and other ways, there was a systematic effort not only to advance the study of ESP on sound lines, but also to meet each challenge to its reliability as it arose.

Then in 1940 came the book *Extrasensory Perception After Sixty Years*, a volume that rounded up all the experimental evidence of ESP to date, along with all the criticisms thus far recorded. Psychology's seven leading critics of parapsychology were asked for critiques of the assembled material, the critiques to be included in the book. Only three of the seven accepted, and their criticisms were answered in the book. From that time on, open criticism of parapsychological research dropped off sharply.

MAIN FINDINGS

The findings of this research period, both at Duke and elsewhere, were substantial. Broadly, parapsychology began to take definite shape as a field, to assume the outlines of an organized whole. The phenomena that were being studied began to show lawful interrelations and even a degree of unity. One by one the major claims, based originally only upon spontaneous human experiences, were subjected to laboratory test and experimentally verified. Independent confirmations both in and out of the Duke center followed during this period.

More specifically, the claim of precognition, or ESP of the future, was established. The original tests have since evolved to a level of methodological control unsurpassed in any division of behavioral study. This advantage, along with the convenience of the techniques, has made it the most extensively used psi research method in the field today.

Furthermore, psychokinesis (PK), "the direct action of

mind on matter," as Charcot originally defined it, was brought into the laboratory. PK lent itself to laboratory testing through dice-throwing experiments which yielded results so objectively conclusive that the Laboratory in 1945 published an invitation to any qualified scientific committee to examine the evidence. The mere fact that the invitation is still unaccepted constitutes a sufficient rebuke to the critics.

Still more important than the findings in each specific area were the emerging outlines of relationships between them, the impression of lawfulness extending from one research to another.

Certain general characteristics of the psi process became clear during this period. The most revealing of these is the subjects' lack of conscious control over any type of psi ability, a characteristic which accounts for its elusive nature. That discovery showed the importance of learning to measure a genuinely unconscious mental process accurately and quantitatively. It was new methodological ground, even for psychology.

Also, we were surprised to find that psi ability is widespread, probably even a specific human capacity rather than a capability possessed only by a few rare individuals as had been the popular belief. Evidence that psi is not linked with illness or abnormality was another welcome advance.

Most significant of all, however, at this stage of our culture was the cumulative evidence that psi communication simply does not show any of those physical relations to the target common to sensorimotor exchange. The case for precognition definitely sealed the evidence which had been accruing in the other branches of the research. Thus there appeared for the first time in history a sharp experimental challenge to the pervading belief that man is entirely physical.

Confirmation of the occurrence of psi was, of course, crucial to its survival. Long before 1892 psi testing was recognized as difficult. It was still difficult in the 1930's and 1940's. Some of those who tried to repeat the tests could not get significant results, while others under the same conditions and with the same subjects were significantly successful. Such differences led to many problems and to the discovery that the subject-experimenter relationships, as well as the test atmosphere, are very important.

Gradually, however, discerning and qualified workers, including some psychologists, began to supply a marginally adequate basis of confirmation for the work initiated at Duke. Some of these experiments produced a higher rate of scoring than the Duke work. The idea that significant research required specially gifted subjects was modified, and at Duke we began to use all volunteers available. Elsewhere some individual experimenters continued to look for exceptionally high scorers, while a few others tried to produce high scorers through training.

Naturally, the search for psychological correlates of psi ability began early, and soon began yielding profitable results.

By 1951, as the period ended, a healthy young science was emerging. The principal basic claims of the field had been verified experimentally and independently confirmed. These findings rested upon no single research center, or school, or profession, or even country.

To be sure, parapsychology still lacked a verifiable theory of the fundamental function involved—but so too did psychology. What counted was that psi research was continuing fairly steadily and showing some progress. A sustained and forthright effort was being made to develop methods that others could follow. This effort was not confined to Duke; independent contributions were coming in not only from the United States at large but from Western Europe as well.

REACTIONS OF PSYCHOLOGISTS

How were the psychologists responding to these findings? When the monograph *Extrasensory Perception* appeared in 1934, the profession showed a lively and genuine interest. While some members were justifiably annoyed by the sensationalism of its reception by a few popular writers, the main reaction was positive. A few older psychologists, among them

Joseph Jastrow and McKeen Cattell, who had been critical of earlier psychical research, now registered skepticism of the new work, it is true. But even some of the leaders of the dominant group, the behaviorists, whose views perhaps most definitely clashed with the findings of parapsychology, took an interest that was meant to be fair; there was serious attention given to the Duke findings.

A number of opinion polls of psychologists' opinions of ESP, notably those by Lucien Warner and C. C. Clark, showed that while very few psychologists were ready to accept the findings, they were overwhelmingly positive on the question of whether the field was a legitimate one for science. In the first survey, eighty-seven per cent of the answers to this question were affirmative.

This did not mean, however, that parapsychology was settled in the field of psychology at this time. The 1934 and later publications brought many criticisms—rather gentle and objective at first, and later more vigorous in tone. The statistics were assailed for a while, but in 1937 the president of the Institute for Mathematical Statistics issued a release endorsing the statistics used in ESP research, which ended serious attacks on methods of evaluation.

The next year, the APA held a round-table session at its annual meeting. Three psychologists criticized the research methods, and three parapsychologists defended them. The huge crowd that filled the auditorium that day represented a large part of the psychology profession, and the applause well indicated that the defenders won the contest. Continuance of the research was approved.

And yet during the next dozen years none of those hundreds of psychologists set up the continuing ESP research programs which their massed attendance and response at the symposium might have led one to expect. Psi research was pursued by psychologists at a few colleges, the most outstanding being City College, New York, after Gardner Murphy himself became chairman of the psychology department. Here and there was a biologist, a physicist, or a psychiatrist doing something in psi research, but departments of psychology on the university level in the United States were almost as bare as parapsychology in 1951 as in 1932 when the period began. Even at Duke, by the time the period closed, the Laboratory no longer had any connection with the Department of Psychology; but that requires explanation.

As far back as 1934, immediately following publication of the monograph, it became evident that the burst of unexpected spontaneous notoriety that greeted the work was not healthy for the department. My reaction was to isolate psi research from the rest of the department, and with Professor McDougall's approval, the Parapsychology Laboratory at Duke was established. The separation widened over the years, and in 1950 I resigned my professorship, which was by then the only remaining bond between the Laboratory and the Duke Department of Psychology. From then on until my formal retirement from the University in 1965, parapsychology at Duke was entirely independent of psychology.

But even in 1950, no one imagined that McDougall's dream of parapsychology as an integrated part of psychology was an illusion. The general thinking was rather that, given the strengthening of the findings of parapsychology normally to be expected, psychology would be prepared to welcome the addition of psi research. As the saying went, the "para" was thought to be only a temporary "prefixation." More psychologists were interested in parapsychology than ever before, even if only a few were doing research. It stood to reason that our findings had to belong eventually to a properly inclusive psychology of man.

ANALYSIS OF THE THIRD PERIOD

What, then, was delaying that stage? First, there was the same old trouble of psi research; it was much more difficult to work in than other areas of psychology. It was still hard in 1950 to say just how a researcher could be certain of getting significant test results. There were individuals, some of them mature, well trained psychologists, who tried but

Psi and Psychology: Conflict and Solution

just did not succeed. Unfairly, but perhaps naturally enough, some of them grew suspicious of the successful work of others.

There had also been far-reaching developments in psychology itself. Its rapid growth as an established academic department naturally increased confidence that psychologists knew what "good psychology" really was. Any body of academic scientific workers needs prestige, recognition, and general approval. One way of keeping these rewards is to avoid open interest in such far-out claims as psi communication. While this conservatism has many advantages for a professional field, it places a degree of restraint on the membership as the organization grows in power and influence. While such restraint was strongest with psychologists, it was by no means confined to them; it is a normal enough professional group response.

But even while this restrictive influence was increasing with the very success of the professional organizations, unrelenting progress in psi research was increasing the pressure on academic psychology. The persistence and vigor of the work in parapsychology had to be reckoned with. Moreover, the growth of intelligent lay interest in the research included active and widespread enthusiasm among students, promising that popular interest in the subject would continue into the future.

The university departments reacted by silence and indifference to the claims of the psi field. They could no longer intelligently criticize the real case for psi, and yet they could not accept it either because, as D. O. Hebb well said, ESP could not be accounted for by physics and physiology. The studied coolness was a natural response.

Beyond a doubt the sensationalism which the work with psi inspired was quite aggravating to many fellow psychologists. It provided an excuse for criticism as if the research itself were to blame for the publicity. Parapsychology had been adopted by the entertainer, the popular writer, the comic-strip artist, and even Broadway, and parapsychologists could do little to regulate this public interest.

The period ended with relations between parapsychology

and other professional fields even less certain than before. Despite all the progress psi research had made, it was a worse time for trying to start a new research center in any university psychology department in the country than when the beginning had been made at Duke a quarter of a century earlier.

FOURTH PERIOD: 1952-1967

The last fifteen years of the APA's history can be covered briefly. Although a time of phenomenal expansion for psychology, especially as an organized system of diversified services to mankind, most of us have lived so closely with this progress that no review of it is needed.

One gets the general impression that emphasis on the applied, the practical, the psychotechnical, and the hyphenated branches of psychology during these later years, has overbalanced the amount of work on the central problems of psychology. It is reasonable to expect, however, that this very disproportion will in time re-emphasize the search for the more basic principles of man's nature.

It is noteworthy that most of the psychologists interested in psi research today are identified with the newer branches of application and specialization which deal more directly with people. The newly discovered parapsychical facts about human personality seem to be of most interest to those who are *not* leaning heavily on the boundary fences of physics and physiology, but who are trying to deal with their science more directly in terms of its own basic realities.

PSI RESEARCH SINCE 1952

Parapsychology has advanced along with psychology during this last fifteen years, although on a necessarily much smaller scale. Most of the developments in psi research are less spectacular than the advances of the preceding period of this field, having more to do with the maturing of organized thinking about the field and its relation to other sciences than with basic new research discoveries.

One of the new aspects is the professional group-feeling

that has developed, even though the workers are still comparatively few and widely dispersed. This group consciousness has been fostered by the Parapsychological Association organized at Duke in 1957, which adopted the *Journal of Parapsychology* as an affiliated periodical. Another reinforcement is a textbook, now in its third printing, prepared in response to the demand created by introduction of parapsychology courses at a number of colleges.

FINANCIAL AID

Viewing the field from the economic side provides another perspective. Not only has more financial aid become available, but the range of sources of financial assistance has broadened. In earlier periods all contributions came from individuals personally interested in the field; in recent years a fair share has come from philanthropic foundations, and some small amounts from government agencies in the form of contracts. Business organizations and industrial research laboratories have also provided small amounts. The main funding however, still comes from interested, generous individuals.

One of the outstanding economic developments of the present period is the establishment of a few special foundations dedicated to the support and encouragement of research in parapsychology and related areas. This development, if sufficiently strengthened, will give the field an order of security—and not only financial—that it has never hitherto possessed, helping to relieve the secondary order of concern over lack of status and recognition.

EXPANSION AND DEVELOPMENT

The spread of psi research in recent years is illustrated by the history of the McDougall Award. This annual presentation was initiated at Duke in 1957 and was adopted by the Institute for Parapsychology when it took over from the Duke Laboratory. The Award is made each year by the Institute staff for the most outstanding contribution to parapsychology published during the preceding year by workers not on the staff of the Institute. British and American researchers have won five of the awards, but the other five were won by researchers in Czechoslovakia, India, the Netherlands, South Africa, and Sweden.

The location of new research centers further illustrates the expansion of parapsychology. A number of these have had the sponsorship of psychiatry, such as those at Maimonides Hospital in Brooklyn, at the department of psychiatry at the University of Virginia, and at the Neuropsychiatric Institute at the University of California at Los Angeles. Others have quite varied connections: one is located at the Newark College of Engineering in New Jersey, another in the department of biophysics at the University of Pittsburgh, and still another in the department of biology at Saint Joseph's College in Philadelphia. Most of the psychology-centered university research in parapsychology is in foreign countries rather than in the United States. Such centers have long existed at Utrecht and Freiburg. More recently research that seems firmly planted in psychology departments has begun at the Japanese Defense Academy and the Universities of Edinburgh, Lund (Sweden), and Andhra (India). In the United States, City College in New York had what may rightly be called a center, and at quite a number of other colleges psychologists are allowed to do psi research. In fact there seems to be an undergraduate movement into the field to be reckoned with if it lasts.

PROGRAMS AND ATTITUDES

There is a healthier self-confidence among psi workers today than in earlier years. At the very beginning of this last period a bold step was taken, back to the raw case studies of what people say happens to them that suggests the operation of psi. We now see that these spontaneous situations can, with careful treatment, enrich the thinking of even the most experimental-minded researcher.

The search for new experimental approaches has also led to the study of animals. First the anecdotal material hitherto swept under the rug by the zoologists was re-examined and found to be highly fruitful when taken with caution. The experimental work that followed has opened a vast new territory for psi research.

The search for a more readily available supply of subjects for testing took parapsychology into the schools, and it will be long in getting out of them, so profitable has been the work. The largest block of psi data on record is that obtained from school children.

Farthest out among the newer steps being taken are the attempts to extend the boundaries of the field. The study of PK, long confined to tests with moving targets such as dice, is now with some success aimed at living targets as well. And very cautiously the attack has begun on the formidable problem of whether PK can influence static, inanimate objects.

A distinctly freer approach has characterized parapsychology of late. There is a feeling that the time has now come to explore wherever the exploring is good, wherever suitable instruments of inquiry and suitable beginning points can be found. Experimental standards and precautions are now solid enough to use as a base for pushing farther on into whatever belongs to the field. The only limitations are the requirements of objective study and the availability of methods.

THE WIDENING GAP

Where now have we left the field of psychology? Or is it better to ask where has psychology left parapsychology?

On the one hand, we can say that more psychologists are openly interested in psi research today than ever before, and more psychology students are thinking of parapsychology as a possible career field than ever in the past.

But to say parapsychology is getting more psychologists does not necessarily mean that psychology is accepting parapsychology. In fact there are indications to the contrary. To begin with, let us look at the McDougall Award again. Of the fourteen researchers who have won joint or single awards, only two were psychologists; three were educators;

three were primarily mathematicians; two, physicists; and four represented biology, biochemistry, medicine, and engineering respectively. Finally, not one of the university psychology departments mentioned above as having recognized centers of research is in the United States.

SOLUTION OF A HISTORIC PROBLEM

As a matter of fact, the existing separation I have described not only suggests the solution of the conflict, it evidently represents the natural adjustment needed as a basis of good relations. All that is required is that the *de facto* separation be accepted for the present and for the indefinite future. There is no need to argue the merits of an ideal but unattainable relationship; a "separation of convenience" has, to all intents and purposes, already come about and needs only to be conceded as the best for the time being for the existing situation.

It helps greatly to see, as we now can, the factors which make for this separation. Let us recall that the Duke work proceeded smoothly in the Department of Psychology for six full years, right up to the eruption of public interest following publication. Even after the storm broke and a distinctive designation, the Parapsychology Laboratory, was adopted for the ESP work, separation was entirely a *policy* move made to maintain good departmental relations. The research kept right on advancing. Popular interest expanded, too, and physical separation from the department came next. Finally, in 1950, complete independence from the Department of Psychology seemed the advisable course.

The point is that none of these steps began with *scientific* disagreements. But in the wake of the manifestation of popular response, tension in the department mounted and some of those who had collaborated in earlier experiments now began to have reservations. If only psi were easier to demonstrate, one thinks, or if it could have been investigated without publicity—but such thinking is unrealistic.

The fact was and still is that psi, unlike the familiar sensorimotor capacities, is *not* easily caught and demonstrated. Furthermore, it *is* theoretically mystifying, as much as consciousness itself, which was all but banished from psychology by the behaviorists. And finally, psi phenomena are boundlessly interesting to most people—as they should be.

These were and still are underlying realities. Moreover the obvious corrective action, separation, is a remedy that has worked; it provided a mutually acceptable ending to the unsuccessful attempt to "integrate" parapsychology at Duke.

The policy of *accepting* independence for parapsychology is now little more than frank recognition of the way things are; there is no need for a dramatic manifesto or a declaration of independence. Seventy-five years is a long enough period for psychology *not* to have included psi research. As an obvious matter of history, parapsychology today stands in essentially the same relation to academic psychology in America as it did in 1892. Time, along with many trials and quite a few errors, has only endorsed the judgment of the APA founders who tactfully decided to leave psychical research to extracurricular agencies and societies.

SOME CONSEQUENCES OF AUTONOMY

The very fact that this new realization of freedom is recognized as a policy move should give assurance that it will improve relations. A long step into professional independence, it should remind us of our inherent dependence upon all our neighbors, of the universal *inter*-dependence of the divisions of natural science. But to say, as I have, that the gains from independence are social and subjective is not to downgrade them. One of the rewards of belonging to a "free and equal" branch of research is the enjoyment of such proper pride as rightfully attaches to progress in the hard work of exploratory science. To trade the fruits of exploration in the commerce of a field unprepared to appreciate them can only bring a low rate of exchange. Rather parapsychology has won its own place in the free market of ideas, and must retain its right to bargain independently regarding the value of its findings.

Recognition of parapsychology's independent status will

correct a number of anomalies. The psi worker will no longer be embarrassed when applying for grants by having his findings referred for evaluation to the "authority" of an essentially alien committee of psychologists. Nor need psychologists be embarrassed by having to judge the value of work outside their field of competence.

Another advantage can be clearly seen: the field of parapsychology has long needed better warnings along its borders against the too easy assumption that whoever has a good training in psychology should have no difficulty in taking over a project in this new subdivision. This assumption is often fatal. Sensorimotor methodology and design do not well fit the situation on the psi side of the line. There is a bigger difference than has yet been appreciated. Now we will at least have a better marked borderline on which to hang counseling signs to guide the entering alien, even as his interest is welcomed.

The main value of autonomy to parapsychology, however, clearly lies in its reorientation value to its own workers. With a truly distinctive field of his own, the psi worker's urge to explore the full range of his territory must gain new impetus. Moreover, he can explore what he finds in its own right, not forever being limited by the terms of a neighboring field. His concept of applicable methods of research and the interpretation of results will take on new dimensions in the perspective of an independent domain.

On the other hand, autonomy underscores the need for self-support. But the fact of the matter is, the psi work has always had to take care of itself anyway. Nonetheless, future support is a matter of concern, especially since university recognition cannot be expected until the new science establishes its own improved basis of admission. Every established branch of science has had to discover its larger usefulness, has had to win appreciation of its potentiality and recognition of its value to some larger discipline. It is this discovery of usefulness that leads to support and advancement. Psychologists have seen what entering the service of human needs has done for the growth of their profession, especially in the last fifty years. My point here is that only when parapsychology feels itself a self-regulated unit among the sciences will it have the self-assurance to identify and extend its own greater role of usefulness and meaning to the life of mankind.

Psi research is obviously of special concern to those interested in the full range of the unexplored nature of man. As has happened already in many of the branches of science, parapsychology is certain to find itself grouped sooner or later with other fields in one or more of those composite sciences which are reshaping the modern structure of knowledge—groupings such as the space sciences, the earth sciences, the microbiological sciences, or such major disciplines as medicine, education, and the like. When the *sciences of man* take a properly pre-eminent position, we should find one of the places around the conference table reserved for parapsychology.

If the findings of parapsychology are as important as they seem to workers in this field, we need feel no undue concern over future recognition by the academic world, by the larger bodies of the sciences, and by other institutions that matter. Instead, our main concern should be with organizing the field of parapsychology for the best exploration and exploitation of its potential that can be given, without regard for its compliance with any other field or framework or even with the basic unity of science. Such considerations are important but must not be primary. Indeed, the more truly independent the explorer, the more he is likely to find those still undiscernible contours and far-off boundaries of the domain of the psi reality that make its phenomena so anomalous at first sight to the academic scientist.

REMY CHAUVIN

Parapsychology and Physics

One of the arguments used by those unwilling to accept the existence of psi phenomena is that the philosophical implications of psi involve contradictions. Many parapsychologists believe that psi research is directly opposed to the general direction of scientific thinking of the last half-century, particularly in regard to the concepts of *mind* and *matter*. To quote Dr. J. G. Pratt, ". . . The battle over the past couple of centuries has certainly been going strongly in favor of these philosophers and scientists who would say that mind has no place at all." Some parapsychologists think, on the contrary, that mind should be the prime concern, and they would be glad to sacrifice matter.

I'm sorry, but I don't believe it would be correct to say that if psi occurs, the mind is "right" and matter is "wrong." There is another way of reasoning. One might try to offer general definitions of words like "matter" and "mind"— definitions which physicists, psychologists, parapsychologists, etc., would all accept. This would almost certainly be impossible and probably uninteresting. The word "matter" is meaningless for the physicist; he is concerned only with protons, electrons, elementary particles, waves and trajectories. On the other hand, who is interested in mind except the philosopher—the psychologist? Certainly not. He studies memory, reasoning, attitudes, emotions, etc., but for him the words "mind" and "matter" are only of philosophical interest, embedded in the dark clouds of metaphysics, useless for the scientists because they are without precise meaning. The use of the terms would darken the light of scientific discussion.

Dinner address at the Autumn Review Meeting of the Institute for Parapsychology, September 13, 1968.

Parapsychology and Physics

It is true that the evidence and conclusions of parapsychology (to divine signals in dark envelopes without using the sense of vision; to walk into the future by precognition; to act upon dice and elementary particles by psychokinesis, without the intervention of any known physical force) do not seem to fit into the panorama of physics today, but we have absolutely no right to say that these facts contradict physical science—"perennial physics" as Aldous Huxley might say. They disagree only with the physics of today. Every scientist knows that science in general, physics in particular, is very young and proceeding at a very fast evolutionary pace, but few realize that this assertion may have drastic consequences. We cannot say what is possible and what is impossible—at least not for the future. Based on our present knowledge, we may be able to say something about today and perhaps about tomorrow—at least tomorrow morning—but it would be foolish to make a pronouncement that the inventory of natural forces in nature has been completed. For example, it has been discovered quite recently that quasars, while no bigger than medium-sized stars, fire as much energy as a whole galaxy. For the physicist and astronomer, however, the mechanism by which quasars produce such energy remains as obscure as the mechanism by which the sun produces energy was to the pilgrim fathers. One cannot assert that what science does not know today will not be known next week. The rapid evolution of our scientific knowledge demands skepticism of so-called impossibilities.

If we are told that the findings of parapsychology contradict the present laws of physics, what is the precise meaning of the word "contradict?" This is not clear, even in physics. Einstein does not contradict Newton, even if many people think so. Rather, in Newton's scale and for Newtonian facts, Newtonian physics and astronomy are true and can be used with confidence; Einstein uses another scale and considers other facts. In regard to parapsychology then, we may affirm only that at the present time we do not know how to reconcile modern physics and psi; we are not entitled to use the word "contradict." The existence of psi does not annul the laws of electrical currents, for on a proper scale and for the facts they regulate, those laws are true. Nonetheless, there may be other facts and other laws not opposing but in addition to them.

It is true that we do not understand the way the nervous system acts to release psi. The instruments of modern physics have not been able, up to the present time, to detect any release of psi energy. But we are just as ignorant of the way the brain moves the body, and this ignorance does not disturb us very much.

If one is asked to extend his arm, he does it at once; in a fraction of a second his nervous system gives orders to contract *musculae extensores brachii* and to release *musculae flexores*, but his conscious (and for that matter, his unconscious) self ignores completely the "how" of what he has just done. Perhaps we will never know, at least not consciously, precisely how it is done. It would even be false to say that it was learned in infancy, for what the infant learns is to "extend the arm," and not to contract *extensores* and expand *flexores*.

So every day we use a power, the nature and mechanism of which we do not understand. A power we call our "will" gives us the ability to order or arrange matter, even living matter—to manage it. The exact way we manage it we do not know, nor are we bothered by not knowing.

This is a process rather analagous to psi, and I am not the first one to remark on this. Who knows what we could learn if we knew more about the nerve mechanism of the volitional act? Or more exactly, about the relations between conscious will and its background of neural mechanisms? But this is a subject almost as obscure as psi.

What could psi change in psychology, in the biological sciences, in physics? In my opinion, it could change everything. This is why there is such a passionate reluctance by so many scientists to accept the findings of parapsychology— the fear of profound change. What change? I believe we are not far enough along yet to really answer this question,

Parapsychology and Physics

but there are two possible directions, as I see it. First, we can find if and where psi is localized or fits in the brain, measuring exactly the psi factor and controlling it eventually. Second, we might be compelled to conclude that psi escapes time and space entirely, eluding the precise measurements of science so that we will never be able to compare psi and other natural phenomena.

I think these two possibilities are before us. I would like the first to be the case rather than the second. The conclusions to be drawn would be revolutionary in either event.

J. B. RHINE

Guiding Concepts for Psi Research

My purpose in the announcement, just made, of my retirement from the directorship of this Institute was partly to ask your indulgence and understanding of my efforts to turn over, as I propose now to do, the keys that have gone with this job. By keys I mean in this case certain guiding ideas which have helped me to open the doors of major difficulties during the decades of research and research directing from which I will soon take formal leave.

In handing them over, however, I dare not imply any guarantee that they will always work for everyone. Some of the working concepts that have served best for me under my circumstances will, I think, seem rather obviously matters of plain common sense, while others will be difficult even to clarify—as they have been to use. But at least if one does feel, as I do, obliged to turn over at such a stage some of the more helpful formulae from his experience, it is good to have such an occasion as this on which to do it.

A First Consideration

The first of these guidelines on my list identifies the quality that I think has most strengthened the parapsychology movement—a key quality in those who have done most for the field. I suspect most people would expect me to say that what parapsychology most urgently requires is "brains." Some, too, would think philanthropic generosity and the capacity to inspire it as of the greatest importance for a research field that is unable as yet to pay its own way. And still others would tend to put first the possession of certain special skills, and above all the ability to get dependably

Address at the Spring Review Meeting of the Institute for Parapsychology, May 3, 1968.

good results in psi experiments. All these gifts are urgently needed, beyond the slightest doubt; but I cannot any longer rank any of these first, as at one time or another I might have done.

Rather, above all these and other contributing qualities and powers, the one I have come to value the most is the trait of *responsibility*. I mean by this the combination of character and perspective that enables the individual to identify himself closely with the field he has chosen. It makes for greater adaptability of the individual to the pressing needs of the field. The highly responsible contributor to parapsychology, whether he is supporting it financially or conducting research in it, wants most to do what is most in need of doing. He measures each step against the larger perspective of the field as he sees it.

This is obviously not unique to parapsychology. Other things being equal, the real social cement of any organization is provided by the members who are most unreservedly dedicated. Such involvement is manifest in many ways. One of the surest marks I have found of the identification of these devoted individuals is their reaction to the contributions of others. To the genuine parapsychologist every good piece of work in the field is important, no matter how unrelated it is to his own personal interest or research. He identifies with the isolated worker and helps him to get on with his work and to find his place in the field.

Such integrative interest is of special importance to parapsychology because the field lacks some of the common inducements most new enterprises furnish. The difficulties of getting financial assistance, of achieving publication, of receiving recognition, and of being able to continue research are all greater than in most other scientific movements of the times. But while some explorers are fully absorbed in their own research corners, a few members here and there have taken the responsibility to raise funds and establish centers for research, to maintain scientific periodicals, and to organize a field of scholarship out of the findings from the largely uncoördinated efforts around the world.

The contribution of these dedicated folk consists of activities easily overlooked, like assisting a new worker to rewrite his paper, supplying the methods for the evaluation of results, help in translation or publication of a report. It has for some individuals involved the drudgeries of editing, of administration, of public relations, or the necessary duties of business and finance—matters little reflected in the published reports. Only at second or third hand are the thrills of new discovery experienced by such "workers in the kitchen." Yet the comforting thought about it is that the devoted worker acquires a rewarding feeling of ownership of it all. Whether or not his name is on the paper, it all belongs to him.

Another value attaches to this high sense of responsibility; it is a beneficently cohesive force as well. The committed individual is not upset by the divisive influences that easily disturb a new and difficult field such as this one. Mere status, even for the field itself, becomes less important except as it may affect research opportunity. Rather, the responsible psi worker especially appreciates what it means to have good organization in the profession and an easy, unstrained exchange between his field and related areas.

Finally, the responsible parapsychologist is relatively independent of circumstance. If he is a research worker, he is not one who must have a grant, a position, or a given apparatus in order to get on with research. If, for some reason, he cannot do research, he will find other ways of participating in the field of study.

So it has been over the years of slow development, and so it must continue. Without those dedicated people who furnish their own ways and means and drives, who find their own stolen moments and borrowed advantages with which to make their contribution, there would not now be any laboratories, any research grants, any periodicals, or even any such meetings as this. It is time, then, to acknowledge that there is, and has had to be, among those who have given parapsychology its beginning, a special order of commitment.

It is the contribution of high responsibility, therefore, which wins my greatest appreciation.

Adequate Perspective

Next in importance on this key ring of guiding concepts is an adequate *intellectual perspective* of the field. I think it is convenient to regard this perspective figuratively as a chart or a map of the territory with which we are dealing—a map of "Psi-land" as someone has called it. Whether one is undertaking a research project or sponsoring one, whether he is writing or editing a report—whatever the job, it is immensely helpful to view that particular work in relation to a comprehensive view of the larger domain of knowledge to which it belongs.

Such a chart, however, needs to show, not only the sections within the field, but likewise what is known about its bordering territories. Like any other map, its usefulness will depend also upon its completeness and its accuracy and especially the extent to which it is kept in line with progressive changes in knowledge.

Again, all of this is obviously common sense. One cannot imagine a responsible surgeon operating without well-mapped anatomy to guide him, or an intelligent traveler proceeding without his geographic maps of the territory involved. It would appear fully as unthinkable that the worker in parapsychology would attempt to progress into his territory without comparably good perspective.

The fact is, however, that a great many of them do just that, to an extent that is appalling. It is rare, for example, for the psychologist to realize that a special perspective of parapsychology is needed when he first proceeds to set up an experiment in it. He will usually design an ESP project along the lines of his own territory, with a plan suitable for a conditioning or a memory experiment. Likewise, the physical scientist venturing into psi research is usually misled by the chart (acquired in his own training) which makes him think that underlying all telepathic exchanges there must be some principle of radiation, and that naturally it must be affected by physical conditions. So he logically enough (for physics) sets up the experiment to fit that perspective. Equally misleading, however, is the conception guiding the newcomer who approaches psi research with a philosophical or religious belief to guide him. Almost certainly his chart of man's nature will have a misconception of psi, at least an untested assumption of its nature; and his cultist map will accordingly lead him astray both in experimental design and in the interpretation of evidence. Seldom, if ever, has anything of value resulted from such misguided explorations. Most of those who have tried to do their psi research in this way have failed to contribute. Happily, not every psychologist or physicist who approaches parapsychology does it so blindly. One consequence of an alien perspective is the rash of irrelevant demands made on psi workers. For example, "What parapsychology needs is a repeatable experiment!" The remark is about as appropriate as saying to a baby who is making good progress in creeping, "What you need is to get up and walk!" Another newcomer to parapsychology will announce, "What you should have is a good theory of psi." Or it may be a "model." This reminds me of the shoe clerk's counsel to "wear these awhile before you put them on."

One reason why so many of those who go into research in parapsychology do so with a poor chart of the new territory is because very little opportunity for training in this field is available. One has to get into the research by his own study and exploration. There is no long-drawn-out university training program to map the field in the individual's mind, as is the case in the established sciences. It is a fact, however, that today the literature of parapsychology is sufficiently available that no one need go far into psi research without a decent opportunity to acquire a reasonably adequate view of the field as a whole.

What does a good map actually mean to the typical worker in parapsychology? One main value is in the better sense of proportion it can provide regarding his own work in relation to the field in general. He is much more likely to develop a long-view objective, even while his current project may properly be a modest one. Identification with a larger design is rewarding in the repetitive routine and daily tedium of the research. And with it too the researcher can better keep his direction through the devious and complex steps. Such orientation can keep the work from becoming choppy and haphazard.

The worker with an adequate view of the field can feel justified, too, in dealing with smaller projects of shorter duration if he is really aiming at a systematic attack on a major problem. Smaller steps are especially wise for the slippery ground that psi research traverses. The shorter the series, the less likelihood it will go stale. The essential atmosphere required for uniformity of conditions can be maintained better this way. In short, good perspective can indisputably do much for the individual worker, for his morale, for his rational appreciation of his successes and his failures.

It is not only the research worker himself, however, who stands to profit from gaining the best possible perspective of the field. It is just as important for those who are interested in any other aspect of the work—whether editing, financing, directing, or just trying to study and evaluate it for their own satisfaction. The very interpretation of the research calls for the same perspective, the same frame of reference, the same backdrop of factuality in order to give the work its relative meaningfulness. The strength of parapsychology depends heavily upon the rational picture that develops from the efforts that went into it. If the psi researcher himself is well oriented, his paper is likely to mean correspondingly more to the reader of his reports. Therefore, the same need for an adequate map exists in every phase of psi research.

It takes time, of course, to catch up and keep up with the advancement of the research, but that is surely no reason to argue the value of doing so. Rather, the progressive charting of the cumulative knowledge is itself a rewarding and stimulating experience. In fact, to look back over the successive sketches of the field at the different stages of its history and observe the various shifts of inner and outer boundary lines, with all the revolutionary changes that are written across these records, can be the most rewarding approach to a present-day perspective of parapsychology.

Objective Approach

Third in this selection of principal guiding concepts is that of *objectivity*. Here again it is helpful to use other words to assist in sharpening the outline of the central idea; for example, objectivity would imply strong emphasis on empiricism in methods, rather than premature theorizing. In parapsychology, it implies intellectual independence of untested doctrines, professional fads or vogues, or ideologies in the conduct of research.

In this field it has always been peculiarly necessary to stress the concept of objectivity. Psi phenomena first came to the attention of science embedded in the existing cultural patterns of the times. The claims of the occurrence of psi were brought into the scientific arena by associations with other areas of interest such as hypnotism, spiritualism, faith healing, and psychoanalysis. It took a long time for a sufficiently distinctive concept of psi phenomena to emerge to permit them to be given specific attention apart from the clutter of beliefs and practices with which they were associated.

Then, unfortunately, in the very transition of the phenomena of psychical research from association with mesmerism and spiritualism, they fell into another cultural sandtrap, that of the philosophy prevailing in the psychology of the time. This was around the second and third decade of this century, when psychology was becoming especially mechanistic and behaviorism was flourishing. At that time, the attempt was being made to try to fit the claims of telepathy and clairvoyance into the university departments of psychology, and it was encountering difficulty. The trouble was that academic psychology, itself still somewhat on trial, had to work with easily demonstrated functions of mental life, whereas (as everyone would recognize today) ESP is not that kind.

Moreover, because of the challenging character of the ESP claims, the researcher who was attempting to work with it in the psychology laboratory was on the defensive. Naturally, the psychologist had to lay down the conditions for ESP experiments if results were to be acceptable to his profession. While the precautions were all to the good, a very disastrous effect resulted from the practice of imposing on psi research experimental designs and test conditions based on the sensorimotor analogy of the easily producible phenomena of general psychology. Test methodology of this type ignored the semispontaneous character of psi phenomena. The psychologist assumed that if ESP ability had once been demonstrated by a given subject, that subject should be able to demonstrate it again and again, even under conditions laid down by a committee of critical psychologists. If he failed, this was grounds for dismissing the claim.

As this growing misunderstanding of the approach necessary to psi research became more obvious, it called for an objective reappraisal of the status of parapsychology—of where it really belonged. At the same time, in spite of the phenomenal growth of psi evidence, very few American psychologists were accepting parapsychology as a proper part of their field. The effort to accommodate psi methodology to current psychological practices and viewpoints had only served to increase the incongruity of the two fields. It indicated that parapsychology did not belong to the prevailing ideology of academic psychology today.

Three major disturbing differences stood out: first, the fact that the psi process is unconscious called for a quite different experimental approach than that used in the measurement of the familiar conscious functions. Second, the psi process is not only extrasensorimotor, but in some essential link, extraphysical as well. This clashed with current rational assumptions in psychology. Third, the psi function had proved to be a very delicate and elusive one, not suited to rigid rules laid down for the easily induced phenomena familiar to the psychology laboratory. Psi ability, needed first to be explored thoroughly for its own principles, and under the special conditions required for its operation. But that was difficult to do under the restrictive conditions imposed by affiliation with an essentially alien branch.

The consequences of the acceptance of the relative independence of parapsychology from psychology are already noteworthy, especially concerning changes in research methods. They have led the parapsychologist to shift major attention rather strongly from the test subject to the psi tester himself. Emphasis is being put on the development of the skills needed to *produce the phenomena* to be investigated. The pressure to acquire testing skill is directed especially at the beginner preparing to do psi research. Sensible as it must obviously appear, this primary emphasis on the responsibility of the researcher to qualify himself (i.e., as one who can get evidence of psi when he needs it) is a distinctive step that had to be taken in the interest of increasing the likelihood of bringing psi under some degree of control. It has been a sort of minor revolution to have to accept the fact (now obvious enough once it is taken) that the parapsychologist first has to learn how to elicit evidence of psi before he can hope to work with it dependably.

Right along with the new pressure on the psi tester goes an equal emphasis on his need to provide the basic operating conditions psi requires—the proper techniques, suitable subject selection, and, of course, the necessary precautions against error of all kinds that always have to be met. Put in its most extreme form, the main burden of responsibility now should be on the tester and his skill, along with the procedures and conditions required for the facilitation of psi communication.

Around this free exploratory preparation, a new design of experimentation has to be developed. It has to provide maximal liberty for learning how best to induce psi to reveal itself and sure methods of confirming its occurrence. A two-step procedure has been found necessary to meet this need. In the first step, the researcher ranges freely in trying whatever procedure he thinks may succeed, exploring every dark corner and testing every half-baked idea. If he does succeed in getting significant results, he must not leap to a conclusion; rather, he must go steadily ahead to see if the first result can be confirmed by an adequately planned experiment—one as close to a repetition as can be designed. If it is confirmed under good conditions, a conclusion may then be allowable. This combination of maximal liberty on the first step and caution on the second is working well to give completely free range to explore at the beginning, and economy of effort, with ample controls, on later research.

It is not only in method, however, that this high objectivity is essential in parapsychology. The same spirit of independence that was needed to turn from psychological criteria for ESP research and develop a distinctive methodology tailored more strictly to the phenomenon itself is just as important when it comes to the drawing of conclusions as to where psi results fit in and where they do not, whether in relation to the academic psychology of today or to the science of physics. The emphasis on the distinctiveness of psi phenomena will help to promote the full exploration of this branch of nature until its main properties are known. We can safely assume, however, that a unifying conception will have to emerge in time which will fully identify psi with the person, the living organism, and, in some principle of interaction, even with the physical system of nature.

Public Understanding

The next key on my ring of major lessons has to do with the educational aspect of psi research, on which the interest of the public largely depends. The word that best represents the idea I shall emphasize is *understanding*—in this case, of course, mutual understanding between the researcher and the audience he needs and hopes to interest in his work. Such understanding would be attained if the interested section of the world at large were able to share appreciatively the objectives, the standards, the findings, and the meaning of the work in parapsychology.

Naturally, the development of any research field depends on a sustaining audience or clientele of some kind. It is an elementary fact of economic life; and since parapsychology is much too challenging and controversial for existing university departments, it has been fortunate to be able to find backing elsewhere. It is well known that parapsychology has owed its very existence to the vigor, extent, and persistence of enlightened public interest. This situation is not unique to parapsychology. As a matter of fact, new ideas in science often seem to germinate best in extramural settings, especially outside of departmental limits.

This very support from the public, however, led parapsychology into its most anomalous and difficult position. The situation was partly a result of the attempt, already mentioned, to establish it in the university departments of psychology in this country. This effort, sponsored especially by Professor William McDougall, naturally led psi research workers to give major attention to the psychology profession and to make comparatively little concession to the need to foster a well-informed and understanding public. It is true, the science writers of a generation ago, especially at the time of the launching of the Duke work, were very coöperative with the Duke Laboratory and did much to present a clear and effective account of the early developments. With their help and the aid of a few books by workers in the field, the public had a reasonably good understanding of the earlier findings on ESP.

But the popular response was extraordinary, considering the meager extent of the research up to that time, and it had an unfortunate side-effect. The exceptional interest shown in the ESP findings stimulated the radio and press to give the subject over-sensational treatment. These excesses greatly annoyed some academic colleagues, especially the psychologists, who were taken to be "nearest of kin," and the resulting antagonism was largely responsible for the negative reaction of many members of the psychology profession throughout the country. Then too, the succeeding generation of science writers, as it came along, followed the academic line and gradually but almost completely dropped the subject of parapsychology.

Guiding Concepts for Psi Research

To worsen the situation still more, a crop of extremely sensational popular writers developed and filled the vacuum of high-pitched public interest; later on, with the advent of television, the subject was even more dramatized and overdrawn than before. The serious writers and workers in parapsychology thus to a large extent lost control of communication with the general public on which the field was (and still is) in reality mainly dependent. Thus it is that today the public and the laboratory staff no longer understand each other very well. A rather serious intelligibility gap has developed.

What is to be done? Obviously, no control of editors and publishers is possible, even if it were desirable. Some of them are interested only in anything that sells books and magazines and unfortunately, the more extravagantly lurid books and magazines are likely to sell better than the soundly factual ones.

One of the deleterious effects of this sensationalism is to drive the person with an inquiring interest to turn his back upon the field. The teacher or counselor is likely to be repelled and to advise his students to avoid the subject. Or an editor may see the public being grossly misled and print a general attack on the field.

The best solution to this situation would, of course, be to help more psi workers to reach the general reader in such a way as to create better understanding. One worthwhile start has been made at the Institute for Parapsychology in the attempt to bring researchers and readers more frequently and more intelligibly together through a new book series. The seasonal review meetings this Institute has been holding every four months in recent years produce three harvests of new research every year; and the resulting papers, with only enough editing to make them understandable, are being assembled in book form to be shared with the general public at suitable intervals. [Editor's note: The first of the series appeared in the fall of 1968; this book is the second.] Through reviews and the aid to writers which these volumes will give throughout the country and in school and public libraries, the reading clientele should be brought closer to the actual research worker than has ever been the case before.

This series of books, however, will not be enough by itself to bridge the gap. Perhaps the time is approaching for the field of parapsychology to sponsor, support, and guide a reliable, interesting, and readable popular magazine designed to promote understanding between those doing research and the interested public. Independent attempts have been made in the past, and new ones are being planned. Eventually one of them may succeed.

Yet, even if and when an effective magazine is published, it is not likely that this objective of creating adequate public understanding will be fulfilled, for the need will also grow with time. It will be necessary to reach out through other existing media of communication to meet the growing desire for information. Over recent years, a phenomenal expression of interest has been shown by the schools and colleges of this country; and in order to meet it, articles in educational publications, recordings, films, lectures, and special books for the student will be called for.

The question arises here whether parapsychologists, so few in number as they are, so burdened already with other problems, so limited in funds and facilities, can accomplish so much on this educational front, important though it may be. If there were any choice in the matter, the answer would be no. But I can see no alternative. To lose still further the general public that is the mainstay supporting parapsychology would be in effect to give up the field and its promise.

Yet, it is not really a hopeless situation. While the editors, writers, and publishers cannot be controlled, the mind of the intelligent layman and student can be helped to make a better choice of educational material if it is available. It is not difficult to believe that the mind of the public can be recaptured through effective presentation of reliable research findings. The effort must be made, since the need of common understanding is very great. It is for the foreseeable future the lifeline of parapsychology as a science.

Program for Personnel

Still another of the guiding values could well be identified, if a single word were to be used, as *coöperativeness*; and the division within parapsychology that is especially involved is a most important one: the research personnel of the field. It is fairly obvious that all aspects of parapsychology as a discipline depend entirely on the people who do the research. Just now I am concerned with the need of improving coöperative interchange between research workers and those who sustain and direct them, with the more general objective of helping to raise the level of production for this field. I wish especially to stress the selection, training, and qualification of research personnel and the relations needed for effective work.

For background on the problem of psi research personnel, I naturally turn first to the past experience at the Parapsychology Laboratory. Before the beginning at Duke, the professional psychical researcher was interested for the most part in the problem of post-mortem survival and undertook his work with mediums on the assumption that no special training was needed. None was available anyhow. But the introduction and continuance of experimental work at Duke did eventually call for training. At the same time, the university setting afforded me the opportunity to recruit research personnel from my own psychology students. It was, in fact, in this way that the Parapsychology Laboratory acquired its research staff during the earlier years, and this went on until the withdrawal of the Laboratory from the Psychology Department in 1950 made the policy no longer feasible.

This change, however, was not as disadvantageous as it then appeared to be. It can be observed in retrospect that the kind of interest a teacher induces in his students, even though strong at the time, can well be a less sturdy one than the rugged road of research in parapsychology requires. Out of the twenty-one of my own early student selectees who participated as assistants in the psi research program, only one is still active in parapsychology today, although another stayed with the field until his death. It is also true, however, that of the other nineteen only one, to my knowledge, is active in any other branch of research.

Admittedly, however, such a look back over the past of the Laboratory gives a poor basis for judgment. Surely, no one else has ever tried to build up the research staff of a laboratory or institute in a new field with so much uncertainty concerning status and future security as that in which parapsychology at Duke had to operate. With no relevant basis for comparison, it only seems profitable to say what appears to have worked best in that situation, and what did not.

One of the first devices tried in training research personnel at Duke was to offer graduate research assistantships to students (my own and others) who had shown interest in psi testing. But after only a few years of trial, it became clear that parapsychology could not compete with psychology in offering the easy, sure-fire results in thesis research that graduate training requires. Psi experiments were too uncertain, and students could not afford to run needless risks. Accordingly, that way of helping them to get training was abandoned.

However, the research assistantship idea was not dropped all at once. At first it seemed possible that an outstanding student could still incidentally get some experience in this field by way of independent study and research in it. But we found that the prior demands of the scheduled work on which the degree depended overshadowed the more informal work in parapsychology too largely to permit this plan to pay off. The "second-table" status was not fair to the subject, and students did not acquire the necessary respect for their non-credit studies in psi research. No permanent workers entered the field via these assistantships, though some hung on for a time. It was a mistake to send them charging against the hard line of academic orthodoxy armed only with the uncertain psi methodology of that period. But on the whole they made a brave attempt.

The abandonment of the use of graduate assistants left the Laboratory with the need to develop its own devices in the selection of personnel. Various types of summer training programs were tried as the years passed, and something was learned thereby as to the better ways to help the candidate get a fair start in the field. As a matter of fact, even though these educational efforts did not yield many qualified workers, they provided a basis for judging the kind of training program needed for the future.

By far the most rewarding idea from the past was the Visiting Research Fellowship Program. It was instituted to bring a few carefully selected individuals from some other part of the country or from another country to spend a period (usually ranging from three to twelve months) at the Laboratory. Those eligible were mainly persons who had already made something of a start at psi research and had already had some success in their experimental efforts. This was quite an important consideration. Today a look around the world at the former Visiting Research Fellows who were aided under this program shows that a large share of the currently active psi research is being done by them. Over the years, there has been cause for very few regrets regarding their selection. It is one program that certainly deserves to be continued.

Probably the most valuable lesson from the past for the personnel program is that it is best to be selective right from the start as to those who can be considered suitable for research involving psi testing. It is a great disservice to parapsychology to encourage an ambitious researcher to venture into the field far enough to feel identified with it, only to have him discover that he can get only chance results in testing subjects for psi ability. Too often in such cases the frustrated individual seeks a perverse satisfaction by becoming a destructive critic of the work of others who succeeded where he failed. In any case, the time, effort, and cost of training can well be a dead loss which parapsychology cannot afford.

What is needed, of course, is a more discriminating plan

of "admissions," and any center that offers opportunities for training can readily provide the assistance needed. The candidate can easily enough be helped to test his ability to produce evidence of psi to a fully acceptable extent before his status is decided. A proper consideration for the good of the trainee (and that of the field, for that matter) will keep in focus the importance to him of an early appraisal of his ability in getting subjects to register significant results.

However, even the greatest care in selecting psi-testing personnel is still not going to take care of all the difficulties. Another area calling for coöperative effort and understanding involves the situation in which the parapsychologist must work. More and more the advantages of belonging to a research center with a group of active co-workers and laboratory facilities have begun to stand out; also much of the research has to be teamwork if the field is ever to deal with its more complicated problems.

Psi workers, however, tend by the nature of their selection to be unusually independent or they would have chosen a more conservative field in the first place. Furthermore, while the academic sciences have a long graduate training period during which the more unsteady students are eliminated and the rest undergo a considerable amount of discipline, parapsychology does not yet have any such training place or program. The absence of such a period when good work habits can be formed and group adjustments made has tended to generate many personnel problems and, consequently, a large turnover in staff. It is hard to see how it could have been otherwise.

The question of how much independence is good is one that calls for considerable tact and mutual understanding. There should, of course, be some general policy at every research center. One laboratory will want each worker to "go his own way" rather freely. This has its advantages, but there would not be much teamwork if the laboratory operated wholly on that policy. In any case, the individual and his stage of development must be considered. Most psi trainees are somewhat like artists who naturally want to work with their own ideas, and they also generally prefer individual work to collaboration.

However, a well planned research institute supported by grants and gifts has to have a long-range master plan of research. Special projects that fit within the larger scheme may still have some independence, but within certain limits. Training projects can be allowed on completely independent lines and some part-time individual projects can be permitted as well, but the major undertaking of the center must have prior claim on those who elect to join in its program. Considerate handling of such problems is needed, however, and compromises must be made. These matters are likely to be a source of strain especially when the research itself turns out to be frustrating, as psi research often does. Parapsychology has special need of the tolerant readiness for the coöperative understanding I am stressing.

But even with all such readiness, membership in a research group makes demands that may be too great for a given individual. This may be because of a trait of character or a dispositional tendency, but in either case it can easily require a shift of employment. But there usually are (and always should be) somewhere within the field, a few research spots for the loners; ideally a research field should help its workers to locate where they can do their best.

This need for a more coöperative effort to help the psi worker find his rightful place has a new urgency today. The entire research program of the future depends on the progress in this essential condition for productive work. Moreover, the manifest spread of interest in parapsychology and its development as a science are naturally leading to the expectation of a growing research personnel. This challenge must be squarely faced: the responsibility for selecting and training psi workers to meet this increasing need will have to be assumed by independent centers for the indefinite future—until the university status of parapsychology is established. Accordingly, though a research staff always tends to be reluctant to assume such training responsibilities, the time has come when the job can no longer be postponed.

The new emphasis on more careful selection of candidates for psi researchers has already put restrictions on progress in staff building, especially in numbers of trainees. But this is a necessary forward step and had to come at some point. At the same time, more areas of psi research are being opened up, and this calls for more diversification and expansion of personnel. One example is the growth of interest in a wider coverage and study of spontaneous psi phenomena. Another is the wide-ranging search for new targets for PK testing, which brings in areas of physical and biological technology. The extension of ESP work into the zone of physiological measurements is another large addition to the territory of psi research. The opening up of related fields such as animal behavior, children of limited potential, and states of altered consciousness has already considerably widened the field. Today, with all these many more areas to study, the psi student stands a much better chance of making a successful beginning than has ever been the case before.

The coöperative approach to the psi student's problem can now be summed up: In fairness he needs to know, before he burns his bridges, whether or not he can work with psi. If he can, he needs, along with his formal education, an opportunity to train and qualify. He has a right then to try working, at least for a time, in a center or location where his maximum potential may be realized, whether in a group or individual situation. The prospects for a satisfactory career, full-time or part-time, should be worked out to the fullest clarification possible for the candidate who is to be the parapsychologist of tomorrow. We must make the way clearer, more inviting, and more properly realistic if there is to be the kind of tomorrow the field deserves.

Development of a Market

A quite different key concept is needed to cope with the problem of financial support. The best way to sum up what I have learned to stress in this connection would involve the familiar expression *business judgment*. Some, perhaps, would emphasize the aspect of "salesmanship," and there are others who would object to both of these terms from the business world as inapplicable to scholarly endeavor. But under our economic system there is no escaping the need to "sell" whatever it is that one produces if he is to get the support to continue producing.

The analogy between parapsychology and business helps to focus on the importance, on the one hand, of facing candidly the interest that people have in parapsychology and, on the other, of assessing forthrightly just what it is that parapsychology has to offer them. While the analogy does oversimplify the situation, it provides some much-needed sharpness and clarity.

Again it is profitable to look backward, first to see what kind of interest in the field led people to support parapsychology in the past. It is well known that the specific interest that led to the launching of the psychical research movement in the beginning and supported it for a long time thereafter lay in the possibility of proving post-mortem survival (PMS) by means of spirit communication. Other elements, such as spirit healing, were mixed with this to some extent, but the financial support of the psychical research societies and even the university investigations (at Pennsylvania, Clark, Harvard, Stanford, and Duke) derived mainly from interest in PMS. As a matter of fact, the very entree of psychical research into American universities was facilitated by the availability of financial aid for research on this problem.

The donors of the university gifts supposed, or at least hoped that, once established on the campus, parapsychology would then hold its own and share the same general support as any other scientific branch. As you already know, this turned out not to be the case. Naturally, as psychologists had already done in accommodating their own subject matter to the university world, those who first undertook to introduce psychical research into psychology departments chose projects that seemed most adaptable to the academic laboratory (telepathy and clairvoyance, for instance, instead of mediumship). But even these phenomena were too fleeting and uncertain for the methods then in use and, as I have said, these early ESP efforts could not compete with those based on the more easily demonstrated natural phenomena from other fields. Finally, the researches in psi in the 1930's brought forth grave doubts that the anticipated case could be made for PMS, and the support for survival research began to fall off.

Other interests belonging to psychical research remained, however, and survived the decline in preoccupation with PMS. For example, attention was given to the probable role of psi in healing; and for a time, this area seemed to offer a promising basis for financial support. But while individual members of the professions concerned showed a readiness for such research, the sources of support were in the hands of men made too conservative by their administrative responsibilities to become associated with the new venture. Besides, the psi research field could only offer promises, and while these were supported by a basis of solid facts, they had to be qualified by recognition of the great uncertainty about the time when application might be realized.

Efforts in other practical directions in connection with government agencies again led up to a similar recognition of long-view possibilities (much as in the case of medicine). But the requirements again called for too much bold money too long in advance of useful application to result in any major investment. The assurance was often given, however, that when parapsychology reached a certain stage it would certainly receive ample help (a stage, incidentally, when it would obviously no longer need to seek buyers). Meanwhile, it was clear in all these searches for a supporting interest that psi research would have to fend for itself.

Eventually, and after more rebuffs than I would have time to review, the idea began to dawn that there was something wrong with the judgment that led to an expectation of support under the circumstances. The item (PMS) for which a market existed was one on which the order could not be filled. For products on which the delivery date was too uncertain (like the practical application of psi) not enough advance orders could be obtained to cover cost of development and production. On the other hand, the kind of psi effects that could be produced and delivered on request were, and still are, too uncertain for any kind of reliable practice or application. (There are, however, highly promoted "psi practitioners" reported to be making fortunes, but that kind of success is no assurance of reliability.)

What, if anything, did this leave to parapsychology which would properly invite support? One fact of great interest stood out: although the principal claim (PMS) for which psychical research had originally been financed had lost marketable status, public interest in the field not only had not declined, it had grown and extended. Some of this interest is doubtless based on highly publicized but unsupported claims, and much of it is due to credulity; but, by and large, I think this public response is based on a generally intelligent curiosity about this puzzling new aspect of man's nature. The concern seems to be too widespread among too many people, young and old, over too large and varied a part of the reading world for it to be dismissed as entirely superficial. It seems instead to come from a deepseated, spontaneous interest of mankind in man himself.

This widespread mass attention, oddly enough, is focused on the very kernel of parapsychology—the primary fact of the field—the fact that psi does occur. Those who are active in the research have long since pushed on to other, more advanced findings, taking the occurrence of psi for granted. But the reflective public, generally speaking, is still only gradually adjusting to the idea. At the same time, this acceptance of the scientific fact of psi occurrence by the average individual is taking place without much knowledge of its significance (we are all waiting for that). But no matter; it must have some great potential, to be discovered eventually. The search for that potential makes an appeal the public can appreciate.

Some tangible evidence of the effect of this appeal can be offered. Only a few years ago the Foundation for Research on the Nature of Man was established without any commitment to the older objectives like PMS. So far as parapsychology is concerned, the basic aim of the FRNM is to see what that science can contribute to the greater understanding of man's nature. Even if there never is any new evidence of post-mortem survival, even if there never turns out to be any practical application of psi ability to the technological, medical, or other needs of mankind, the aims and purposes of the Foundation could still be met to the full and without default.

Yet this generalized objective has drawn more support for the FRNM than all the former objectives in all the preceding years yielded for its predecessor institution, the Duke Parapsychology Laboratory. This support has come from a small, but not unrepresentative, membership of the intelligent public that has held on faithfully to an interest in finding out what parapsychology can reveal about the peculiar make-up of man.

The fact is that in the findings of parapsychology we do already have a product that is salable, and it is one on which we can deliver immediately. The scientific establishment of a firm case for psi makes that much difference to the human situation of today. I think, therefore, that a sustaining public interest is fairly well assured to psi research as long as men want to understand their own nature to the fullest extent possible.

It is true, as I said on an earlier topic, that a large gap still exists between public knowledge about psi and the present status of parapsychology, just as a large gap of financial inadequacy still remains. In fact, the two gaps are quite closely related. But knowledge about the psi process is only the beginning; more pressing still is the need to appreciate the crucial bearing of psi research on human life and affairs. The "simple fact of psi" raises questions that will have to be answered if public interest is to continue. Most assuredly, it would be good business to study the supporting public and realistically appraise its higher-level interests and its requirements with regard to the psi research potential for human society.

Recognition of the fact that public interest supports psi research should in itself have a unifying impact upon the all-too-disunited factions of this field. Nothing could more favorably impress the world watching the progress of parapsychology than to present to it an image of professional solidarity, along with a reasonably well integrated scientific program for the subject as a whole. For that matter, there is no good reason why the professional organization of the workers should not concern itself with this practical problem of looking after its "public image." The coördinating effect of such concern on the forces behind the "front" could hardly be anything but salutary.

However, marketing the product of psi research in today's world presents complications that did not exist for the founders. The work has become more "professional." The way in which research gifts, grants, contracts, and such are handled is no longer as simple at it was a generation ago. The research worker more often than not needs to have someone else to present his case if he is to obtain the assistance that will enable him to continue his work. It is almost necessary that a sort of general clearing house be established for exchange between those who can produce and those who can support such production. This seems a worthy idea, at least for some point ahead, but the field is not ready yet for such coördination. It would need to be preceded by a well developed common understanding among psi workers; and such agreement comes hard among individualistic explorers. And yet, the awareness of pressing common needs can well reverse the rule and actually facilitate a community of interest, just as business competitors can learn to combine.

One final point remains: changes in the status of parapsychology, especially in its independence of university departments of psychology, may affect its financial policy considerably. Such a change of identity will call for a new survey of the field, a fresh analysis, and a modified plan of development. The buyer of research is, of course, purchasing the future and he will want to be able to visualize that future as clearly as possible. To win supporting interest, the psi research center must find common ground with the agencies showing the best understanding of the research field. There is no special need for university intermediation; the research institute may work even more efficiently without it by coming into direct contact with the agencies that are in need of its findings.

In short, "good business" for parapsychology could well begin with a new prospectus showing the independent territory of psi research, first listing currently conceived projects and the latest plans for the development of unexplored areas. A second section might picture the range of possible coöperative exchanges with bordering sciences and disciplines, looking both for potentially remunerable services and for meaningful new links with neighboring fields.

It is time for parapsychology to shake off the welfare mentality of an academic and professional dependency, candidly identify with the world-wide interest that has already given it support and, exercising its newly acquired independence, make common cause with the great human search for a self-knowledge that men can really use. Indeed, if this new branch of science can now launch a forthright search for its own destined usefulness, it will surely be marking off a new era in its own history.

Sound Organization

The last of these special fruits of experience which I will discuss here is focused on the organizational problems of the field, on the question of the institutional character best suited to parapsychology. The key word to be stressed in this connection is *realism*. By this I mean a combination of candor, practicality, and sincerity in dealing with organizational problems. The opposite of this concept of realism would be pretentiousness, status seeking, inflated affectation, and visionary fantasy.

My first point concerns what I have called the new independence of parapsychology. I can feel more strength in being identified with this small autonomous field, in spite of its lack of recognition, than I could if it were prematurely affiliated with any other field, department, or scientific organization. By prematurely, I mean before its association is logically appropriate and intellectually harmonious. After having seen the futility of the efforts to invade academic psychology, and having studied the reasons for the failure, I now consider that in the world as it is, it is better for parapsychology that these efforts did fail.

If and when the reasons become good enough for parapsychological research to return to the university, the change will, of course, be welcome. Until then, such a return would put the field in a position where the wrong thing would be expected of it and where it consequently would be disadvantaged in more ways than it would profit. Parapsychology needs first to explore and exploit its own natural potential and peculiarities and then seek linkage where it can best be found. Its rightful connections with other fields will come about naturally enough in due course.

Both in and out of parapsychology, some apprehension was genuinely felt over the complete change of status of the Duke Parapsychology Laboratory in its transfer to the FRNM and its conversion to the Institute for Parapsychology. The question was: Does it not mean *something* to be a part of a good university—something especially for a still growing and adjusting branch of science? The answer has been: Yes, it means a great deal. Intellectual exchange with fellow scholars is of first importance. And so are mathematical and other technical aid, a good library, access to a computer, the possibility of student volunteers as subjects, and so on through a long list of important services which university facilities can provide. But after all, they do not necessitate formal linkage. For the present, therefore, it seems to me that the the independent research institute offers the ideal arrangement (among a number of alternatives) for this branch of science.

Within the field of parapsychology itself, however, there are other, and probably more important, organizational relations to be considered. One of these is the need for unity.

It is not good for one institute to be too isolated from other centers and workers. A number of agencies have functioned to bring workers together, perhaps the best of these being the Parapsychological Association. In time, the research centers themselves, or most of those that survive the rigors of initial development, may link up into something like a "United Centers for Parapsychology." Some such federation of scattered units could do much to coördinate efforts in setting up training centers, organizing meetings and publication to best advantage, and even perhaps adding efficiency in an overall public relations program.

Judging by the history of other scientific groups, we must also anticipate a fair amount of specialization within the field as it grows. This should be a welcome development, although when it starts, it may easily run wild for lack of an organized developmental program. A highly specialized interest (such as the problem of post-mortem survival almost proved to be) backed by big enough money, could easily convert what should be a mere application of psi research into an overgrown monstrosity and unbalance a rounded-out development of more general research. Who and what could stop such a development or keep the general operation of the field from its danger? Several agencies like the PA and the societies for psychical research should be of some help, but there is need, too, for a stabilizing organization or confederation on the administrative level, something like the "United Centers" just mentioned. The independent institute, like the FRNM, could also be a stabilizing force with its broad and long-range commitment of aims and purposes, but only through coöperative action.

In general, however, specialization is more to be encouraged than feared. Each division becomes a growing point in itself, capable of unlimited extension—and even a stimulating challenge to the rest. Accordingly, as the number of workers increases, there should be some overall planning to assist those concerned with a limited area of problems to get together for uninterrupted treatment of their own special problem area, at least within certain limits and part of the time.

There is one more of these organizational problems that seems to me even more important. When we look around at the other sciences, we see that some of them developed as more or less pure sciences, like astronomy, let us say; but others have become practically engulfed by a large field of application right from the start. Physiology will illustrate this latter trend. Still others have had a divided existence, one branch perhaps located in the school of medicine and another in the department of biology or chemistry. We need not try to predict which way parapsychology will go, but we may concern ourselves with the question: Which way would be better to try to have it go? My vote would be for the analogy with physiology. It was originally the obvious relevance of physiology to medicine that sky-rocketed it into enormous usefulness and support. Then basic research on the problems relevant, not only to medicine, but to the whole of life made it into a province of its own.

I need hardly say that, whether one likes it or not, parapsychology will have to start looking for its most likely kind of application. I pointed out earlier in my remarks that it has to make an effort to sell itself and show its usefulness and significance, and so to insure support. Would it not be logical to turn to disciplines already making use of psi ability? And of these, which could be more obvious than religion? (I have indicated in an earlier lecture that the entire communication system assumed by the world's main theologies translates literally into psi communication and even into the special types of psi as now established.) To some extent, religionists themselves are turning their attention to parapsychology, at least to some of its border claims and associations. The greatest difficulty for such interest lies in the fact that religious leaders in general are not scientifically oriented; they tend not to welcome experimental research as an ally. But the medical profession of Pasteur's day was not, as an institution, seeking his experimental assistance either. Nonetheless, his findings eventually revolutionized it.

For that matter, the parapsychologists themselves (most of them) will not take any more easily to the idea of putting their science at the service of the problems of such a declining and "non-scientific" discipline as religion. But the answer is that these attitudes do not realistically bear on the question raised: Has parapsychology a relevant and possibly useful bearing on the problems of religion—that is, those problems of religion that can be stated as questions of fact concerning man's nature and destiny? There will, I suspect, be a few persons in both fields, religion and parapsychology, who will be drawn to this application as its importance becomes clear. They will be encouraged to recall the parallels which the history of science offers in the case of other disciplines as they underwent their scientific revolution.

Just now, no one wants to turn to see how much his culture still owes to the ethical "engineering" that in the past was supported by the structure of a "supernaturalistic" interpretation of man and his universe. Not many are yet ready to consider seriously (as Sir Alister Hardy does in his "Gifford Lectures") a scientific reconditioning of the speculative structure of theology to see to what extent modern experimental parapsychology is verifying principles hitherto only assumed on the basis of authority and faith. I think it is fairly predictable, however, that the time *will* come when, in one way or another, man will be constrained to see whether the wholesale rejection of the religious approach to man's nature, such as that represented by a materialistic philosophy, offers a more factually reliable solution than the effort as a scientific examination via parapsychology could produce. Some inquirers will want to try a reconstruction of the system of human personality, utilizing and extending the psi researches to see what man can do to build a structure of ethical guidance on tested findings of man's nature. If so, they will want a structure that, like the modern system of medicine, can be counted on more dependably than its prescientific heritage to stand the pragmatic tests it must meet.

This is why I would favor attempting to make parapsychology—ideas and all—immediately and as far possible, useful. But I think it might be wise to make "applied parapsychology" one of those special subdivisions of the field which I mentioned above, in order that those who think of themselves as more puristic parapsychologists need not on every occasion have to commingle with those who, let us say, are looking for a possible relation between psi ability and ethics. One branch may conceivably develop the application of psi to practical affairs, and another, hardly less practical, could become parapsychosomatic medicine. Still a third section could explore the role psi has played in the religions. This could be a study of the parapsychology of religion.

I think that if enough institutional realism is applied, the natural divisions which accommodate to differing interests can be allowed while avoiding the kind of divisiveness that goes with too much concentration on the same point or issue. It seems to be true that the more people divide into natural groups and keep themselves relatively independent in this way, the more ready they are when necessary to recombine in larger relationships that do not force them to give up their requirements for individual identity.

Never before has parapsychology been far enough along in the accumulation of sound research findings to take a position of unaffected independence. But if, as I now enjoy thinking, we do not have to have identification with any other organization or group in order to proceed with our work, a certain proper self-respect can be spontaneously generated by the appreciation of this branch of study as a separate section of inquiry. It need not be a matter of pride, but it can hardly be less than a cause for satisfaction. This acceptance of more or less complete self-management is one around which all responsible and understanding parapsychologists can readily unite, as far as they need to be united, and still, for the most part, enjoy their individual preoccupations.

These are some of the keys I would turn over to those who may wish to try them in the locks that will from time to time give difficulty. I cannot acknowledge all the sources of contact from which I have obtained them or even estimate how much they are worth. It does not really matter. The best real valuation of the past comes in the tests of the future; and it is for use in those tests that, with mingled gratitude and confidence, I now hand over to all who may care to try them, the ideological keys I have described. They symbolize, I would like to think, something of the combined responsibility and vision this Institute and its work have helped to develop.

Appendixes

APPENDIX A

Position Effects

The mere location on the record sheet of the trials in a psi test has been found to influence the rate of success. These variations have been found to show significant patterning in many researches and are called position effects (PEs). The most common PE is a decline of scoring rate in the column on the record sheet representing a run. Often, however, the scoring rate will go up again at the end of the run, giving a U-curve when the hit distribution is plotted.

PEs are likely to appear in various structures of the record sheet depending, of course, upon the type of record sheet used. In a sheet composed, let us say, of ten vertical columns, or runs, the run may show a decline or U-curve, but the page may show a decline from left to right. With both a lateral and vertical decline, a diagonal decline will result.

Or again, if the runs are broken into segments, let us say five segments of five trials each in each column, the segments are likely to reflect the general patterning of the column as a whole.

These PE hit patterns are now recognized as the result of the subject's reaction to the structure of the test as reflected in the record sheet. If the subject has no awareness of the position of a trial in the run or other series, position effects are not to be expected.

For more information on this topic, see "Position Effects in Psi Test Results," by J. B. Rhine, *Journal of Parapsychology*, June, 1969.

APPENDIX B

Selecting Precognition Targets

The general procedure worked out at the Institute for Parapsychology for selecting precognition targets includes a ten-step method for finding an entry point into a random number table. In the example given below, the entry was to a book called *A Million Random Number Digits*, but the procedure can be modified for any random number table.

1. The research assistant shakes a covered box containing three ten-sided dice of different colors and sets the box down.

2. The experimenter opens the box and records the uppermost digit of the red, white and black dice, in that order, to obtain a three-digit number.

3-4. The first three steps are repeated twice to obtain two more three-digit numbers.

5. The first two numbers are multiplied, and the product multiplied by the third number to obtain a number of approximately eleven digits.

6. The last ten digits of the number obtained in Step 5 are reversed to obtain a ten-digit number.

7. The square root of the number obtained in Step 6 is taken to six places (ignoring a decimal point and not rounding off the last digit) to obtain a six-digit number.

8. The first digit of the six-digit number obtained in Step 7 is changed to 1 if it is odd, to 0 if it is even, and the fifth digit is changed to 5 if it is odd, to 0 if it is even. The sixth digit is dropped off, leaving a five-digit number.

9. The index number of a horizontal column in the random number table corresponding to the five-digit number obtained in Step 9 is found. (Each such column contains ten five-digit numbers.)

Appendix B 297

10. The sixth digit of the six-digit number obtained in Step 7 (which was dropped off in Step 9) determines which of the ten numbers in the column identified by Step 9 is the entry point.

The five-digit number obtained in Step 9 is then written in the upper left-hand corner of the first record sheet followed by a hyphen and the single digit used in Step 10.

To obtain a set of random targets, the five digits in the random number determined by Step 10 are copied one below the other in the order in which they occur in the random number table number, followed by the digits in the subsequent four random numbers, to give a column of 25 single digits. This column of digits is then translated into the five ESP symbols according to a code:

    1s and 6s become ESP symbol O
    2s and 7s become ESP symbol +
    3s and 8s become ESP symbol ≈
    4s and 9s become ESP symbol ☐
    5s and 0s become ESP symbol ☆

Each column of 25 single digits thus provides a block of 25 randomly ordered ESP targets. If more blocks of randomly ordered ESP targets are needed, the subsequent numbers in the random number table are used to provide them according to the same code.

For a discussion of the reasons for using such a complicated procedure and results of a related experiment carried out by Robert Morris, see *Parapsychology Today*, p. 75. For a more general statement see pp. 162-163 of Parapsychology, Rhine and Pratt, (Thomas) and for a simpler procedure, see p. 151 of the same.

APPENDIX C

Psi-Missing

It has been found that under some psi-test conditions the person (subject) being tested manifests ESP or PK ability by avoiding the target instead of hitting it. When this avoidance occurs to a significant degree, it is identified as psi-missing. Such results can be regarded as evidence of the operation of psi quite as well as if the scoring rate had gone to a similar extent above mean chance expectation.

Early experiments that showed psi-missing have indicated a connection of this result with some stress or conflict on the part of the subject. In some cases there were long, tedious test runs in which the scoring would drop well below the chance line at the end.

Later it was observed that if a subject had two types of tests confronting him (perhaps with two types of targets that were being compared or two test conditions) he tended, without consciously attempting to do so, to score positively on one and negatively on the other. This effect became a familiar, as well as useful, result known as the psi differential effect.

Psi-missing was at first associated with extreme declines (see Position Effects, Appendix A), but later research has indicated the two effects to be different in principle, although they sometimes occur together.

For more information on this topic, see "Psi-missing Reexamined," by J. B. Rhine, *Journal of Parapsychology*, March, 1969.

APPENDIX D

Stacking Effect

When several subjects try to guess the same series of targets in an ESP test, there is a possibility that some similarity of habits or preferences among members of the group will "stack" the results. Such a stacking effect may influence the rate of success, changing the value of the results as evidence of ESP. Methods of evaluation to correct for possible stacking are discussed in the *Journal of Parapsychology*, June 1970, but wherever possible, each subject should have a separate set of targets.

Of course an experimenter testing a class of students may, for motivational reasons, want to have them all guess at the order of a single deck of cards so that scores can be checked immediately by the students. Or it may be an almost impossible task to provide separate targets and check the results when a test is administered to thousands via the mass media. If, for these or other reasons, a number of subjects guess at the same target order, the experimenter should use a statistical method that allows for the possibility of stacking in analyzing the results.

To understand the possible difference, consider this hypothetical situation. A hundred subjects take a test which requires them to guess at the symbol order in randomly assembled decks of ESP cards. Because of some psychological factor common to the group, most of these subjects tend to call stars more often than the other symbols. If one subject's randomly selected target deck happens by chance to have more stars than other symbols, his score will probably rise above chance level, not because of ESP but because his calling bias dovetails with the symbol favored by chance in the randomly selected deck. Not many of the different randomly selected decks for the other subjects will have a preponderance of stars, and some will have fewer stars than other symbols, so that pooling the scores cancels out the star bias, and deviations can be attributed to ESP.

But if all hundred subjects are guessing at the same deck, and the deck happens to favor the target they tend to call, the effect of the coincidence will be multipled by one hundred, or stacked.

APPENDIX E

The Variance Test of Significance

The variance test is a standard means of evaluating the fluctuation of scores above or below the level theoretically expected by chance. It measures the extent to which such fluctuation is unusual.

The mean variance expected by chance can readily be computed. Comparing that mean with the actual variance in a set of psi test data gives a measure of the extrachance significance of the results.

Run scores are the most common units used in evaluating variance, but the calculation of mean variance and the comparison can be based on the total scores of an individual, the record page, segments of runs, or various other subdivisions.

The test most frequently used in ESP research is to have subjects guess the order of the symbols in a deck of ESP cards. Since each of the five symbols occurs approximately five times on the average in the 25-card deck, an average of five hits in each run can be expected by chance alone. Even when a subject's score over a number of runs averages exactly five, some slight fluctuation is to be expected by chance in individual runs. Either a large variance of scores (on either side of the mean), or a very small fluctuation (that keeps close to the mean) can give evidence of psi by means of the variance test if the effect is persistent enough to be acceptably significant. For example, a subject may score 10, 0, 10, 0 on four runs for an average run score of five, which is exactly mean chance expectation. The score for each run, however, deviates considerably from chance, which would lead the experimenter to suspect that something other than chance was operating. Another subject might score 7, 3, 6, 4, also an average run score of five, but the variance is quite small since the individual run scores depart very little from mean chance expectation.

If the data from a proper experiment show either significantly large or significantly small variance, the variance itself serves as a useful test of significance, whether or not the usual methods of evaluating total scores show significance.

The formula for the variance test can be found in Rogers, D.P. *Journal of Parapsychology*, 1966, Vol. 30, pp. 151-159, or by writing the Institute for Parapsychology. It is important to use the theoretical mean chance expectation.

Glossary

AGENT: The "sender" in tests for telepathy; the person whose mental states are to be apprehended by the percipient. In GESP tests, the person who looks at the target object.

CALL: The subject's guess (or cognitive response) in trying to identify the target in an ESP test.

CHANCE: The complex of undefined causal factors irrelevant to the purpose at hand.

Mean Chance Expectation (also *Chance Expectation* and *Chance Average*): The most likely score if only chance is involved.

CLAIRVOYANCE: Extrasensory perception of objects or objective events.

DEVIATION: The amount an observed number of successes varies (either above or below) from mean chance expectation in a run, series, or other unit of trials.

DT (DOWN THROUGH): The clairvoyance testing technique in which the cards are called down through the entire pack before any is removed or checked.

EFT (EMBEDDED FIGURES TEST): A psychological test in which the subject is asked to isolate a geometric figure within a complex pattern.

ESP (EXTRASENSORY PERCEPTION): Experience of or response to a target object, state, event, or influence without sensory contact.

ESP CARDS: Cards, each bearing one of the following five symbols: star, circle, square, cross, and waves (three parallel wavy lines). A standard pack has 25 cards.

Closed Pack: An ESP pack composed of five each of the five symbols.

Open Pack: An ESP pack made up of the ESP symbols selected in random order, thereby being composed of no fixed number of each symbol.

EXPECTATION: See *chance*.

EXTRACHANCE: Not due to chance alone.

GESP (GENERAL EXTRASENSORY PERCEPTION): ESP which could be either telepathy or clairvoyance or both.

MCE (MEAN CHANCE EXPECTATION): See *chance*.

PARAPSYCHICAL, PARAPSYCHOLOGICAL, PARANORMAL: Attributable to psi.

PARAPSYCHOLOGY: The branch of science that deals with psi communication, i.e., behavioral or personal exchanges which are extrasensorimotor—not dependent on the senses and muscles.

PDE: See *psi differential effect*.

PERCIPIENT: The person experiencing ESP; also, one who is tested for ESP ability.

PK (PSYCHOKINESIS): The extramotor aspect of psi; a direct (i.e., mental but non-muscular) influence exerted by the subject on an external physical process, condition, or object.

PLACEMENT TEST: A PK technique in which the aim of the subject is to try to influence falling objects to come to rest in a designated area of the throwing surface.

PRECOGNITION: Extrasensory perception of future events, i.e., random events the occurrence of which cannot be inferred from present knowledge.

PSI (PARAPSYCHICAL, PARAPSYCHOLOGICAL): A general term to identify extrasensorimotor exchange with the environment. Psi includes ESP and PK.

PSI DIFFERENTIAL EFFECT: Significant difference between scoring rates when subjects are participating in an experiment which has two comparative conditions (such as two types of targets or two modes of response).

PSI-HITTING, PSI-MISSING: Exercise of psi ability in a way that hits (psi-hitting) or avoids (psi-missing) the target the subject is attempting to hit.

PSI PHENOMENA: Occurrences which result from the operation of psi. (See *psi*.)

PSYCHICAL RESEARCH: Original term used for parapsychology.

RANDOM ORDER: Chance

Glossary

RUN: In psi tests, a standard group of trials. In ESP tests the run is usually 25 trials based on the deck of 25 ESP cards or symbols; in PK tests the standard run consists of 24 single die throws regardless of the number of dice thrown together.

SCORE: The number of hits made in any given unit of trials, usually a run.

Total Score: Pooled scores of all runs.

Average Score: Total score divided by number of runs.

SERIES: Several runs or experimental sessions that are grouped in accordance with the stated purpose and design of the experiment.

SESSION: A unit comprising all the trials of one test occasion.

SIGNIFICANCE: A numerical result is significant when it equals or surpasses some criterion of degree of chance improbability. The criterion commonly used in parapsychology today is a probability value of .01 or less, which means odds of at least 100 to one.

SPONTANEOUS PSI EXPERIENCE: Natural, unplanned occurrence of an event or experience that seems to involve parapsychical ability.

STIMULUS: See *target*.

SUBJECT: The person who is tested in an experiment.

TARGET: In ESP, the objective or mental events to which the subject is attempting to respond; in PK tests, the objective process or object which the subject tries to influence (such as the face or location of a die).

Target Card: The card which the percipient is attempting to identify or otherwise indicate a knowledge of.

Target Face: The face on the falling die which the subject tries to make turn up by PK.

TELEPATHY: ESP of the mental state or activity of another person.

TRIAL: In ESP tests, a single attempt to identify a stimulus object; in PK tests, a single unit of effect to be measured in the evaluation of results.

VARIANCE (THEORETICAL): A measure of the dispersal of a

group of scores about their theoretical mean (*Mean Chance Expectation*).

Large Variance: Fluctuation of scores beyond mean chance variance.

Small Variance: Fluctuation of scores below mean chance variance.

Mean Variance (theoretical): The expected variance of the theoretical mean score.

Run-Score Variance: The fluctuation of the scores of individual runs around the theoretical mean.

Subject Variance: The fluctuation of a subject's total score from the theoretical mean of his series.

Name Index

Backster, Cleve, 103
Balounova, Marie, 15-16, 62-66
Barrett, William, 239
Barry, Jean, 70, 118-21
Bechterev, Vladimir, 17
Bernheim, Hippolyte, 237
Bhadra, B. H., 145-46
Binet, Alfred, 237
Brier, Robert M., 15, 36-52, 63, 71, 102-17, 118, 128, 129-35, 149, 161-70
Buzby, Dallas, 181-82, 183, 184-91

Cadoret, Remi, 36, 54, 56
Carington, Whately, 229, 233
Carpenter, James C., 93, 183, 203-14
Cattell, McKeen, 247
Charcot, J. M., 245
Chauvin, Rémy, 218, 258-61
Clark, C. C., 247
Coover, John E., 240
Cormack, G., 80
Cox, W. E., 69, 71, 80, 97-101, 102

Dale, Laura, 78
Duval, Pierre, 14, 17-27

Ebbinghaus, Hermann, 237
Eccles, Sir John, 84

Feather, Sara, 69, 71, 86-96, 127, 128, 129-35, 145-51
Few, William Preston, 243
Forwald, H., 80
Foster, A. A., 37
Foster, Esther, 13, 18, 24
Freeman, John, 128, 139, 163, 170, 182-83, 192-202

Gengerelli, J. A., 127, 128, 152-60
Gibson, Lottie, 77

Grad, Bernard, 103, 118
Gurney, E., 221

Hall, G. Stanley, 236
Hallett, S. J., 36
Hansel, C. E. M., 225-26
Hebb, D. O., 249
Hitzig, E., 237
Honorton, C. H., 213
Humphrey, Betty M., 86, 91, 96, 213-14
Hyslop, James, 236

James, William, 236, 239
Janet, Pierre, 237, 239
Jastrow, Joseph, 247
Jones, Joyce N., 127, 128, 145-51

Krippner, Stanley, 160
Kuhn, T. S., 225-27, 233

McDougall, William, 239, 240, 242, 248, 272
McMahan, Betty, 77
Martin, Dorothy R., 138
Montredon, Evelyn, 17-27
Moss, Thelma, 127, 128, 152-60
Münsterberg, Hugo, 237
Murphy, Gardner, 247
Myers, F. W. H., 221

Nash, Carroll B., 186
Nash, Catherine S., 186
Nielsen, Winnifred, 92, 93
Nowlis, V., 203

Osis, Karlis, 13, 18, 24

Pasteur, Louis, 70
Pratt, J. G., 138-39, 230, 233, 258
Price, G. R., 225

Rhine, J. B., 3-9, 13-16, 69-71, 73, 82-83, 125-28, 181-83, 221, 223, 236-57, 262-92
Rhine, Louisa E., 69, 71, 72-85, 86-96, 102, 128, 171-78, 217, 223
Richet, Charles, 5, 237, 238
Richmond, Nigel, 17, 103
Rogers, David Price, 92-93, 94, 203-04
Royce, Josiah, 236
Ryzl, Milan, 15-16, 38, 62-66, 138-39, 224, 233

Schmeidler, Gertrude, 127, 150, 230
Schmidt, Helmut, 14, 28-35
Shackleton, Basil, 223
Sidgwick, Henry, 237, 238, 239
Smythies, J. R., 84
Soal, S. G., 229

Stanford, Birgit, 53-61
Stanford, Rex, 15, 53-61, 128, 136-44
Stepanek, Pavel, 138-39, 224
Stevenson, Ian, 223
Stewart, Mrs. Gloria, 139, 230
Stribic, Frances P., 138

Thouless, Robert H., 82, 83-84, 217, 221-35
Tyminski, Walter V., 15, 36-52

Ullman, Montague, 160

Vasse, Dr. and Mme. P., 103
van Helmholz, H., 237

Warner, Lucien, 247
White, Rhea, 53

Subject Index

Affect
 defined, 203
 negative and positive, related to ESP run-score variance, 203-14
Alpha rhythm in ESP studies, 7, 53-61
American Psychological Association, 236
American Society for Psychical Research, 78
Animals, ESP in, 252
 experimental work on
  cats, 18
  dogs, 17
  mice, 4, 13, 17-27, 218
  paramecia, 17, 103
 homing, 17
Anpsi; see Animals, ESP in
Apparatus used in psi tests, 15, 19-23, 55, 80, 87-88; see also Electrical and electronic devices
Application of psi ability, 4-5, 36-52, 183, 282-83
Attitude; see Psychological variables affecting ESP; Belief in ESP
Automatic recording devices in psi tests, 21-23, 28, 30-31

Belief in ESP, effect of on psi tests, 152-60, 173-75; see also Sheep-goat differences
Beta rhythm, 54
Binary choice response bias, 138-39

Call balancing, 58-60
Call-column preferences, 139
Call frequency, 38, 138
Call patterns, 139

Casino, psi research in; see Gambling
Census of Hallucinations, 237, 238
Checker, effect of on scoring rate, 126, 129-35
Children as subjects, 37, 77, 253
Chi-square goodness-of-fit test, 166-67
Cognitive variables affecting ESP
 spatial *vs.* verbal ability, 192-98
 tests of
  Embedded Figures Test, 184-91
  Thurstone Primary Mental Abilities Test, 193-98
Computer cards as ESP targets; see *under* Target variables
Conscious control of psi ability; see Application of psi
Consistency test, 174, 176, 201
Controversy between parapsychology and psychology, 236-57
Conviction and ESP scoring, 143
Correspondence ESP tests, 149-50, 161-70
Creativity; see *under* Personality variables
Critical ratio, 125
Criticism of parapsychology, 224-25, 247

Direction of scoring, prediction of
 by first trials, 113, 114
 by interest inventories, 213
 by primary and secondary responses, 200-02
 by sampling, 36-52
 by sex and PMA scores, 192-98
 by subject's conscious expectations, 135
Displacement, 229-30, 233

Draw-a-Man Test; *see under* Personality variables, tests of
EEG (electroencephalogram), 5, 15, 53-61
Electric shock, use of in psi research, 19, 21-22
Electrical and electronic devices in psi research, 4, 14, 28, 29-31, 97-98, 102-03, 118
Electroencephalogram; *see* EEG
Embedded Figures Test; *see under* Personality variables, tests of
"Emotional episodes" in ESP tests, 152-60
Evolution and ESP, 229
Experimental controls, 110-19
  for dice bias, 73, 91
  for fraud, 63, 65
  for sensory cues, 88, 104
  for skilled throwing in dice tests, 74
Experimental Psychical Research, 217
Experimenter fraud, as counterhypothesis to psi phenomena, 224-25
Extra-Sensory Perception, 221, 243, 246
Extra-Sensory Perception after Sixty Years, 224, 244

Financial support for parapsychology, 251, 256, 263, 280-86
Focusing effect, 231, 233
Foundation for Research on the Nature of Man
  aim of, 284
  establishment of, 283
Free associations in ESP tests, 152, 158-60
Freeman Word Reaction Test; *see under* Personality variables, tests of

Galvanic skin response; *see* GSR
Gambling, psi research in, 5, 14-15, 39-52
GSR (galvanic skin response), 7

Habit patterning in animal research, 18
Hallucinations, 136, 237
Healers (healing), 118, 268, 281-82
Help-hinder PK tests; *see under* PK
Hidden Channels of the Mind, 223
High-scoring subjects, 32-33, 35, 224
Historical reviews of parapsychology and psychology, 236-57
  during last quarter century, 221-35
Hypnosis, 16, 62-66, 238-39, 268
  by telepathy, 224

Impromptu testing, 171-78
Inhibition in ESP tests, 228-29
Institute for Parapsychology, 3
Intelligence, relation to ESP scoring, 192-98
Interest in ESP as related to scoring level vital *vs.* casual interest, 184-91

Journal of Parapsychology, 75, 82, 219, 223, 244, 251

McDougall Award, 13, 15, 181, 251-52, 253
Majority vote technique, 37-52
Mass ESP tests, 161-70
Mechanical behavior, 24, 110
Mediums (ship), 31, 73, 239, 275
  as subjects, 31-33
Mental states and ESP; *see under* Psychological variables
Methodology in psi research, 271
Mind Over Matter, 69
Mood, effect of on psi tests, 69, 87, 92-96, 183, 203-14
  moderate *vs.* extreme, 207-14

Index

Target variables in psi tests
  baccarat cards, 39, 45-48
  colored lamps, 28-35
  computer punch cards, 16, 62-66
  dice, 44-45, 87-96
  ESP cards, 55
  pennies, 36
  roulette wheel, 39-44
  slides, 152-60
  words and symbols, 163-70, 182, 193-98
Thurstone Primary Mental Abilities Test; *see under* Cognitive variables affecting ESP, tests of

Unpleasant mood experiment, 92-96

Variance, 53-61, 125, 147-50, 168-70, 184-85, 187, 188, 201, 231-32
  decline of, 203-14
  in PK tests, 89-96
Visiting Research Fellowship program, 277

Water droplets machine, 80

135, 168, 212-14, 228, 229; *see also* Displacement; Quarter distribution
Post-mortem survival, 241, 281-82, 284
Primary process material, 158-60
Psi
  and physics, 218, 258-61, 266
  and psychology, 217, 236-51
  direction, 125
  efficiency, 125
  guiding concepts for research in, 262-92
  in conflict with mechanistic theory, 83-85
  nature of, 6-8, 125, 136, 223, 230, 245, 269
  operation of, 260
Psi differential effect; *see* PDE
Psi Experience Questionnaire, 146
Psi-missing, 7, 77, 80, 109, 125, 126, 228
  in application attempts, 36
Psychical research, 221-22, 237-42, 268
Psychokinesis; *see* PK
Psychological Abstracts, 219
Psychological variables affecting psi, 29, 37, 76, 77, 81, 184-91; *see also* Mood
  attitude, 78, 79, 86, 127, 128, 145, 174, 177, 181, 198
  mental states, 7, 53-54, 57, 182
Psychosomatic medicine, 85
Public interest in ESP, 249-50, 254, 271-74, 283, 284

Quantum processes in psi research, 28-35
Quarter distribution, 69, 75

"Radar test," 140-41
Random behavior, 13, 18, 24-25, 26
Random target selectors, 20, 28
Rapport, effect of in ESP tests, 157-58

Reincarnation, 223
Repeatability in psi experiments, 222, 266
Research centers, location of, 252, 254
Response bias, 126-27, 136-44; *see also* Call frequency
Review meetings, 3, 273

Sampling technique, 36, 40-52
Second International Congress of Psychology, 237
Selection of subjects, 108, 128
Sensationalism of ESP, 273
Sensory cues, elimination of in psi tests, 25-26
Sequential bias, 139
Sex differences in ESP scoring, 7, 127-28, 161-70, 182, 192-98
Sheep-goat differences, 7, 127, 150, 230-31; *see also* Attitude
Shin, 84
Soal-Goldney experiments, 223
Society for Psychical Research, 224
Specialization in parapsychology, 288-89
Spiritualism, 241, 268
Spontaneous ESP, 53-54, 127, 128, 136-37, 152, 172, 221, 223
  as related to ESP test scoring, 145-51
Spontaneous physical phenomena, 6, 72, 85, 102
Stacking effect, 66, 161, 172, 174, 176
Static behavior, 24
Structure of Scientific Revolutions, The, 225
Stuart Interest Inventory, 210-14
Subject-experimenter relationships, 246
Subject variables affecting ESP, 153
  artists *vs.* non-artists, 157
Survival; *see* Post-mortem survival

Index

Mood scales, 92, 93
  adjective check list technique, 203-14

Novelty, effect of on ESP scores, 177-78

Objectivity, necessity of in psi research, 268-71

Parapsychological Association, 288
  organization of, 251
Parapsychology
  and conflict with psychology, 8-9, 272
  and philosophy, 266
  and physics, 9, 258-61, 266
  and religion, 266, 289-90
  independent status of, 254-57, 270, 285
  organizational problems in, 286-92
Parapsychology Today, 3, 5, 7, 70
PDE (psi differential effect), 7, 80, 198-202, 230, 231
  as related to conscious expectations, 125, 129-35
Pearce-Pratt experiments, 223
Personality variables affecting ESP
  affectable vs. unaffectable, 210-14
  creativity, 231
    global vs. analytic perceivers, 184-91
  likers vs. dislikers, 182-83, 198-202
  tests of
    Draw-a-Man Test, 181, 184-91
    Embedded Figures Test, 181, 184-91
    Freeman Word Reaction Test, 198-202
    Rorschach, 231
    Stuart Interest Inventory, 210-14
Personnel for psi research, 219, 275-80
  available training for, 266
  development of skills, 270
  necessity of responsibility in, 263-65
  need for diversification, 280
Perspective, necessity of in psi research, 265-68
Phantasms of the Living, 223
Physics and parapsychology; *see under* Parapsychology
Physiological studies and ESP, 7
PK (psychokinesis), 5, 6, 69-71
  development of tests for, 73
  early studies, 244-45
  effect of on animate objects
    fungus, 70, 118-21
    germination of seedlings, 103, 118
    paramecia, 17, 103
    plants, 5, 70, 102-17, 253
  effect of on inanimate objects
    mechanical devices, 5
    pendulum system, 97-101
    static objects, 76, 84-85
  history of, 217
  in help-hinder situations, 6, 69, 86-96
  in light-dark situations, 77
  nature of, 76-82
  physical forces involved, 81
  physical vs. psychological influences, 81
  placement tests, 76, 79-80, 97
  relationship to ESP, 79
  relationship to mass of target object, 76-77
  survey of, 72-85
  theories of
    atomic theory, 81
    kinetic theory, 79, 80
    loading theory, 79, 80
    origin, 82-85
Placement PK tests; *see under* PK
Plant perception, 70, 103
Polygraph, use of in psi tests, 55, 102-17
Position effects, 38-39, 48, 75, 134,